Collision Course

rell Ph.D

.999

Trinity College of
Vermont

Collision Course

Conflict, Negotiation, and Learning in College Composition

Russel K. Durst
University of Cincinnati

National Council of Teachers of English
1111 W. Kenyon Road, Urbana, Illinois 61801-1096

Staff Editor: Zarina M. Hock
Interior Design: Tom Kovacs for TGK Design
Cover Design: Carlton Bruett
NCTE Stock Number: 07427-3050

It is the policy of NCTE in its journals and other publications to provide a forum for the open discussion of ideas concerning the content and the teaching of English and the language arts. Publicity accorded to any particular point of view does not imply endorsement by the Executive Committee, the Board of Directors, or the membership at large, except in announcements of policy, where such endorsement is clearly specified.

Library of Congress Cataloging-in-Publication Data
Durst, Russel K., 1954–
        Collision course: conflict, negotiation, and learning in college
        composition/Russel K. Durst.
            p. cm.
        Includes bibliographical references (p.   ) and index.
        ISBN 0-8141-0742-7 (paperback)
        1. English language—Rhetoric—Study and teaching.   I. Title.
    PE1404.D87 1999
    808'.042'071—dc21   99-12766
                                                                    CIP

To my family—
my wife, Siusan,
and our sons,
Alexander, Jacob, and Isaac

Contents

Acknowledgments

Researching and writing a book can be painful work, but writing the acknowledgment section is closer to pure pleasure. Part of the enjoyment, of course, comes from the knowledge that most of the hard labor is done. But the bigger part comes from thinking back upon—and thanking—the many people who contributed in such different ways to the work.

First of all, I want to thank two extraordinary teachers, Sherry Cook Stanforth and Nan Reitz, for allowing me over the course of two academic terms to observe their composition classes, talk with them at length about their teaching, and work extensively with their students. This was no small favor. It's not always fun—I'm not sure it's ever fun—to have a curious, critical observer poking his nose into one's teaching. But Sherry and Nan graciously let me into their classrooms and their work lives. I thank them for their generosity and for teaching me so much about teaching. I also thank Sherry for her own perceptive contribution to this book, Chapter 7, and for her very helpful feedback on the manuscript as a whole.

In addition, I wish to thank Sherry and Nan's composition students for letting me observe them in class, interview them, read their papers, and interview them some more. The more I talked to these students, the more I liked and respected them. Busy with classes and jobs, adjusting to a new and demanding phase of life, learning how to be college students, they spoke candidly about their experiences, attitudes, and approaches in the composition class. As will be evident from the book, I learned a great deal from these students, and that knowledge has helped me in very direct ways to develop curriculum for the University of Cincinnati English Composition Program.

Many colleagues also helped in the creation of this book. My writing group partners and fellow University of Cincinnati English professors, Maggy Lindgren and Lucy Schultz, read numerous drafts and provided wonderfully detailed responses, even though constantly pressed by the demands of their own work. I am grateful not only for their help but for their friendship. At two points in the writing, Tom Newkirk of the University of New Hampshire gave the developing manuscript a careful review and made excellent suggestions. Stuart Greene of Notre Dame read a late draft and helped me think through complex notions of critical pedagogy. Ellen McIntyre of the University of Louisville read the manuscript thoroughly and helped make every chapter stronger. Early in my thinking and writing process, Steve North of SUNY Albany and Barbara Walvoord of Notre Dame gave encouragement and direction as I planned the overall structure of the book. Friend and former Cincinnati colleague Marjorie Roemer, now of Rhode Island College, taught me about curriculum design and the politics of teaching. The anonymous reviewers for NCTE provided useful criticisms and suggestions.

Thanks to a sabbatical leave made possible by the University of Cincinnati, I was able to spend the 1995–1996 academic year at the University of Oviedo in Spain, analyzing my data and writing a first draft of the book. While in Spain, I was helped immeasurably by the late Patricia Shaw Fairman, the department head who provided me with office space, library and computer privileges, and the finest hospitality. I will always remember her kindness and that of her husband, Millan Urdiales Campos. And Lioba Simon Schuhmacher, a friend and faculty member from this same department, helped me and my family spend a wonderful year in the north of Spain, an experience I would recommend to anyone.

Back home in the University of Cincinnati English Department, Sandi Nieman provided expert clerical help with the transcripts of student and teacher interviews. And along with Associate Director of English Composition, Maggy Lindgren, she kept the Program going whenever I was distracted by my work on the book.

I would also like to thank the Charles Phelps Taft Memorial Fund for granting me several summers of research funding for work on this project. And my editors at NCTE, Michael Greer and Zarina Hock, have been exceptionally helpful through all phases of the writing.

1 Introduction

The first-year college writing course has been a site of conflict since its very inception at Harvard in the late nineteenth century, with debates over the nature and function of the course continuing up to the present day. In recent times, disagreements have concerned such issues as whether overtly political content should be part of the course (e.g., Hairston, 1992; Brodkey, 1996); whether personal narrative should have a prominent place in the curriculum (e.g., Elbow, 1995, Bartholomae, 1995; Newkirk, 1997), even whether the first-year requirement should exist at all (e.g., Crowley, 1991, 1995; Petraglia, 1995). Fittingly, in these contentious times, in a field characterized by such conflicting views, the composition classroom itself is frequently positioned as a scene of disagreement, debate, and confrontation. Berlin's *Rhetorics, Poetics, and Cultures* (1996), Fitts and France's *Left Margins: Cultural Studies and Composition Pedagogy* (1995), Gale's *Teachers, Discourses, and Authority in the Postmodern Composition Classroom* (1996), and Sullivan and Qualley's *Pedagogy in the Age of Politics* (1994) are but four examples of influential contemporary works that depict the classroom as an arena for various kinds of conflict. These books and many others explore the theoretical and pedagogical underpinnings of classroom conflict, with an emphasis on the ideological issues that guide teaching decisions. The field is replete with works that examine the role of politically charged subject matter in composition theory and in the classroom. However, none of these works applies theoretical notions of conflict to an extended empirical analysis of classroom work in first-year composition classes.

Collision Course does just that. In the book, I examine teaching and learning in classrooms that embody the emphasis of current composition theory on situating writing instruction in a larger social and political context. The book is based on a reflective qualitative study, grounded in theories of critical pedagogy, classroom discourse, and writing development. In particular, I examine a teacher and her students as they work, interact, and frequently conflict over two quarters of composition instruction. The study contributes to the ongoing discussion of composition teaching an examination of the complex relationship between theory and

1

classroom praxis. The book also contributes to an ongoing professional conversation regarding the nature and purpose of the first-year writing course. Such work takes on particular importance, given the pervasiveness of first-year college writing, taught at several thousand institutions around the country and serving more than half a million students per year. At the large, urban university in which this research took place, first-year writing is the only course sequence required of all students.

The Book's Central Premise

Collision Course is based on the overarching view that students and teacher often have very different—and in many ways opposing—agendas in the composition class, that these differing agendas lead to significant conflict and negotiation throughout the course, and that a greater understanding of the nature of these disagreements and how they are or are not resolved can enhance both the theory and practice of composition teaching. This view has been shaped by my fifteen years of experience as a teacher, researcher, and administrator, but more specifically, by my recent two-year study of students and teachers in first-year writing classes. The study is qualitative, using ethnographic methods of classroom observation, teacher and student interviews, and analysis of students' texts and course materials. The thesis I explore in the book is a qualified one, based on my work at a large public university in the Midwest, and certainly not applicable to all students and teachers in all composition classes at all institutions. But I believe the thesis is a compelling one nonetheless. My argument is that first-year students typically enter composition with an idea of writing and an understanding of what they need to learn about writing that are dramatically at odds with the views and approaches of the teacher.

The core difference I have observed can best be described as follows: On the one hand, most students in first-year college composition are career-oriented pragmatists who view writing as a difficult but potentially useful technology. These students would generally prefer to learn a way of writing that is simple, quick, and efficient; applicable in all or most situations; and either reducible to a formula or straightforward set of rules, or free from rules, prescriptions, and restrictions. Experienced consumers of a wide range of products, students see writing as a technology which, like most technologies, should be designed not to complicate their already stressful, busy lives, but rather to make their lives run more smoothly. In preferring such instruction, students are not necessarily being lazy, misguided, reactionary, grade-grubbing, or otherwise difficult, as teachers may sometimes assume them to be. Instead, students who wish to learn a form of literacy that will both make their lives easier and help them become more successful in their careers are following in a long tradition of American pragmatism. This tradition was commented upon as early as 1835 by de Toqueville in his classic study, *Democracy in America*, and has been discussed at length by later distinguished commentators such as Dewey (1916), Hofstadter (1963), and Rorty (1979). Recently, Jeff Smith (1997) has pointed out that the vast majority of his composition students at UCLA "volunteer college-related career goals—and mention jobs, careers, or some form of the phrase 'being successful'—when asked an open-ended question about their principal reason for being in school" (p. 303). Smith's students wanted their composition class to be more explicitly related to such goals.

But while students may hope for a pragmatic approach to composition, teachers of contemporary college writing classes typically stress much more complex and demanding notions of critical literacy. I would argue that such notions are in many ways incompatible with students' wishes. As first articulated by Paulo Freire (1970), and later developed by such figures as Patricia Bizzell (1992), Henry Giroux (1983, 1988), Ira Shor (1996), and John Trimbur (1994), critical literacy approaches ask students to examine their relationships to language and other cultural tools in an attempt to understand their role as actors in history and to realize their potential to create change on both a small and large scale. Influenced by Freireian pedagogy as well as continental literary theory, critical literacy approaches in composition emphasize self-reflection, multi-perspectival thinking, explicit consideration of ideological issues, rigorous development of ideas, and questioning of established ways of thinking. Influenced by cultural studies, feminist theories, and Frankfurt School Marxism, current approaches also foreground awareness of social and political inequities and consideration of ways to resolve them. And influenced by writing process pedagogy, critical literacy approaches promote extensive invention and revision, careful consideration of audience, and sensitive reading and re-reading of one's own and others' texts. Notions of writing advanced by teachers employing critical literacy approaches are designed to complicate rather than simplify students' lives and to inculcate ways of thinking and acting in the world whose benefits, while evident to teachers, may be quite unclear to students. Markedly divergent conceptions of education, culture, and politics underlie the different classroom agendas of critical literacy teacher and pragmatic student. In my opinion, much of what is most interesting in a composition class happens at least in part as a result of the interaction between these conflicting agendas and world views. And what students

learn in composition class about reading, writing, thinking, and learning is much affected by these conflicts in ways that the book will detail
and reflect upon.

In the book, I investigate the conflicts in first-year composition through
a conceptual framework that places the writing class with a critical literacy orientation in a larger institutional and social context. One of my
guiding assumptions is that the class focuses on much more than "just"
writing. A key underlying purpose of the class is to help beginning college students develop what are, for many, new ways of thinking or dispositions of mind. Hence, the teacher promotes a pedagogy of interpretation, critique, meta-awareness, and dialectic types of intellectual work
that constitute the hallmarks of a critical literacy orientation, while students wish for a simpler, more straightforward, and less conflictual approach. Moreover, in many critical literacy classes today, composition is
taught within a framework that emphasizes political and cultural awareness as a cornerstone of students' education and intellectual development. Accordingly, this book analyzes the political focus of recent composition pedagogy as a way of teaching critical disposition of mind,
studying the impact of this political orientation on the curriculum of a
first-year writing program through the experiences of one teacher and
her students. At the same time, as director of the program under examination, rather than the impartial observer assumed in traditional models of research, I discuss my own complicated stake both in the curriculum and in this study. In my analysis of classroom interactions, I look at
teacher and student responses to a curriculum partly of my own devis-
ing, a curriculum that is intended to challenge long-held beliefs, assumptions, and habits.

Composition's Social Turn and Teaching Students to Write

One impetus for the study is my interpretation of the current, more explicit emphasis on political and cultural issues in composition, as depicted in much recent scholarship. This movement in composition studies has been called "the social turn" (Trimbur, 1994), and it refers to
widespread attempts in the field to open up instruction and theory at a
variety of levels to issues of justice, oppression, and diversity. I am interested in the relation of the social turn in composition to the more traditional concern in the field with the teaching of writing, as in strategies, approaches, and techniques that students can use in producing texts.
I see unresolved, even unacknowledged tensions between these areas
of concern. I believe that, for teachers, a focus on the political implica-

tions of writing instruction helps to clarify what we do in the classroom and to critique inequities in the institutions in which we work. And I think that students can benefit in similar ways from more explicitly political composition instruction, not least through becoming more aware of their own cultural situatedness.

However, I would also argue that, as we in the field have become more concerned with larger issues of politics and culture, we have not yet formulated new understandings about the role of such issues in teaching students how to write, or even been explicit about what it means to teach writing in these new pedagogical frameworks. Indeed, most of the recent discussions of what has been called "the social turn" in composition studies say very little about the teaching of writing in the more traditional sense of examining ways in which one might develop, think through, and structure an argument or interpretation. Much current work focuses instead on helping enhance students' awareness of political and cultural issues. A few authors discuss ways of teaching students about the intellectual work involved in producing an essay, such as Kurt Spellmeyer in his 1993 book *Common Ground*. This book focuses on the role of the composition class in helping students develop more theoretically and politically sophisticated understandings of themselves and of their worlds. However, Spellmeyer's and other such works generally disparage work concerned with teaching writing strategies for an emphasis upon "mere" skills, and as work that betrays an "instrumentalist" orientation (p. 18), suggesting that such pedestrian matters as writing strategies are beneath the consideration of serious thinkers.

There is indeed a strong tendency now in composition studies to focus discussion almost exclusively on ideological matters such as students' political beliefs; race, gender, and class inequalities; the oppressiveness of our institutions; and how we might effect change. These issues are no doubt crucial ones for the field and for society, and well worth taking up in the classroom, but it is not immediately clear how they map onto our role as teachers helping students improve their writing. I am not arguing against the politicization of composition as an important influence both on theoretical discussions in the field and on classroom practice. Rather, I am in substantial agreement with those who argue that the curriculum has always been political, if not explicitly so; that there is no "value-free" education; and that a focus on the political can be a critical part of students' intellectual and moral development.

At the same time, however, I also believe that an important part of what we do in the classroom involves helping students become more effective, intelligent, and reflective writers, whatever their political be-

liefs may be and however we in the field of composition studies choose
to define these terms. Though I believe in and teach a critical literacy
approach that locates students in a larger cultural and historical context,
my goal as a teacher and program director is not to turn first-year students into critical intellectuals and political activists. In any case, very
few of our students have an interest in becoming Frankfurt School style
intellectuals. I would argue that, when they enter the composition class,
most students, given their pragmatic orientation, have the goal in mind
of improving their writing to be more successful students and career-
seekers. Moreover, I believe that this goal is a reasonable one, given students' purposes in attending college, and that, as composition specialists—while we should not focus exclusively on this goal—we should be
more supportive of students' instrumentalist desires if we wish the
course to be a productive one.

In my view, we can best teach critical literacy in first-year composition not by denying or trying to undermine students' careerism. Rather,
I believe we can best teach critical literacy by accepting the pragmatic
nature of most students' approach to the first-year writing course, by
taking students' goals into consideration when designing curriculum,
and then by attempting to build a reflective, intellectual, politically aware
dimension into this instrumentalist orientation. Thus, my goal in teaching is to develop a critical literacy approach that accepts the careerism
which so many students bring to the classroom, yet uses that careerism
not as an end in itself but rather as a beginning point on which to build
greater awareness and sophistication. Given this goal, one key purpose
of the book is to place the teaching of composition—as in consideration
of such issues as "What do we mean by good writing, given the many
different contexts in which writing takes place, and how do we help students become good writers?"—back into the professional conversation.
I wish to bring back a concern with the teaching of writing not by returning composition studies to a mythical past in which we taught by
objective standards agreed upon by all and in which politics was not a
part of what we did in the classroom. Rather, I hope to integrate a focus
on the preparation of students *as writers* within the context of the field's
social turn. The book will argue in favor of a pedagogy which, while
politically aware, still makes the teaching and learning of writing—as a
critical intellectual tool—a central, defining focus of the composition
class. Framed by this discussion, the book explores what it means to teach
writing and to learn to write in a critical literacy classroom when, in a
great many cases, teacher and students have fundamentally different
outlooks and goals.

:udy

search project focused on teacher-student interactions in first-year
osition classes. For two academic years, I sat in on composition
s with permission from the teachers and students. At the univer-
here the research took place, there is a composition sequence with
two required ten-week quarters of instruction for all students. There is
also a third quarter of instruction in the sequence, but not all students
are required to take it. Consequently, the research focuses on only the
first two quarters of the composition sequence. The first course of the _Comp I_
sequence focuses primarily on writing from personal experience and
knowledge; it is intended to help students move toward analytic, self-
reflective modes of writing. The second course consists of critical read- _Comp II_
ing and writing about cultural and political issues, along with a research-
writing component. Individual instructors may depart somewhat from
the established curriculum in developing their own teaching styles, but
they are asked to keep their approaches as consistent as possible with
the overall philosophy underlying the curriculum.

    In carrying out the research, I wanted to see, in part, how individual
instructors reinterpreted the curriculum, and how students subsequently
came to grips with the reinterpretations. Accordingly, for one year of the
study, I observed the first two quarters of a class taught by Nan Reitz,
an experienced adjunct instructor with a doctorate in literature, a background in journalism and business writing, and a pedagogical approach
emphasizing lively, readable prose. During a second year, I observed the
first two quarters of a class taught by a theoretically and politically engaged doctoral student, Sherry Cook Stanforth, whose work focused on
composition studies and who was particularly interested in looking critically at her own ways of interpreting and teaching an established curriculum. In studying each teacher's classes, I took detailed field notes of
my classroom observations; spoke regularly with the teacher; conducted
frequent interviews with case study students chosen to represent different levels of writing ability, gender, and socioeconomic backgrounds; and
photocopied all student writing and class handouts for later analysis.
(See Chapter 2 for a detailed description of the research methods.) For
the book, I ultimately chose to focus on Sherry and her students, with
only a few short references to Nan's classes. I did so because Sherry's
teaching was much more influenced by contemporary composition
theory, politicizing the classroom and emphasizing critical self-reflection.
I wanted to examine the relationship of this theory to classroom practice in light of students' attitudes and approaches to composition instruction.

how does
personal
socialization come in to play
in The writing
classroom.

Research Questions

In examining directly the deep-seated differences in teacher's and students' agendas in the composition class and the ways in which such differences influence the inner workings of the class, this book addresses several key issues in composition scholarship. The first concerns the uses of critical pedagogy and cultural and political approaches in the composition classroom. The book investigates with copious examples, drawn from long-term empirical study, the timely issue of the conflicts between teacher and students to define and carry out the agenda of the writing class. A second important issue concerns the difficulties students encounter in the college writing class, particularly working-class students who have traditionally faced considerable obstacles in higher education. The book offers portraits and analyses of two such students in composition, contrasted with the experiences of more traditional middle-class students. Finally, based on an awareness that people, ideas, and events cannot be well understood when studied in isolation, the book examines the experiences of individuals and classrooms within the framework of the broader institutional and social contexts in which they are embedded. The study investigated the following research questions:

1. What attitudes did students have toward writing at the beginning of the course sequence, and what did they hope to learn in college composition?

2. How did the students approach the critical thinking demands of the first-quarter course, which was designed to help them learn to take a more analytic stance in writing?

3. How did the students engage with the political and social content of the second-quarter course, along with the critical thinking and argument aspect of the course?

4. How did students relate their own political views and understandings to those embodied in the textbook, writing assignments, and other aspects of the second-quarter course?

5. How did the teacher approach the requirement of using the "official" syllabus? In what ways did she adapt the prescribed curriculum to fit her own teaching preferences?

6. In what ways did students' approaches to the course conflict with those of the teacher, and how did students attempt to resolve those differences?

7. How did the teacher attempt to resolve the course conflicts, and how did students react to these efforts?

8. What understandings about literacy and culture did students take away from the writing courses?

9. What are the implications of this research for the teaching of composition?

The Book's Organization

The next chapter discusses the context, participants, and methods employed in the research. In Chapter 3, "The Enigma of Arrival," I look closely at the initial ideas about and attitudes toward writing that students brought with them to the first-year composition classroom, primarily through an examination of self-reflective essays written on the first day of class. The following three chapters investigate different types of student resistance to the writing instruction they received. Chapter 4, "Ground Rules in College Composition," uses a sociocultural frame to examine conflicts that arose during the first quarter of the composition sequence when students were instructed to employ a complex and elaborated composing process. Chapter 5, "Flashpoints: Developing an Analytic Stance," examines student resistance to the interpretive, self-reflective approach to subject matter emphasized in the composition curriculum. Chapter 6, "Persuasion, Politics, and Writing Instruction," focuses on conflicts that arose when culturally and politically conservative students wrote in response to a textbook, writing assignments, and curriculum grounded in a left/liberal ideology. Following Chapter 6, Sherry Cook Stanforth contributes a chapter responding to my interpretation of her teaching and her students. The concluding chapter of the book discusses student learning in the composition sequence and puts forward the idea of "reflective instrumentalism" as a means of teaching critical inquiry and social awareness in the composition class while at the same time respecting and incorporating a concern for students' more pragmatic, career-oriented goals.

2 The Research: Contexts, Participants, and Methods

My primary purpose in the study was to examine the ways first-year college students make sense of, engage, resist, and learn from the critical literacy approach practiced in the composition program. I wanted in particular to investigate the relationship, or fit, of this teaching approach with the attitudes and goals that students brought to the class. I wanted to examine students' receptivity to the composition instruction and to see how their orientation toward the subject matter evolved over time. My goals for the study led me to adopt an ethnographic methodology. In conducting the research, I combined classroom observation, case-study interview, and qualitative analysis of student writing and teacher's course materials. This approach allowed me to examine the teacher's and students' decision-making processes, to look closely at students' interactions with one another and with the teacher, and to investigate individual students' writing and learning within the larger classroom and programmatic setting. In this chapter, I will present a portrait of my research site, introduce the teacher and students studied, detail my data sources and analytic frameworks, and describe my procedures in carrying out the study.

On Campus: Scenes for Writing and Learning

After touring the United States in the late 1940s, the Welsh poet Dylan Thomas described with ironic awe "the great midwestern university factories" at which he read his work in vast lecture halls. He could have been talking about the University of Cincinnati, a school which in many ways fits that distinctive image. Located in southwestern Ohio close to the Kentucky and Indiana borders, Cincinnati is a city of about one and a half million, including the surrounding suburbs, and is noted for its conservatism and pro-business environment. Sinclair Lewis did research in Cincinnati and used the city as a model for the midwestern town of Zenith in *Babbitt*, his classic novel of crass materialism, philistinism, and "boosterism" for which he won the Nobel Prize (Schorer, 1961). Several years ago, when a local museum planned to exhibit the photography of Robert Mapplethorpe, the city tried, unsuccessfully, to close the show down. Even more recently, after the city council voted to expand an anti-discrimination ordinance to protect homosexuals, the citizens of Cincinnati, after a well-funded nationally financed, "pro-family" campaign, overturned the part of the ordinance referring to gays. The city is home to a number of large corporations and industries, including Procter and Gamble, Federated Department Stores, Chiquita, and the American Financial Corporation, all of which maintain fairly close ties to the University of Cincinnati, particularly to its College of Business Administration.

The University, which both defies and reflects the city's conservatism, was founded in 1819 as the city-run McMicken College of Arts and Sciences, the first municipal college in the nation. Over time, it has become part of the state university system of Ohio, and, with a total of almost 40,000 students, has grown into its second largest university behind Ohio State. Along the way, the University has expanded into a system of fourteen undergraduate colleges, three of which are open admission, two-year branches and the other eleven of which offer different professional specializations at the baccalaureate level, including engineering, design and architecture, business, education, health sciences, social work, and music and drama. In addition, there are several graduate-only colleges such as law and medicine. The original College of Arts and Sciences remains the University's largest, with twenty-three academic departments and programs ranging from Anthropology to Women's Studies. One of the college's most important functions is to serve as the site where students in the professional colleges take their required liberal arts and general education distribution courses. With a unionized faculty, the University has undergone bitter labor disputes in recent years; several faculty strikes have taken place over issues of money and governance, as serious cuts in higher education at the state level reduced the budget, eliminating some programs and shrinking the rest (except for intercollegiate sports). Few new full-time faculty have been hired in this decade, as the University has increased its reliance on part-time instructors. Though clearly second fiddle to Ohio State, the University of Cincinnati strives to maintain a national profile as a research university. It is one of eighty-eight designated Research One universities nationally, according to the most recent Carnegie Report, based on scholarly productivity, library holdings, grant funding, and graduate-student placement, and boasts the eleventh largest endowment of any public university in the country.

But the University's greatest strength and most important priority, according to the administration, remains undergraduate education, in particular the professional colleges. And the greatest strength of its professional colleges is the University's program in cooperative education, which attracts many of the best undergraduates. UC was the first college in the country to develop a program of cooperative education almost a hundred years ago, and it still has the nation's largest. Under this program, students in the professional colleges, after their first year, take full-time, off-campus positions with companies in their fields, alternating between work and study. Students work off-campus every other academic quarter until graduation, at which time many new graduates are hired permanently by the companies they worked with while students. These co-op positions place students in numerous foreign countries and practically every state of the union. They provide opportunities for significant professional experience and income prior to graduation, and are a major reason why students from outside the Cincinnati area, and outside Ohio (including international students), about 40 percent of the total undergraduate population, choose to attend the University. These students in the University's top professional colleges include most of the undergraduates with the best academic records from high school, and many cite the co-op program (as well as the relatively low cost of tuition) as strongly influencing their choice of college. The professional colleges with the most competitive admissions are Engineering, DAAP (Design, Architecture, Art, and Planning), and CCM (the College Conservatory of Music).

Thus, for many undergraduates, especially the academically stronger ones who gain admission to the more competitive colleges, the main attraction of UC remains the opportunity it offers for focused professional development and on-the-job training in the student's area of specialization. Most students enter the University with a major, a curriculum, and sometimes even an idea about where they might like to co-op already picked out. As will be seen in later chapters, many of these students, even in the freshman year, are clear about *not* wanting a broad-based liberal education, preferring the more pragmatic and marketable, professionally oriented programs of study. This pre-professional emphasis affects virtually every aspect of undergraduate education, including the first-year college writing program. For some students, such as string players in the College Conservatory of Music, the first-year writing sequence is the only set of classes outside their college that they are required to take. As at many state schools, a high percentage of UC students have jobs. The Office of Student Affairs estimates that well over half of the undergraduates work at least ten hours a week, with many working forty hours or more. According to the Office, first-year students work as much as more advanced undergraduates. A general education program has been in development for a number of years, a long, at times heated process of planning and negotiation, and has been accepted by some but not all of the professional colleges. This program requires students to take core courses in the arts, humanities, social sciences, and sciences. Thanks largely to the efforts of composition and Writing-Across-the-Curriculum specialists on the faculty, general education courses involve a significant writing component. Resistance to this initiative continues to come from the pre-professional colleges, which have traditionally offered a much more specialized curriculum. And it is in this context of a school with a liberal arts mission in some ways overshadowed by and in conflict with its pre-professional mission that the first-year writing program can best be understood.

Operating as part of the English Department, the program consists of a year-long sequence of writing courses, is the only set of classes required of every baccalaureate student in the University, and is therefore the largest program of its kind on campus. It is in many ways a standard, large-scale college composition program, with about 2,500 students per quarter enrolling in first-year writing courses. Indeed, the English Department offers more first-year composition courses than all other types of courses combined, including literature, linguistics, journalism, professional writing, and creative writing, at both the undergraduate and graduate levels. As a large program, it is heavily administered by university standards, with two full-time faculty members serving as director and associate director, and an advanced graduate student working as their assistant. The directors work to develop curriculum, devise and coordinate ways of evaluating student writing programwide (currently a portfolio assessment), hire new instructors, train new graduate teaching assistants, conduct ongoing workshops with instructors, choose textbooks, teach graduate seminars, make up the teaching schedules, work to improve job conditions for instructors, communicate with the rest of the university, and handle the steady stream of issues and problems that need to be dealt with on a regular basis. The first-year writing courses are staffed by a combination of adjunct instructors (about 65 percent of the faculty), graduate teaching assistants (about 25 percent), and full-time faculty (about 10 percent). Since this study was completed, the university administration has agreed to the department's proposal to upgrade positions for composition instructors, with new positions offering better pay, full benefits, and long-term contracts. A committee consisting of composition teachers as well as the program directors makes policy decisions for the program, along with the occasional interest and advisement of the full-time English faculty as a whole. The program sponsors an annual essay contest and publishes a collection of essays written by first-year students which is used in classes.

The program has benefited from the attention of the composition scholars and teachers who have helped to shape it over the years. Past directors include James Berlin, Joseph Comprone, Patrick Hartwell, Marjorie Roemer, and Lucille Schultz. I directed the program from 1993 to 1998, having inherited a curriculum developed primarily by Schultz and Roemer. The first-year writing curriculum has evolved from its original literary orientation of genre classes, one quarter each of poetry, fiction, and drama, to its current critical literacy focus grounded in contemporary composition theory and scholarship. This focus, and the program as a whole, are described in detail in a document written initially by a committee overseen by Schultz and Roemer but revised and expanded over the years. The program's overarching purpose, as described in the mission statement, "is to empower students to become confident and responsible writers, both in college and beyond" (1993). More specifically, the mission statement lists as goals, "to teach students that writing is a way of thinking and that in the very act of writing about a particular subject for a particular audience, the writer will discover new knowledge," "to let students know that writing is something they can learn to do and that frequent writing is one of the best ways to become a successful writer," and "to show students that writing and reading are interrelated."

The program attempts to accomplish these rather lofty goals over three ten-week quarters, only two of which are required of all students. There is a standard curriculum that has taken years to develop and that is always evolving. While some may see a standard curriculum as authoritarian, the directors (of whom I was one) have justified it as the theory-based product of long, careful thought and planning by professionals who have devoted their lives to the teaching of writing and as particularly useful in introducing the large number of new teaching assistants to theoretically-grounded notions of pedagogy. The directors also see the standard curriculum as flexible, open to new ideas and input from all who teach in the program, and therefore continually in process. Beginning instructors are asked to stay within the parameters of the curriculum, while experienced teachers have more flexibility in that regard and may teach in the way that is most comfortable for them as long as they do not depart from the overall goals, course framework, and curricular sequence laid out in the mission statement. While an overarching conception of the uses of writing and the role of writing in a university education ties the sequence together, the three courses are very distinct in terms of their goals and the theories which underlie each.

The first course in the sequence owes much to the dictum that, as composition teachers, we should "start where the students are." It attempts to help students who enter with "one-draft" notions of writing to develop a more complex, flexible, and expanded composing process as well as a more sophisticated sense of audience and purpose, and a larger personal stake and presence in their writing. There is an emphasis upon prewriting and revising, with invention and multiple-drafting built into every writing assignment, and with students encouraged to keep a journal as a way of getting more comfortable with the act of writing and developing ideas for essays. The course curriculum also draws upon the "abstractive scale" notion of James Moffett (1968), later adapted as a research tool for categorizing student writing by James Britton (1975) and his colleagues (T. Burgess, N. Martin, A. McLeod,& H. Rosen) in the United Kingdom. This curricular approach moves from narrative and summary writing to analysis, argument, and theory, from self-examination to investigation of a wider frame of reference. In an attempt to allow students to begin their college composition instruction writing with authority and confidence, the first course focuses primarily on writing from personal experience and knowledge. The primary texts for the class at the time of the study were thus students' own writings, supplemented by a book of some of the best essays from past first-year writing students and by a limited number of essays from published authors. The course made use of a textbook, *The Concise Guide to Writing* (1993) by Axelrod and Cooper, the book on the market which most fits the theoretical underpinnings of the course in its assignment units, containing a wealth of in-process activities, clear explanations, and sample essays by students and professional writers. It was also one of the least expensive books on the market, and its small size fit well the ten-week format.

The course (English 101) consisted of five major writing assignments, with approximately two weeks devoted to each, though students were encouraged throughout to revise previous essays. The writing began at a personal level, with the first assignment to write an essay relating a significant event in the student's life and explain its importance. The second assignment was to explain a concept the student knew something about and was interested in. The third assignment was to discuss a problem, preferably one that the student him- or herself had some experience with, rather than a complex and distant world event, and to propose some possible solutions to the problem, while also considering the limitations of possible solutions. The fourth essay asked students to construct an argument concerning an issue they cared about. And the final essay was a profile, based on field research, of a person, organization, place, or activity they found interesting. While these were obviously not totally self-selected topics, students had quite a bit of choice within the overall framework of the assignment. More in keeping with the envi-

ronmental approach of Hillocks (1995), these assignments asked students
to do particular kinds of thinking and writing, and to become progres-
sively more analytic in their approach. Throughout the course, there was
a programwide portfolio evaluation of student essays, with students
choosing their best work at mid-quarter and again at the end of the quarter for pass-fail assessment by another teacher in the program. Teachers
worked in trios evaluating the writing of each others' students, and in
cases of disagreement, sent the student writing to a third reader; they
negotiated the pass-fail status of particular disputed portfolios. Students
whose portfolios were failed by two readers, their own teacher and another, were asked to retake the course, though they received a non-pu-
nitive grade of N which did not count against them in their grade point
average. About ten percent of students were typically asked to retake
101.

Most students thus moved immediately into the following course,
English 102, which shifts the focus from writing about primarily personal
experience and knowledge to reading and writing about larger cultural
and political issues that help to shape contemporary thought. There was
also a research-writing component in this course. The course was based
on a cultural studies and critical pedagogy framework applied to composition, drawing upon the work of Giroux (1983, 1988), Harkin (1991),
McLaren (1994), and other politically and socially oriented perspectives.
Emphasis in the class was on self-reflection, critical analysis of one's own
positions and those of others, and development of increased understanding of the rhetorical and political power of texts not just to communicate but to shape thought. However, the 102 curriculum made every effort to retain the personal investment and orientation of the previous
course, while placing the personal in a larger cultural and political context and thus moving students toward issues about which they are often less knowledgeable and less interested than they were about the
subject matter they chose in 101. There was a strong tendency for students to want to shift into the depersonalized expository and argumentative modes they seemed to be more familiar with from their high school
writing, and which used to characterize the 102 curriculum as well, never
employing the first person and drawing primarily, and often uncritically,
on the content of their readings.

The focus in 102 at the time of the study was on constructing arguments and interpretations on issues of larger interest (though not always
of student interest) based on critical reading and analytic reasoning. Students were asked to locate themselves and their own positions through
a process of reading about issues, reflecting, discussing them in class,
and writing about them. They learned how to work with texts in differ-

ent ways, as material for agreement or disagreement, as opportunities for exploration and consideration of their own understandings and subjectivities. The emphasis was thus on interpretation and on consideration of a range of possible ways of thinking, rather than on the development of pro/con arguments. The intention was to help move students beyond consideration of their own immediate situations and black-white understanding of issues to more complex, sophisticated, multi-perspectival ways of thinking and writing. Accordingly, in the research component, students were asked to pick a subject of personal interest and to investigate it in a larger context through library investigation of many types of relevant readings, interviews and other types of field work, observation, and reflection. The course thus challenged students to examine more carefully their own closely but often uncritically held beliefs, not so much to change students' opinions and not to radicalize them, but rather to help them become more aware of the nature and sources of their own beliefs and the existence of other perspectives.

Consistent with this emphasis on self-reflection and location in a social context, the recommended textbook for the course at the time of this research was *Rereading America*, by Colombo, Cullen, and Lisle (1992), which offers readings that attempt to go against the prevailing, commonplace views, or cultural myths, as it terms them, on such subjects as the American dream and notions of success, racial and ethnic difference, the media in our society, gender roles, the family, and the educational system. Students often complained that the book bullied them into adopting left-wing positions that conflict with the more conservative views held by the majority of students. Yet instructors were asked to be careful not to use the book or their own views, and their authority in the classroom, in pushing a particular ideological agenda. Rather, they were asked to use instances of disagreement as opportunities for consideration of the sources of and intellectual bases of differing views. The course consisted of four major writing assignments, each pegged to a particular unit in the textbook. While experienced instructors could choose different units and develop writing assignments accordingly, the standard syllabus asked students to read and write about the nature of family structures, the issue of money and success as reflected in the American dream, and aspects of prejudice, discrimination, and group membership. For the research writing unit, which was given twice as much class time and twice as much weight in the course grade as other units, students were asked to pick a topic from the book not covered in class and to find an area of personal interest within that topic, then to research that topic in the ways described above. They were asked to find ways of bringing themselves and their own interests, opinions, and understandings into the research, rather than uncritically stringing together a series of quotes from experts without laying their own interpretive framework onto the material.

The third and final course of the sequence focused on writing in response to literature. The course, rooted in the reader-response theories of Bleich (1978), Fish (1980), and Iser (1989), attempted to begin with the individual student's response and then to move toward an examination of larger cultural influences on readers' understandings of literary texts. There was also a multicultural component in the selection of readings and in the nature of writing activities, with students exposed to readings from a variety of different cultures. The sequence as a whole was intended to be transformative in helping students make the move from high school to college not just in their ways of writing but in their overall approaches to education. It emphasized active, critical learning, in opposition to the more passive, non-participatory amassing of information in the lecture hall environment characterizing much of the college curriculum of the large university. In the words of the program's mission statement:

> Because the sequence stands as the students' initiation into the discourses of the academic community (and because it is one of the few small classes that undergraduates have at the start of their studies), certain features of this course are crucial. It is a class that must involve active participation; the processes of critical thinking, reading, and writing must be experienced, exposed, and critiqued, and this struggle must be the business of the course. Community is also central here. Students need to see that culture in general, and texts in particular, are made and shaped by people and by various voices in conversation. This give and take and active shaping by dialogue is central to the way we understand the writing process and its place in the world of work and thought.

The Research Participants: Teacher and Students

Official documents such as this mission statement speak with an authoritative voice of the overall goals and underlying purposes of the first-year writing program. Yet the people teaching in the program, while no doubt influenced to some extent by official statements and ways of thinking, are also individuals with their own understandings about the nature of writing and its role in a college education, their own ideas about teaching, and their own styles of interacting with students. For this research, I looked at two exemplary teachers in the program who also represented rather different approaches and orientations while working within the basic parameters of the program. I chose to study exemplary teachers because I did not want to enter the class as an administrative evaluator judging the quality of instruction, but rather as a colleague looking at patterns of interaction. I also wanted to work with teachers who were very interested in teaching, who wanted to examine their own teaching more closely, and who would have enough confidence and interest not to mind too much having an outside observer present to help with that examination, particularly one who was also the program director. Another reason I chose to work with individuals whom I and others considered to be strong teachers was because, quite frankly, it is a great pleasure and a source of much fascination to observe and analyze talented teachers at work. The teacher whose work I focus most closely on is Sherry Cook Stanforth, a doctoral student interested in critical theory, feminism, composition studies, and creative writing, all of which interests find their way into her teaching.

Sherry Cook Stanforth is a graduate student and composition teacher with many interests and talents. In a doctoral program where specialization is the norm, one might call her "a bit all over the map" because her interests are so varied. But she has found considerable success in diverse areas. While still preparing for her preliminary examinations, she had already published a short story in a respected literary journal, a scholarly article on multiethnic literature in an MLA periodical, and a co-authored chapter in a collection of essays on composition research published by NCTE. She had given a paper on grief narratives at an international conference in Paris that was under review by an international folklore journal. She had also co-directed a film on approaches to teaching while working as a graduate assistant for the writing-across-the-curriculum program at our university. Outside of school she was an accomplished Appalachian folk musician, singing, playing flute, harmonica, and penny whistle, and performing in a band with members of her family. Along with the rest of the band, she had just completed a compact disk of their music. Despite these many interests, she was a particularly focused teacher. She put in long hours of preparation time for her teaching, while at the same time taking a full schedule of graduate classes herself. In her spare time, she and her husband, an equally busy medical student just beginning his residency, enjoyed hiking, playing tennis, and rollerblading. Sherry was considered by the faculty to be one of the finest doctoral students in the department. As a teacher, she had consistently strong evaluations and was highly respected by her peers for the classroom activities and exercises she designed and freely shared. She was beginning to write a dissertation in composition studies and planning to become a professor of composition, a goal which I encouraged her to pursue. I had taught Sherry in two graduate courses and supervised her teaching for several years, finding her to be an independent-minded, confident, creative teacher and scholar who was not afraid to speak her mind and who followed her own convictions in the classroom. For all of these reasons, she seemed an ideal teacher for me to work with in this study.

In her own composition teaching, Sherry emphasized critical engagement and creativity. She wanted to challenge students to move beyond unreflective acceptance of commonplace notions. But at the same time, she wished to provide an enjoyable and engaging classroom atmosphere, in her words "to invite first year students rather than bully them with a 'you're in the academy now' ethos." She wanted the class to focus on exploration and experiment, risk-taking, rather than on finding correct answers, learning proper formats, and keeping safe. Her teaching goals were to help students

> explore relationships with literacy, with their own reading and writing processes. While helping them develop a pre-writing habit, I strongly emphasized invention. I have become increasingly convinced that this is a critical part of literacy most students have not been taught to value or explore. I also tried to help students become aware of their own subjectivity, competing authorities, and some of the complexities involved in taking a 'creative' approach to an assignment.

While recognizing a legitimate role for correctness in writing, she tried to move students away from what she saw as an overconcern with surface features:

> I wanted my students to leave 101 understanding correct (standard English) grammar as a tool which would lend them authority with many audiences, especially academic audiences . . . . But, because I did not want students to fixate on surface 'correctness' as the end-all of writing, I directed most of my emphases, in grading and in discussions, on content. Students in 101 are still experimenting with the amount of energy it takes to write an effective piece; if that energy was being distributed by writers in a limited resource fashion, I wanted them to direct most of it toward critical thought and development of ideas.

Another emphasis in Sherry's teaching was to help students make connections between their academic work and other parts of their lives. Out of a belief that students engaged much more deeply in a school task when it sparked a personal interest, and out of her own experience as a student from a strong Appalachian background alien in some ways to the university culture—sensitive to students in a similar position—she wanted students to find "some common ground between 'home' cultures and academic cultures. I think my concern for this particular relationship influences my teaching style significantly. I attempt to utilize connections between orality and literacy as much as possible." On the whole, she had an ambitious vision of the first-year writing class, one informed by extensive reading in composition, rhetoric, literature, and critical theory; by her own commitment to writing; and by her belief in the power of education. I sat in on her classes over two quarters, during which time we talked regularly about what she was doing and how students were responding to it.

In addition to working closely with Sherry, sitting in on classes and debriefing regularly, I also regularly met with and interviewed four of her students over two quarters of writing instruction. While I examined the writing of every student in the class, and talked informally with many over the course of the study, I focused in greater depth on the particular experiences of these four students. In choosing case-study participants, I wanted to get to know the range of students we see in first-year writing classes at UC: male and female; strong, average, and weak writers; students from privileged, middle-class, working-class, and poor backgrounds; and people from diverse ethnic backgrounds—as much as possible, given the rather homogenous student body. I wanted to work with students who represented typical kinds of problems or conflicts with teachers that are found in the composition classes, such as students who resist process; students who like narrative but resist analysis and argument; students whose writing skills, in terms of standard notions of organization, development, and surface conventions, are weaker than average; and students with better developed skills who try to "coast" without challenging themselves to develop new strengths. I also wanted to work with successful, engaged writers who did not seem to resist the pedagogy. Based on these interests, and on my initial observations of students during class, I asked a number of students if they would participate as case-study students in my research, meeting with me to talk about each paper they would write for the class and about other issues arising from the class. Most agreed, and I was able to work closely with a total of four students. To encourage candor, I promised the students that what they told me would be confidential until the research was written up. In addition, I told students I would be willing to help them with their own writing, not just as an inducement for them to participate, but also to give them something in return for their participation. So, with most of the students, in addition to interviewing them as a researcher, after the interview part of our meeting I used my experience as a composition teacher and writing center tutor, on occasion, to help them generate ideas, develop, and revise their papers. These case-study students, who, along with Sherry, form the primary subject matter of Chapters 4 through 7 of this book, are introduced below. All students' names are pseudonyms.

Cris

Outspoken, with shoulder-length hair of an orange-ish hue, bright lipstick, a taste for 60s fashions, and a quick wit, Cris established herself on the second day of class as a possible case-study student. During the first classroom activity, in which the mainly self-conscious students in the circle tersely introduced themselves, Cris interrupted the pattern of a diffident identification of name and intended major, often accompanied by blushing, mumbling, and looking down at the desktop. She boldly proclaimed herself both a feminist and a writer, said she had already completed sixty pages of a book "about men, what they're like, what creeps they can be, based on my many personal experiences over the years," and pointedly did not mention her intended major. Her comments clearly unsettled some of the male students in the class, not the last time that that would happen during the quarter. Here was a student who clearly enjoyed writing, liked talking about issues and about herself, and had some provocative ideas as well.

What I learned about Cris after she agreed to be a case-study student was no less interesting than what she had told the rest of the class. Brought up in a large industrial city near the East Coast, Cris had experienced a very difficult life. Her father died of a work-related injury when she was twelve, and her two older siblings, though according to Cris very intelligent, had dropped out of a tough urban high school while her mother struggled to support the family. She had graduated from that same high school. Cris had been sexually assaulted by an acquaintance in her early teens, an incident that still troubled her a great deal and that she chose to write about for two of the course papers. She had come to UC because her boyfriend, about five years older, was working as a chef in town, and because her best friend from high school was at UC studying design. Cris had also wanted to study design, but was not admitted to that highly selective program, yet she had decided to come to UC anyway and to work toward a degree in art education instead. On a shoestring budget, she had scraped together tuition fees through loans, savings from past jobs, and some money from her family, and was living with her boyfriend to save on room and board. But she still needed a part-time job in a daycare center to make ends meet, and occasionally borrowed small sums of money from me or from classmates for busfare or lunch.

Besides art, writing was a major interest for Cris. She had been involved in a high school writing workshop and had published several pieces in its journal. Her favorite kinds of writing, the kinds she felt she did best, were "telling stories, sarcasm, and humor." She had taken two English classes in 12th grade, one on creative writing and one on literature, and gave the appearance of real confidence in herself as a writer. But she also worried about her grasp of fundamentals, saying she "wished they'd stressed grammar and punctuation more in high school." Moreover, though she was politically opinionated, and in class discussions seemed more sophisticated than most of her classmates about social issues, Cris had little expertise, and even less interest, in writing that involved the development of a more serious argument. She recalled writing only one such paper in high school, a major research project discussing similarities between the gods of Hindu and Greek mythology. Her writing preferences were quite evident in her course papers. When she could rely on lively narrative, description, and humor, as in essays about tattooing and about an offbeat coffeehouse, her papers were among the strongest in the class. But when she wrote two issue-oriented essays about date rape, a subject which she was uncomfortably close to, the writing was much less fully developed.

Joshua

Conspicuous for his southern accent and almost courtly way of participating in class discussion, Joshua was a student in the selective College of Engineering, who enjoyed using language in both speaking and writing. He came from a fairly affluent suburb, and his father was a corporate executive who had "worked his way up." Wiry, of average height, with wavy, mid-length brown hair and sensitive blue eyes, he chose his words carefully and did not mind—in fact liked—using the occasional obscure word or expression, such as the archaism "whilst," which he told me he had found in a poem by Tennyson. But he said he employed unusual language not to impress others but to say what he wanted to say in his own preferred style. His classmates seemed to like and respect him, and to enjoy his writing, rather than finding him pedantic. However, the next year when one of Josh's essays was read and discussed in other classes, I recall one student finding the language pretentious, though this was not the impression he gave in class. On the one hand, Joshua was very bright, concerned about the plight of less fortunate people, and open to new ideas, but on the other hand, he was often very traditional in his attitudes, conservative in his politics, and religious almost in a fundamentalist sense. He enjoyed reading poetry and novels, liked studying math and science, and took pleasure in learning about nature and history. His writings and class comments revealed that he was sensitive about issues of gender and race, he spoke thoughtfully about poverty in the developing world, and—very unusual among undergraduates these days, it seems—he said he was not interested in making a lot of money, but rather considered it more important to be a good father and husband and to serve the community. At the same time, he could espouse much more conservative views about male superiority and government waste, and even claimed to have written a paper in high school "disproving evolution" and supporting the creationist view. Outside of school, he was an avid mountain bicyclist, not only riding whenever possible but also belonging to a biking organization, subscribing to related magazines, and working as a repair and sales person in a bicycle shop.

As a writer, Joshua was relatively highly skilled and deeply engaged, particularly when writing about a topic he felt close to. He maintained a high level of engagement in English 101 by writing almost exclusively about issues related to mountain biking for his course papers, turning the subject into a quarterly theme tying his work together. For his end of term portfolio, he even supplied photos of mountain biking to go with his essays. Throughout the quarter, Sherry, his teacher, wondered if she should encourage him to change topics and take on some different challenges with new material, but she ultimately chose to let him stay with his chosen subject of interest and was pleased with the result. However, the following quarter, when it was no longer possible for him to work biking into his essays, Joshua, while still successful, had a harder time finding the same high level of engagement and accomplishment he had achieved in his earlier work.

Louise

A returning student in her 30s, married with three young children, Louise wanted to become a nurse and, because she had mainly taken vocational/clerical track courses back in high school, needed to do well in her first-year classes to gain admission to the College of Nursing. With short auburn hair and large eyes that seemed to register her feelings, she was direct and outspoken, like Cris, but politically conservative and religious, like Joshua. She described herself as coming from "the wrong side of the tracks" as a kid, but through hard work and education her family had become much more middle class. She also described herself as "set in her ways," particularly in religious and moral matters, was suspicious of the "liberal views" that seemed to her so prevalent on campus (and, it seemed, particularly in her English class), and had an "I want to get on with my work here, so just tell me what to do" attitude toward her assignments.

Some years earlier, her husband had come back to school for a two-year associate's degree in a technical field, studying nights while working full-time over four years to complete his program, which allowed him to qualify for promotion at work. Now, according to their plan, with the children all in school, it was Louise's turn to study. But from the beginning she had to struggle hard to stay afloat academically while retaining most of her responsibilities at home. She had a very limited background in school writing, had done little reading or writing since graduating from high school about fifteen years earlier, spoke somewhat nonstandard English, and was very busy with her life outside of school. All of these factors made it difficult for her to keep up with her work in first-year writing. But at the same time, Louise was goal-oriented, fiercely determined, and hard-working. She became convinced that Sherry's standards were unreasonably high when her first paper, an account of meeting her husband when both were in high school, got a highly critical evaluation. Yet, though angry, she reacted not by complaining or giving up but by redoubling her efforts and scheduling regular appointments both with Sherry and at the Writing Center. As a result, she essentially brought herself up to the level of the good, solid writers. In class, she could be rebellious, frequently spoke her mind, and often took a leadership role in expressing conservative views during discussions, especially in English 102. She remembered being less than enthusiastic when her husband had returned to school and it had been difficult to keep their long-term goals in mind.

> I was not supportive at all. I hated it! I was pregnant. He was working swing shift, a different shift every week. He was going to school three nights a week. We never saw each other. We didn't have any money, and it was just rough. But now it's worth it; it's paid off in the long run.

Now she herself was experiencing the difficulties of being a student, while taking care of three children and running a household, and, in writing class, she was having to overcome some of the limitations imposed on her by a weak academic background. At the same time, she brought to her work a maturity, clear goals (which were somewhat in conflict with the goals of the course), and life experiences beyond those of the typical first-year student that would provide powerful subject matter for her essays in the composition courses. She battled on and off with Sherry throughout the two quarters, but the two eventually developed a grudging respect and affection for one another. One of Louise's favorite leisure time activities was country line dancing—she wrote her "author of the day" piece about it and even invited Sherry to attend a session with her—and the two have kept in touch since the class. Sherry said recently of Louise,

I still feel proud of her for the effort she put into making progress with her writing. She managed to hang tough through both quarters out of sheer determination and by putting in what I suspect to be decidedly more effort into the course. Her written work didn't stand out or surprise me too often, but her commitment did. Even while she periodically dominated discussions, Louise lent the class a certain contagious enthusiasm, and sometimes, she engaged peers in challenging discussion without my prompting.

Rachel

According to the demographic profile of the University's freshman class, she was the most typical of the case-study students from Sherry's class. Rachel was a recent graduate of a parochial school for girls in Cincinnati, majoring in nursing with the goal of becoming an obstetrical nurse. Both her parents were trained as nurses, and her father worked at a local hospital. With short blonde hair and rosy cheeks, Rachel was rather tall and big-boned. She approached the first-year writing class with more than the usual amount of trepidation. While accustomed to writing rhyming poems in her free time about personal aspects of her life, which she tended not to share with others, Rachel did not like the reading or writing associated with English classes and rarely read on her own. She preferred math and science classes, in which she typically got B's and A's, saying she had been a C student in English and only an average writer in high school. The year before, her sister had been a first-year nursing student at the University and had almost failed the first quarter composition course, a fact which contributed to Rachel's anxieties. In addition to her studies, she had a part-time job at a local amusement park that consumed ten to twenty hours a week of her time.

Overall, Rachel had been a hard-working and successful student in high school, in honors classes for every subject except English. But she was determined to do well in her college English classes. She listened carefully to Sherry's advice about writing, and more than any of the other case-study students, she followed directions closely about the importance of prewriting and revising, taking to heart the pedagogy. She volunteered whenever possible to have other students in class critique her writing and give her feedback. She also participated earnestly in class discussions and activities. Even when others occasionally joked around and undermined the seriousness of an activity, as in a role-play discussion about teen pregnancy that will be considered at length in Chapter 4, Rachel tended to stay focused and sincere. She admitted being resistant to moving away from the comfortable narrative of her first paper, which was about the time a snake crawled into her sleeping bag during a family camping trip. She was hesitant about the move toward analysis and exposition in her following papers, which were on such topics as multiple personality disorder, procrastination, and the inevitable euthanasia. Yet she dutifully did what she was told and ended up faring better in the course than she had expected.

Data Collection and Analysis Procedures

I began this two-year qualitative study in my first year as Director of the Composition Program. At the outset, my broad-range goals for the study were twofold, reflecting my dual and somewhat conflicting roles as both researcher and program director. As a researcher, I wanted to examine the nature of students' resistance to writing instruction, which I saw as an interesting and quite pervasive phenomenon, not just in our program but in other programs I had worked in, limiting the effectiveness of the composition sequence. I wanted to see in what ways that resistance was related to our particular curriculum and to investigate how teachers worked with and tried to overcome and/or make use of student resistance. As a program director, I wanted to find ways of improving the curriculum by better understanding how teachers and students negotiated it, that is, how the curriculum was realized in actual classes.

I began the study upon taking over as Director of the Composition Program, after having spent the previous year as Associate Director. For the five years before that, I had worked as Director of the Writing Center, which offered tutoring help and was closely aligned with, but not exactly a part of, the composition program, though over half the students who used the center were taking first-year composition courses. I had never set out to direct a large writing program, had indeed not been attracted to the position in light of the well-known difficulties of adequately funding, staffing, and coordinating such a program. But having observed the workings of the program, as well as participating in developing curriculum and helping to train new teaching assistants, I had become more interested in directing the program. Moreover, there was no other obvious candidate for the position in the English Department, and I felt an obligation to do my share. But I knew that I would be most interested in directing if at the same time I could examine the workings of the program by doing research on it. I also felt such work would ultimately help strengthen the program.

In part, then, my desire to study intensively what was going on in writing classes was motivated by my interest as an administrator in keeping the program strong and in further strengthening it. In this sense, I wanted to do some up-close and personal program evaluation, in addition to the ongoing larger-scale forms of evaluation that had been carried out for some time. My sense from working with this curriculum in my own classes and from frequently observing other classes was that, while teachers generally liked it to varying degrees, or at least professed to liking it, many students were less enthusiastic, though in general they dutifully did what was asked of them. Indeed, while fulfilling course requirements, many students seemed to resist the program's most basic premises, which were intended to encourage critical thought, analysis, interpretation, use of an extensive writing process involving invention and multiple revision, and of a thoughtful, reflective approach to the reading of complex texts. I wanted to look more closely at that resistance, to see ways in which it may have functioned, in Giroux's (1983) sense, as a productive move, an attempt to accomplish something in a mindful way rather than as just an attempt to avoid doing something else.

I also knew, from previous research, such as Langer and Applebee's 1987 study of writing and learning in secondary school content areas, and from my own observations of composition teachers over the years, that an "official" curriculum changes significantly depending on the approaches and understandings of the teacher enacting the curriculum. Moreover, I sensed that students' approaches and orientations—the ways in which they were or were not prepared or inclined to work—also deeply affected the nature of curriculum in the classroom by leading instructors to modify their initial plans for teaching. Thus, in carrying out the study, I wanted to observe other classes in the program, rather than focusing on my own teaching; that is, I wanted to investigate other teaching approaches working with the same material. While not its primary architect, I had had a hand in developing the curriculum, and therefore I wanted to see how the courses worked when taught by teachers who had not helped to create the curriculum and who might have very different approaches to teaching. Teachers in our program, after the first year, were allowed to choose their own textbooks and develop their own assignments, but most chose to stay with the "standard" curriculum, and I was very interested to see how this curriculum was interpreted by those teachers who had not had a hand in shaping it initially. If I were to continue developing curriculum, I wanted, indeed felt I needed, to have a better sense of what was happening to that curriculum as it spread throughout the program, what sense teachers and students were making of it, what changes it was undergoing, and how these changes affected student learning. Through my regular classroom observations of teachers, I achieved some of this understanding, but to go more in-depth,

I wanted to study a particular teacher or teachers more intensively, and not for the formal evaluative purposes of my usual observations.

What I had in mind for this study was not merely program evaluation in this fairly traditional though important sense. I also wanted to explore questions of broader concern in the field of composition studies, questions regarding the ways in which teachers of first-year college composition help students develop critical, analytic writing abilities in a class governed by principles of critical literacy, including the awareness of writing as embedded in political and cultural concerns. As I discussed in the previous chapter, my sense over the years—as a teacher, a researcher, and an administrator—was that the sort of writing we stressed in the classroom went against the grain for many students, that there was a certain amount of resistance to the intellectual demands, and the political and cultural context in which those demands rested, which we tried to place upon students in our writing courses. I wanted to see if this resistance was indeed taking place among students, what it consisted of, how teachers attempted to overcome or otherwise work with it, and how students reacted to teachers' efforts. Stated in political terms, as I was aware that the majority of students appeared to be fairly or very conservative, I wanted to see how they responded to a curriculum that was more liberal or even radical, that encouraged questioning of established ideas and beliefs.

Moreover, I had noticed over the years that students from wealthier backgrounds, who had been to strong private or suburban secondary schools, tended to outperform the students from less exclusive inner-city or rural schools. Our program worked with students from a great variety of academic backgrounds, since the different colleges in which students were enrolled had very different admissions standards. There was clearly a high correlation between academic success and class background, at UC as well as nationally and even internationally, as Bourdieu (1974) has argued, and I wanted to investigate the influence of class background on student performance. Such effects are obviously variable, with excellent as well as weak students coming from all backgrounds. But in general, students from higher socioeconomic class backgrounds seemed to be better prepared for the work required of them in the first-year writing class, and I wanted to see how teachers were able to work with students who had been less well prepared. Moreover, I was interested in seeing how students from a variety of class backgrounds interacted in the classroom, whether or not class-related tensions developed, and how such conflicts affected individual students and the class as a whole. All of these questions helped to shape the design of this study.

Data Gathering

For two academic years, I sat in on first-year writing sections over two quarters with permission from the teacher and students. During year one, I observed English 101 and 102 sections, in fall and winter quarter respectively, taught by an experienced adjunct instructor with a Ph.D in English literature from the department and experience as a journalist and business writer. I sat in on twenty 75-minutes sessions out of a total of forty. During year two, I observed English 101 and 102 sections taught by a theoretically sophisticated and politically aware doctoral student in English. I sat in on thirty-one 50-minute sessions out of a total of fifty-eight. In each case, I took detailed field notes of my classroom observations, recording as much as possible all that was happening in class. And I kept a reflective journal in which I attempted to interpret what I was viewing in class and to pull out salient themes for further analysis as well as evidence for or against the tentative interpretations I was beginning to form (Spradley, 1980, p. 71). After being introduced as the Director of the Program who was studying the effects of the curriculum on how students learn college writing, I asked for and received permission from students to sit in on and study the class. I tried to make my presence as inconspicuous and comfortable as possible for teacher and students, and for this reason did not audio- or videotape class sessions, but rather took handwritten notes. I requested permission to examine student writing and in-class comments, and only a few students declined to allow me to use their written work. When requesting volunteers to serve as case-study students for more intensive study, I offered to help or talk with any student who wanted assistance. I occasionally participated in class discussion and small group activities.

In addition to the classroom observations, I also conducted biweekly, audiotaped, semi-structured one-on-one interviews (Bogdan and Biklen, 1982, p. 136) with the teacher and with the case-study students, whom I had chosen to represent different socioeconomic backgrounds, academic interests, and relationships to literacy. To prepare for these interviews, I put together an interview schedule, a list of typed questions concerning the particular writing assignment or aspect of the course students were currently working on, but I departed from the protocol depending upon the drift of the conversation, relevant topics the interviewee wished to discuss, and interesting possibilities that presented themselves. My questions to the teacher generally concerned her understanding of course assignments and activities, her purposes in assigning the coursework, and her sense of how students were doing with the material. My questions to the students generally concerned their understandings of the material and why it was part of the class, their interpretations of what was happening in class, their approaches in carrying out coursework, and their attitudes to the work. I transcribed the taped interviews with both students and teachers for a total of 40 half-hour to one-hour interviews averaging eight typed pages each.

Additionally, I collected and photocopied all student writing and class handouts for analysis. My data therefore consist of extensive field notes from more than fifty class observations; over forty transcripts of interviews with case-study students and with teachers; curriculum statements, course descriptions, and other class handouts; the official program description, and nearly 500 student essays from over the two years of classroom instruction. My intention in collecting so much data was to allow for triangulation (Miles and Huberman, 1994), or cross-interpretation, of varied data sources as I attempted to draw meaning from these disparate materials: what teacher and students said in class, what they said in one-on-one discussion with me, what students wrote in their papers, what they wrote for other class assignments, and what course materials the teacher distributed throughout the quarter.

For this book, I have chosen to focus closely on only one of the two teachers and her composition students over two quarters of instruction. I chose to write mainly about Sherry Cook Stanforth and her students, with only a brief discussion of Nan Reitz's classes, because I wanted to look in as much depth as possible at a specific classroom situation. I also did so because Sherry's teaching most exemplified the critical literacy approach I wished to examine in the study. As much as possible throughout the book, I try to let Sherry, the case-study students, and the rest of the class speak in their own words from their writing, interviews, and class comments. Following the discussion in Chapters 4 through 6, which focus on her 101 and 102 classes, respectively, the book includes a response to my interpretation written by Sherry.

Because I was Director of the Program and one of the authors of the curriculum, I wanted to work in the classes of experienced, confident, and successful teachers who were also interested in the research and who would not mind so much my being in the class. Indeed, the teachers seemed interested in my presence and encouraged me to work with them. I saw the research as collaborative in this sense, with the possibility of exploring issues of teaching together with the teachers as the issues arose from the study. These were not classroom evaluations in the traditional sense. I wanted to see how these teachers adapted the curriculum to reflect their own diverse perspectives—the explicitly political, critical literacy classroom and the more traditionally liberal-humanist approach is how I initially contrasted them. And I wanted to be clear that I was not observing their classes in a supervisory capacity. The students in both teachers' classes were middle- and working-class freshmen, fairly homogeneous ethnically with few minority or international students. Like most students admitted to the University, they had mainly been solid students in high school, graduating with a B average or better. They were almost all just out of high schools in Ohio, with a scattering of students from out of state. All had enrolled at this large midwestern state university which emphasized pre-professional education. The case-study students I worked with represented a wide range of social class backgrounds, from first-generation college students from very poor families and inner-city schools to more privileged, middle-class students from strong suburban and private schools. I believe this focus on students from varying social class backgrounds is of particular importance because, while current composition theories stress the importance of empowering students from less privileged backgrounds, classroom approaches have often marginalized such students and kept them at a disadvantage.

Data Analysis

Gathering information from a variety of sources and perspectives allowed me to question and reflect carefully on my own evolving interpretations of the classes under scrutiny. After observing a class and hand writing extensive field notes, I typed the notes onto the computer within a day or two, adding commentary, questions, and expanded descriptions of the events and interactions observed while the memories were still fresh in my mind. If questions remained, for example, concerning the nature of comments made in class, I asked the students involved for clarification at the end of class or the beginning of the next class, or in a case-study interview, or I consulted with Sherry. In the field notes, I focused closely on the teacher and the case-study students, while attending as much as possible to the activities of the class as a whole.

Bi-weekly interviews with the case-study students served primarily as opportunities for students to talk with me about their understandings of and approaches to the essay assignments, and for me to check my own developing interpretations with the students. However, I also used the interviews to discuss what was happening in class, focusing, for example, on students' perceptions of the relationship between a particular class activity and the concurrent essay assignment. Or, I would ask for feedback about the usefulness or applicability of specific course handouts or reading assignments. Similarly, my interviews with the teacher centered upon her own intentions and approaches in classroom lessons and writing activities, frequently examining the ways in which her own teaching related to the "official" approach laid out in the program description and curriculum guide. After transcribing the audiotaped interview, I examined the transcription carefully and added bracketed annotations, summaries of my reactions to and interpretations of what had been said. Also, in reading through the transcripts, I high-lighted discussion that related most closely to my developing interest in goal conflicts, misunderstandings, and other sources of resistance between teacher and student. At the same time, I tried to look closely for counter-examples, instances in which the teacher and the students' intentions seemed to be compatible or reasonably close.

In examining student writing, I first read through the entire class set of essays, usually consisting of about twenty-five pieces. These were the "final" draft essays handed in for an evaluation, although students were encouraged to revise their writing after it had been evaluated. My analysis of class sets focused upon the topics chosen; the structures students employed in their writing; the analytic thinking evident, such as the uses of generalizations, supporting points, counter-arguments; and the ways in which students seemed to resist the assignment or to employ a substantially different approach than that suggested by the prompt. After reading and making notes on the entire class set, I would then focus on the writing of the case-study students. In most cases, I had already interviewed the student about the writing by this point. And for the case-study students, I examined not only the "final" draft but also earlier drafts and notes, in order to obtain a more comprehensive picture of how these students understood and approached the papers. I examined the type and extent of revisions undertaken in the evolution of the paper, and I considered carefully the nature of the critical thinking displayed in the paper. My analysis of the writing provided numerous questions which I could ask students and issues for further discussion during the regularly scheduled interviews.

At the end of the data-gathering process, I carefully studied all my sources of information in relation to one another in order to highlight what were emerging for me as the most important themes of the study. At this same time, I worked to crystallize, refine, and develop these themes as they related to issues of broader discussion in the field of composition studies. The deep-seated, almost fundamental resistance on the part of students to the critical literacy approach employed by their teacher was such a salient and constant finding, and seemed to be a relatively ignored phenomenon in the professional literature and theory, that I decided to focus primarily upon this issue for the book. Readers should keep in mind, however, that my interpretations have no doubt been strongly influenced by my perspective and responsibilities as Director of the Program and an architect of the curriculum. I have been careful throughout the study to generate, solicit, and keep in mind alternative understandings about the experiences, goals, and attitudes of Sherry and her students, and to let my research participants speak for themselves. However, my perceptions have filtered through my own beliefs as a composition specialist and an adherent of critical literacy concerned that many students seem to resist this approach and interested in finding out more about this resistance, yet at the same time eager to tap into the substantial energy, drive, and optimism that I believe students initially bring with them to the composition class. The remainder of the book details my findings and reflects upon their significance in understanding the nature of teaching and learning in a large state university's first-year composition program. The following chapter interprets students' first day of class essays describing themselves as writers and discussing their goals for the composition course.

3 The Enigma of Arrival

The title of this chapter comes from a painting by the Italian surrealist Giorgio de Chirico; it's also the title of a novel by V. S. Naipaul (1987). The painting depicts a port shrouded in darkness, the site of an ambiguous meeting between two shadowy figures. Naipaul describes the scene in his autobiographical novel:

> A wharf; in the background, beyond walls and gateways (like cutouts), there is the top of the mast of an antique vessel; on an otherwise deserted street in the foreground there are two figures, both muffled, one perhaps the person who has arrived, the other perhaps a native of the port. The scene is of desolation and mystery; it speaks of the mystery of arrival. (p. 99)

We generally think of opening day in a first-year college composition class as an exciting time, students arriving with new notebooks and pens, eager to please, anxious to succeed. And yet, when I saw a reproduction of the Chirico painting, and, again, when I read about the painting in Naipaul's novel, I immediately connected it with the beginning of fall term in composition. The painting's haunting and poetic title (in fact, the title was created not by the painter but by the surrealist poet Apollinaire) and its depiction of a vaguely foreboding situation resonated with my strong feeling that the composition class is shrouded in mystery for both students and teachers.

I argue in this chapter that beginning college students often come into composition with little idea of what will be expected of them, and, more important, with views about writing and notions of what they wish to gain from the class that are surprisingly different from—and in many ways seriously at odds with—those of their teachers. This basic incompatibility has been touched upon but not well-developed in the composition literature. For example, Brooke's study (1987) of "underlife" in the classroom revealed that surface cooperation on the part of students can mask a variety of oppositional attitudes and behaviors toward the "official" pedagogy. Similarly, discussions of student resistance to curriculum and class norms by Chase (1988), Giroux (1988), and Shor (1996) suggest that students motivated by feelings of disenfranchisement and alienation often try, subtly or not so subtly, to subvert or work around the goals of the teacher, and that such resistance can often be quite justifiable. Nelson's examination of students' often ingenious ways of avoiding extended critical thought in research-paper assignments demonstrates how a desire to save time and effort, and an interpretation of the assignment as one of summary rather than analysis, led students to short-circuit the "writing as learning" process envisioned by their instructor. And my own earlier investigation (1994) of beginning college students' approaches to writing theory-based essays revealed that many students, intimidated and confused by the complex demands of the assignment, sought and found ways to avoid engaging their subject matter theoretically. These studies all hint at a basic difference of approach between teacher and student. Yet I would suggest that such incompatibility is not an isolated instance but a fundamental feature of the college composition class, raising serious challenges to the work of both students and teachers.

This chapter provides another layer of empirical evidence for my argument about the mismatch between students' and teachers' ways of conceptualizing composition, and the effects of this mismatch on students' and teachers' work in the course. In the chapter, I examine beginning college students' writing through autobiographies completed on the first day of class, and contrast students' understandings, attitudes, and aspirations about writing with those embodied in their composition curriculum. The purpose of the chapter is to examine the mind-set of students as they enter first-year composition, taking into consideration that the data under scrutiny are timed, first-day essays for their instructor in which students may be trying as hard to construct the right kind of persona as they are to describe their writing practices and beliefs. I investigate students' constructions of themselves as writers and students of writing in the context of the written work and other intellectual activity that will be expected of them in the course. After briefly describing the writing curriculum's theoretical and pedagogical foundations, I will explain the context in which students wrote their autobiographies and the assumptions underlying my reading of them. In the following section, I will discuss the overall tone or mood of the essays, then move on to analyze the specific ways students discussed both their own writing and writing in a larger sense. Next, I will examine what students said they hoped to learn in first-year composition. Finally, I will contrast students' views with the goals of the composition curriculum.

The argument I wish to make from these opening-day essays, which I develop in later chapters through my interpretations of the student and teacher interviews, classroom observations, and student essays, is that, as teachers, curriculum designers, and theoreticians, despite our advocacy of student-centered pedagogies, we have not been sufficiently aware of students' attitudes and prior knowledge about writing, nor of how their attitudes and knowledge affect the way they approach composition instruction. Therefore, if we indeed wish to take students' concerns as seriously as we say we do, we would be well-advised to re-examine our own approaches.

The composition curriculum at the University of Cincinnati emphasizes what has come to be known as "critical literacy." While there is obviously a good deal of variation in the way this term is understood and in the kinds of curricula that have been set up in its name, primary features of a critical writing pedagogy are generally agreed upon. As Sullivan and Qualley describe this approach in the introduction to their book, *Pedagogy in the Age of Politics*, "teachers who once invited students to master or to transcend the strictures of written discourse now call upon students to participate critically in the discourses that shape their lives. Pedagogies that once aimed at self-actualization now aim at social transformation" (1994, p. ix). A critical approach to literacy thus emphasizes certain broad dispositions of mind, including reflectiveness about self, about one's wider society, and about one's roles in that society.

A critical literacy approach also stresses awareness and appreciation of group differences, multi-perspectival consideration of ideas, and the questioning of established ways of thinking. The postmodernist ideas that reality is socially constructed and truth rhetorically determined are fundamental assumptions of this pedagogy. In terms of actual writing and reading strategies, a critical literacy approach emphasizes rigorous development of ideas, the opportunity for feedback from a number of different sources, extensive invention and revision, and careful reading and re-reading of one's own texts and those of others. This pedagogy therefore combines complex and demanding aspects of academic, civic, and personal literacy with the aim, not just of improving students' abilities to communicate in writing, but of encouraging in students a reflective, questioning intelligence and a willingness to use that intelligence as fully participating members of a critical democracy. In brief, ambitious as they may seem, these are the overall goals of the first-year composition curriculum. In the pages that follow, I will demonstrate the ways in which entering students' assumptions about writing, and their aims for what they hope to learn in first-year college composition, appear strongly opposed to these curricular goals.

On the opening day of Sherry's 101 class in fall quarter, students receive a copy of the course description, go over what they will be doing for the next ten weeks, and find out about my presence in the class as a researcher who also happens to be the Director of the Writing Program.

But first, according to departmental policy, she asks students to write a brief essay "not for a grade, but to let me know a little about you as writers." She explains that if anyone's essay reveals serious problems in writing, they could be placed into a developmental section designed to meet their particular needs. But she reassures students that such a move is very rare because they should already have completed a placement essay during orientation, on the basis of which they were placed into her section. In any case, knowing her supportive attitude toward students, I strongly suspect she would be reluctant to move even a very basic writer out of her class unless that person particularly wanted to go. The essay assigned today is in two parts; it asks students, first, to describe themselves as writers and, next, to say what they hope to learn about writing in college composition. A group of students in Nan Reitz's 101 section also write a first-day essay on this same prompt, making a total of 48 responses.

I make no claims about the representativeness or generalizability of these essays to other groups of beginning college students around the country, though the descriptions and attitudes depicted are typical of entering students in the 1990s at this large, midwestern state university and seem not unlike those at similar schools as described by colleagues around the country. I will let others make their own judgments about the essays' typicality or applicability to their own situations. Moreover, as alluded to earlier, in interpreting the essays it is important to keep in mind the complex rhetorical situation in which students find themselves here. As Postman and Weingartner (1969) among others have argued, one of the most important lessons students learn in school is how to present themselves to various types of authority figures, particularly teachers, in as safe and positive a way as possible. We therefore cannot take students' comments about writing at face value as accurately and unambiguously reflecting their attitudes and experiences. Rather, such essays can be regarded as rhetorical constructions designed, at least in part, to make a favorable impression upon an as yet unknown teacher. Presumably, in their introductory writing, students want to appear serious, mature, and committed, confident but not cocky, knowledgeable but not know-all; to perhaps give a sense of themselves as individuals; and possibly most of all, not to be thrown back into a lower-level writing course. Quite likely, responses to the prompt would be framed differently, showing more cynicism and less deference toward the subject matter, were students seated around a table in the Student Union's Rhine Room, eating pizza and talking with friends.

Still, despite these important caveats, I believe, as David Bartholomae (1985) suggests in "Inventing the University," that students try to fulfill such assignments to the best of their abilities, as candidly as they can under the circumstances. I also believe that a careful analysis of the essays can reveal a good deal about these students' knowledge and attitudes about writing, its role in their schooling and in their lives generally, and what they hope to learn in the class, shedding light on the specific understandings and expectations students bring to college composition. Though a limited data source, these essays are valuable nonetheless in providing self-reported information about forty-eight students, far more than I could have interviewed. In addition, so as not to place undue or exclusive emphasis on what students wrote about themselves as writers in a pressurized, rhetorically complex, first-day-of-class situation, in the following chapter I will compare students' expressed attitudes and experiences to the case-study students' initial comments about writing, about learning, and about themselves as writers, which they made privately to me during interview sessions early in the school year.

Some of what I say here could possibly be interpreted as "bashing" students by presenting certain of their ideas in an unflattering light. In particular, I suggest among other things that a degree of what could be described as anti-intellectualism is evident in many students' comments, and that this attitude in its various manifestations conflicts fundamentally with the goals of the composition program. However, I can only say that it is not my intention here to disparage or complain about students. On the contrary, what I am trying to do is to better understand the students, to take students' ideas and aspirations seriously, to examine them closely, critically, and as sympathetically as possible in light of the curricular demands that we, as composition specialists, have set up for them. Throughout the book, I try to look just as closely and critically at the ideas and aspirations portrayed in the composition curriculum statement, notions that are widely endorsed throughout the field as a whole, and to consider how we might better accommodate students' more pragmatic goals in their composition classes. Thus, I discuss student writing here not as incriminating evidence of deficiencies but, in the words of Joseph Harris (1994), "as expressions of views that call for our serious consideration and response," with the larger purpose "to revise and contest some of the assumptions and pronouncements of theory" (p. 8).

The Students as Writers: Self-Critical Views

What views, then, do students express? A study by the Educational Testing Service (Lapointe, A.E., et al., 1989) of elementary and high school students' mathematics knowledge received a good deal of attention in the national press for a seemingly paradoxical finding (discussed in Jacoby, 1994). On the one hand, American students scored near the bottom on the exam itself. On the other hand, in a separate "attitude survey" that was part of the test, the American students reported *feeling better* about their math knowledge than students from any of the other countries, boldly but fatuously assuming their math skills were very strong, though their performance indeed suggested the opposite. This apparent confidence was seized upon by the press as a sign that schools are emphasizing "feel-good" values over tough academics.

Students' confidence was indeed surprising, partly in light of the difficulty of math in school and the lack of success many have with it, especially compared with other areas of study, including English. According to the National Center for Educational Statistics, for example, grades in math courses are consistently lower than grades in almost all other classes at all levels of schooling, including English and writing courses. Moreover, in school districts that do competency testing, failure rates on the math section of these exams are generally twice as high as those on the writing section. At my university, failure rates for the introductory calculus course required for many freshmen are much higher than those for first-year composition. In the context of such information about the greater difficulty of math in school as opposed to writing, and the corresponding knowledge that, in spite of this difficulty a national sample of students tended to feel very positive about their math abilities, it seems reasonable to suppose that students' views about their writing ability would also be, at the least, fairly positive. Remember, too, as was stated in the previous chapter, that we are focusing in this book on a group of successful students who, for the most part, carried a solid B-average or above in high school. However, at least for the forty-eight freshmen whose essays I read—eight of whom I talked to in greater depth as case-study students—such an assumption about their attitudes would be badly mistaken. As a group, with not many exceptions, the students appear unconfident and self-critical about their writing.

Let me elaborate on this point. A third of the students (sixteen of the forty-eight) portray their writing in an entirely negative light. Another third describe themselves in a rather negative way as mediocre or average writers; half of these students (one-sixth of the overall sample) have nothing at all positive to say about their writing, or about writing in general. The other half offer a more balanced picture, saying they are good at or enjoy some aspects or types of writing but bad or even very bad at others. Of the remaining third, about half (again, a sixth of the total group) do describe themselves as good or successful writers, or as people who like—in a couple of cases even love—to write. The others offer no assessment of their writing abilities, instead discussing in a nonevaluative way the types of writing they have done and/or the strategies they have used.

It is noteworthy that so many of these beginning college students sound so negative about their writing because the prompt did not actually ask them to assess their own abilities, only to describe themselves as writers. The negative tone is also surprising because one might expect students to present their writing more positively to their future evaluator. (The mechanics of doing so would, however, be rather complicated. A student believing him- or herself a weak writer might well feel unable to offer a positive self-assessment, because that assessment would have to be made *in writing*, thus possibly revealing the very weaknesses the student may wish to conceal.) Moreover, the institutional pressure bearing down on students as they begin college, the knowledge that they are now playing in a new and presumably tougher league, may work as an intimidation factor leading to more negative self-assessment, just as the bright lights of an interrogation may lead to a confession of guilt. That is, a student who proclaims him- or herself a confident, successful writer may be risking the teacher's close scrutiny. It is safer perhaps to claim a lack of skill. Then the teacher can either confirm the accuracy of the assessment or else judge the student as better than he or she thinks. But in any case, these student essays are detailed and direct; taken together, the displayed lack of confidence in the essays can make for rather depressing reading, though the self-appraisals, especially the negative ones, are in many cases also quite lively. As one representative student, Bob, writes:

> To describe my writing skills, it doesn't take many sentences. I'm sloppy, unfocused, and all over the place. I procrastinate till the night before, and rarely follow a straight line to tell my reader(s) what it is that I want to say . . .

Often going along with such self-assessments is the expression of a deep dislike for or fear of writing. Another student, Rita, begins by saying she's "always hated to write." Then, after describing one senior year paper she "thoroughly enjoyed writing and did an excellent job on," an argument in which she took the role of a prosecuting lawyer convincing a jury to send a man to the electric chair for murder, Rita reflects on her problems with writing:

> I don't know if I exactly "hate" to write because sometimes I come up with good ideas. It just looks so stupid when I put it on paper. I don't know if it's my lousy grammar, my terrible spelling, or just my ugly handwriting. But I have never liked my writing style. For instance, once I had to write a paper on my most valuable pocession.

> I decided to write about my family, how they are the most impor-
> tant people in my life. I thought it was a good idea at first, but when
> I got finished with the paper I hated it. It was long and drawn out
> with a ton of grammatic errors.

Indeed, a number of students pinpoint precisely this problem of having "a good idea" or even a great idea, on a topic of genuine interest and
importance to them, but then writing a very disappointing paper that
does not say what they wanted it to say. About a quarter of the students
describe receiving "process" type writing instruction and show considerable familiarity with such aspects of that form of instruction—prewriting, peer response, student-teacher conferences, and revising. However, almost without exception, students describe the development of
their ideas as largely if not wholly separate from the act of writing. The
notion, practically ubiquitous in the field of composition, that writing
might itself be a way of organizing and developing ideas, of learning, is
virtually absent from the essays. This notion was presumably not a point
of view students were exposed to in their previous education, or if exposed, it did not stick. Rather, ideas are depicted as coming to students
quickly, almost instantaneously, to be then transferred to writing or "put
down into words." Students cite the difficulty of doing so as causing
much of their frustration with writing. The issue seems to involve putting ideas or a creative and exciting plan into words, in the process of
which the writing bogs down; the excitement and creativity somehow
get lost, leaving only the flawed and error-ridden ramblings of a vulnerable adolescent. In these accounts, the writing seems to take on a life
of its own and to spin out of control. Writing is never conceived as a part
of a larger thinking process. Shawna explains:

> I may begin with an incredible thought, but by the end my writing
> doesn't make any sense. I'm disorganized when it comes to putting
> all my ideas together. In fact, sometimes I think I'm writing in a
> foreign language.

What students cite as the main cause of their problems with writing
is rather depressingly predictable. While a wide range of problem areas
are cited, including disorganization, lack of motivation, and inability to
express and/or support an opinion, by far the largest number of problems mentioned have to do with sentence- and word-level issues of grammar, punctuation, vocabulary, and spelling. Curiously, even those students such as John, below, who complain about an inability to coordinate
their writing from an initial "idea" stage through to completion—a classic
"process" problem—generally attribute their difficulties primarily to
shortcomings in word choice, grammar, or usage:

> I have never been able to express myself well on paper; this is due to the fact that I understand very little about proper grammar.

In addition to labeling themselves as bad writers, a number of students question whether they could be considered writers at all. This view is not surprising, given the prevailing notion of a writer as a literary, intellectual type who makes a living by producing books. In her book on the writing of successful women academics, Gesa Kirsch (1993) points out that even those women who published regularly and to considerable acclaim often did not think of themselves as writers and in more than a few cases did not even credit themselves with the ability to write (p. 70). Students both male and female display a similar lack of confidence in their writing. Moreover, students make clear that their previous education has not encouraged them to think of themselves as writers. Only two students in the entire sample describe writing as having anything like such a central role in their lives or identify strongly as writers. However, of equal concern is that several students not only reject the possibility that they might be considered writers, they also reject the very idea that their written work for school could even be considered writing. As Bart puts it:

> Describing myself as a writer is hard for me to do because I don't really consider myself as a writer. In high school I had to write many essays and narratives, but I wouldn't consider that writing because it was always specified as to what I needed to write about . . . I like to write about topics that interest me, and I don't find it to be worth the time to write about something that I really don't care about.

The above essay is noteworthy in part because it shows an independent spirit, resisting the dominance of the teacher, throwing down the gauntlet, so to speak, in announcing a preference for self-selected topics and for pursuing one's own interests. The writer does, however, become more accommodating as the essay goes along, as if reacting against the implicitly confrontational stance taken earlier. This essay later offers a toned down form of the original argument, stating: "I prefer to know what I am writing about, or at least have an understanding of the topic discussed." Even in such a mild form, however, I found that overt resistance to the terms of the assignment or to the possible expectations of the teacher was very rare. In fact, even when broadly defined to include any statement of preference as to what students will be expected to do in the class, such resistance can be seen only in a few other essays. The most direct of these, written by Jack, begins without mincing words: "If I had to describe myself as a writer, unmotivated, uninterested in writing, and quick to the point are the first things that come to mind. Yet, when forced upon to write, yes it can be done." The student concludes, "In classes I've previously taken, form and 'length' were emphasized. Writing should be more open and carefree. You shouldn't have to worry about how long something is." This essay is noteworthy in being one of a very few in the entire sample (along with Bart's essay just cited above) in which the writer challenges the authority of the teacher, presuming to stand on anything close to an equal footing. Yet even this writer is careful to preface the expressed views on form and length with a disclaimer, "Not to disrespect you in any way, but writing isn't my thing."

Of course, it would be misleading to focus only on pieces emphasizing the negative representations of writing and of the students as writers, even though such pieces dominate the sample. As mentioned earlier, a sixth of the students do describe their writing in positive terms, and another sixth offer a more or less balanced assessment of strengths and weaknesses, though the majority of the "balanced" views do give greater weight to the negative. However, a close look at even the positive accounts raises some troubling questions about how comfortably these students will adapt to the curricular orientation of first-year composition. Three of these positive assessments were indeed extremely enthusiastic, as in the following example by Megan which places a great value on personal uses of writing:

> I love writing. I love writing about me. It's part of my being. I always need to put my thoughts down on paper, either in the form of letters, or scribbles, or often writing in my journal. I write a lot about facts which help the reader understand the situation I'm talking about, but because I think facts are a bit tiring and boring, I try to express mostly my feelings and deeper thoughts.

Another enthusiastic student, Carl, is one of only two who actually self-identifies as a writer (in addition to case-study student Cris, with her book-in-progress about her experiences with men). Carl cites successes at creative efforts and a desire to learn how to get future work published:

> I've won three writing awards at school, an honorable mention from a national story contest, as well as placed in the Cultural Arts Writing Contest. I have discovered and developed my style of writing, which is made up of the fantasy side of nature, like talking beavers and also children's books.
>
> The key factor to my style of writing is my imagination. Nobody usually uses characters such as Hypercolor beavers and vampire squirrels, so my writings can be easily identified by people who have read others of mine before. Using this imagination is why I have won so many awards, since one of their requirements was creativity.

A third student, case-study student Rachel, cites her enjoyment at writing poetry for herself and letters to friends. Yet none of these students, despite expressing very positive attitudes about writing, mentions any particular affinity for the academic, analytic writing that makes up the great majority of the composition curriculum. Rachel specifically contrasts the enjoyment she gets from writing poems and personal letters with the pain and difficulty she experiences in school writing. Several other students who portray their writing in positive or balanced terms cite a particular teacher or class that helped them to develop and overcome earlier problems in writing. Two such essays describe "workshops" in which students were allowed, even encouraged, to read and write whatever they wanted, and cite these courses as leading to their improvement in and greater enjoyment of writing.

What all these students appear to have in common are strong, positive feelings about personal and imaginative uses of writing. However, such writing is *not* emphasized in first-year composition. Rather, the main focus in the program is on helping students to construct analyses, primarily arguments and interpretations, in other words, on academic, analytic forms of writing. True, there is a strong personal component built into almost all assignments, guided by the assumption that interpretation starts with a writer's own understanding and is grounded in that person's individual and cultural contexts. And, of course, imagination, or creativity, is also important; how often, after all, do we tell students that "all writing is creative"? However, the program attempts primarily to develop students' critical and reflective abilities in writing. Thus, as a teacher, I would be excited to work with these positive-sounding students in a first-year writing class—they seem bright, lively, enthusiastic, personable, hard-working, even interested in writing. But I also recognize that these students have expressed no particular interest in doing the sort of written work I will be laying out for them. The kinds of imaginative and personal writing that they express interest in, the kinds that they describe doing successfully, though not unrelated to what they will be doing in first-year composition, are rather significantly different. And, on the whole, the students suggest that these academic forms of writing are also significantly more difficult.

Similarly, other essays, even ones in which the writers express views about writing and about themselves as writers, suggest students that one would be delighted and honored to work with, as much as one can tell from a decontextualized essay written in thirty minutes under stressful circumstances. Thus, the news is by no means all bad. Many students express some satisfaction with their past writing instruction, including in one case a tribute to a class taught by a published poet in which every student had a poem published somewhere and the writer describes gaining a new appreciation for poetry. Several students voice pride in their overall growth as writers and in particularly successful or memorable pieces they have written, such as a comprehensive research paper effort. The vast majority of students depict themselves as conscientious, ambitious, hopeful, and hard-working, eager to do well; they seem like a pleasant and engaging group. Perhaps by way of putting the best foot forward, only a few students portray themselves as lazy or lacking in effort, and even these students should perhaps be praised for their candor.

Yet all in all, the balanced and even the positive essays offer a reading of the student that, as a teacher looking carefully over this first-day writing, I might indeed regard with some concern. Most of these pieces (and for that matter, most of the pieces in which students portray themselves as bad, even terrible writers) do not strike me as badly written in the conventional sense of the term, for students just coming out of high school, despite the timed, one-shot nature of the assignment. They address the prompt's questions; provide specific, often intriguing details; convey emotion; reveal the presence of "thinking" individuals with opinions and personalities behind the page; and use grammar, punctuation, and mechanics that are generally correct, and even when incorrect do not impede understanding. However, in some pieces the words themselves belie the student's attempt to portray him or herself as a proficient writer, reflecting the ability of the written word to "betray" the student and act as a kind of shibboleth separating the students who belong from those who don't. Paradoxically, these are pieces in which the writers say they write well, but the words themselves say they don't. A few essays, like Larry's below, show the pugnacious or defensive quality seen in Jack, the resistant student's essay above, combined with an oral, conversational style that does not work well as written prose:

> In describing myself as a writer, I feel that I know just as much as all the students in this class will know. Possibly a little less or a little more knowledge. Some of my writing experiences in high school consisted of creativity, personal, hobbies, and research reports, also reading stories from various authors. Doing this in high school helped me become a better righter as the years progress. It not only prepared me for college but also reality.

Other such pieces reveal a somewhat naive notion of writing that might lead a teacher to anticipate some potential difficulty. Amy writes:

> As a writer I am very creative. During high school we were given writing time and I used to close my eyes and just imagine. Anything at all. As far as stories or real personal experiences. I enjoy

free-writing because you can be your-self and write about whatever is on your mind.

Finally, the small number of students who do report success at and/
or enjoyment of critical or research writing generally emphasize aspects
of such writing that are very much at odds with the program's approach
to composition. These students either pledge allegiance to one or the
other of the rigidly structured five-paragraph theme formats (several are
mentioned in the essays) or assert a dubious ability to write "factually."
Yet another way some students mention to avoid the oppressive demands of rigorous and careful thought is the time-honored, romantic
tradition of spontaneity. Damon, a self-confident student who appears
to have known success in the past, defends this approach with evident
sincerity, and is also savvy enough to demonstrate knowledge of the
"correct" way to write, but simply prefers not to:

> Upon examining my previous writing experiences, I would be char-
> acterized as an excellent composer of research papers and literary
> criticisms. Although . . . I believe I work better under the pressure of
> a deadline. I almost always wait until the last minute to write a
> paper, and I have always abhorred writing rough drafts. Admitedly,
> my papers would be improved if I were to take the proper steps to
> writing a paper (brainstorming, forming an outline, composing a
> rough draft, etc.). I suppose, however, that the absence of these steps
> is what defines my style of writing. It gives my papers a sort of
> spontaneity and freshness. True, I could improve by preparing more
> extensively, but I have also found that under the confines of things
> like rough drafts, my style becomes muddled.

These few essays, which present the student's own preferences and
challenge the "official" pedagogy, may stem from a lack of tact or savvy
on the part of the student. Yet such essays are refreshingly bold, suggesting an independent-minded student who, from a teacher's point of view,
might well prove unconventional, nonconformist, or otherwise interesting and enjoyable to work with in the class. Paradoxically, the essays that
portrayed the writer, and writing in general, in a more negative light were
often among the liveliest and most interesting to read. Those pieces that
offered a positive slant were more often general, insipid, lacking in conflict, distinctiveness, drama, or intensity. Perhaps, just as Dante's *Inferno*
makes for much livelier, if more harrowing, reading than the blander
Paradiso, so the more negative accounts with their depictions of pain,
failure, and disappointment are more engaging than the rather compla-
cent and conventional positive accounts. Certainly those positive accounts are more affecting that place the student's success in writing in
the context of a long and difficult struggle to overcome problems and
deficiencies.

While as a group students seem highly critical of themselves as writers, they aren't particularly critical of their past English classes, perhaps to an extent not wanting to offend the English teacher who would be reading and evaluating their work. In fact, many students express satisfaction with at least some aspects of their high school writing instruction—a particular teacher, a certain approach, a specific essay or story. And as I will discuss more in the following section, students generally report seeing writing as an ability that will be important in their lives. Yet the essays as a group, while offering both positive and negative appraisals of students' writing abilities and attitudes toward writing, lean decidedly toward the negative. Vulnerability, lack of confidence, and feelings of nonmastery of a written code that can quickly betray one's shortcomings dominate the sample. Moreover, as we have seen, even the more positive descriptions depict approaches to writing that are largely inconsistent with the critical form of literacy emphasized in first-year classes. It is difficult if not impossible to know just how honest and open students were being in these essays. However, there would seem to be little benefit to students in presenting a greater aversion to writing than they genuinely felt, or a more negative assessment of themselves as writers than was really the case. The following section of the chapter presents a similar interpretive dilemma. Here we move away from the study of student attitudes to examine how students described to the teacher their own goals for the class.

What Students Hope to Learn about Writing: A Counter-CCCC

The second part of this first-day essay assignment asked students to discuss what they hoped to learn about writing from the composition course. And just as in the previous section, a basic conflict is evident between what the students say and what the curriculum emphasizes. There are some points of overlap, but these are largely overshadowed by the areas of divergence. I want to begin by giving the overall flavor of students' responses to this part of the prompt. As I have said, I was quite struck earlier by the extent of students' negative cast of mind about their writing. Not surprisingly, many of their concerns and worries carried over to their responses to the second part of the prompt as well. Specifically, in examining students' comments, I was impressed by both the importance they attach to writing and the corresponding pressure they report not only to do well in the course, but also to improve the quality of their written work. Students want to improve their writing for a variety of reasons, most of them very pragmatic. Clearly, the stakes are high for students in first-year composition. There is some, but very little, casual talk from the most confident-sounding students about brushing up on previously learned skills and branching out adventurously into new areas. More common, though, are remarks like the following, from Melissa, one of the many students coming into college, and entering composition, uncertain and more than a little frightened:

> In this class I hope to learn how to be more creative. I need to know how to get things flowing so that I don't just stare at a piece of blank paper. I see people around me just writing and writing and I sit here thinking and thinking; what am I going to write? I shouldn't be nervous I should be confident and ready to write, and I should know what to write about.

By the word *creative*, this writer seems to mean able to get words down on the page, productive, rather than imaginative or inventive. Half a dozen other students show similar symptoms of writer's block, or fear of writing, and the desire to overcome it. But even students, such as Penny, who do not express an inability to get words on the page admit deep worries about their prospects in composition class, and in college generally:

> All I want to learn about writing is the proper way to write. I want to express myself in a way that the reader will find enjoyable; moreover, I don't want to write a paper that has a lot of neat stuff being boring because of bad grammar.
> I also want to become a better writer to help me through college. I have been told by a number of people that I would be doomed in college because of my writing skills; I want to change my skills so I won't be doomed.

Another student, who earlier reflects on whether she actually "hates" to write or perhaps is merely ambivalent, concludes, "I want to learn how to have fun with writing and not dread doing it or coming to class."

Doom and dread. These students' comments are only the most extreme representations of an attitude expressed by many of the essays. These essays seem to depict writing instruction as an unpleasant and even dangerous activity most noteworthy for its ability to get a person in trouble at school. Yet students also depict writing as a necessary activity, like taking a harsh medicine needed to cure an illness, but medicine of a curious type. For the medicine is not so much worthwhile in itself. Rather, it is the courage and character required to steady oneself and take it, the very act of taking it, that makes the medicine worthwhile. A steely stoicism permeates these essays, reflecting not just the common notion that nothing worthwhile is easy, but also the idea that writing and writing instruction are worthwhile precisely *because* of their difficulty. Some students justify writing instruction the way Latin instruction used to be justified: as an important form of mental discipline, boot camp for the mind. Reading these essays gave me the strong feeling that students were trying hard to convince the teacher that they could do a good job in the course, but also to convince themselves that the composition class, however unpleasant, would be good for them. Such a sentiment comes through clearly in the following essay by Mike:

> This is going to be a very important course for me. I have never been interested in or even liked english classes in the past. It is necessary for me to take this class not only to develope my writing style, but also to see if I can learn to like and do well in a class that otherwise I wouldn't have taken.
>
> This class should help me become more rounded as a student and as a person. I'm going to put my mind to it and try hard so I can prove to myself that I can do things that are difficult and things I don't enjoy as well. This should be an indicator to show if I have what it takes to succeed in college and in life. I'm going to have to face it; life isn't always going to be fun. If I keep a good attitude and work hard I think I can do well.

This stoical "I know it must be good for me" stance and the emphasis on keeping "a good attitude" permeates the essays: composition class as a character-builder; writing instruction as hard, dirty, uninteresting work, the doing of which will make me a better person. On the one hand, such attitudes should not be altogether discouraging to us as teachers. We want students to have a strong work ethic and to believe that composition class will be useful for them. On the other hand, such attitudes should concern us greatly. When students express so little interest in, indeed so much distaste for our subject matter, we of all college teachers need to sit up and take notice. For as composition specialists, we have been among the major advocates of student-centered learning in the university, priding ourselves on giving students as much autonomy and authority in the classroom as possible. Therefore, we must look beyond students' general willingness to do what we ask of them, in order to examine how their approach to composition may be affected by their own goals and aspirations, their own relationship to our curriculum.

Springing from students' metanotions about composition are a number of more focused goals for what they hope to learn in the class. One finds very little variation in the overall goals students express. Their aspirations are overwhelmingly pragmatic and utilitarian, far more focused on attaining practical skills and achieving career goals than on critiquing current society or developing reflective capabilities. This pragmatism reflects a strong tendency in American culture that has been noted and discussed since the early nineteenth century. Starting with de Toqueville (1835), the discussion has continued with Dewey (1916), Rorty

(1979), and other thinkers, and shows no signs of abating in the present day. Punctuated by brief periods such as the late 1960s in which idealism was widespread and practicality unfashionable, especially among the young, a pragmatic, largely materialistic spirit has dominated American culture and served as a key component of schooling. Hence, the domination in many universities, including the one in which this study is set, of pre-professional, career-oriented education. With few exceptions, the goals students express reflect a powerful desire on their part to develop writing skills that will help them do well. They want to learn skills that will help them, first and foremost, in the composition sequence itself, a distant second, in their other coursework, particularly their majors, and a remote third, in their careers and later lives generally. The humanistically oriented goals of a traditional liberal education as they relate to writing—to convey one's ideas persuasively and eloquently, to develop a greater appreciation for and understanding of the best that has been thought and said, to live the examined life—are not mentioned as part of most students' desired repertoires. Nor are the more explicitly political goals of critical literacy—to use writing and reading in order to better reflect on and understand oneself, the larger society, and one's relations to that society; to prepare for participation in a democracy; to foster a desire to work for social justice. Such concerns, important as they may be in shaping the composition curriculum, seem far from the minds of students as they begin college composition, at least as indicated by these opening-day essays. Perhaps students were not exposed to these ideas in their previous education, and their goals mirror the kinds of teaching they have experienced, the classrooms they have inhabited.

Indeed, the first and—for many students—only stated consideration centers on their anticipated performance in the course. Such grade consciousness and performance anxiety have been cited by Ehrenreich (1989), Horowitz (1987), and others examining the culture of contemporary college students as springing from a perceived fear of falling, of not doing well enough academically to attain the good job which is the primary reason for attending college in the first place. According to such an interpretation, this anxiety combines with, and to a large extent causes, a lack of deep interest in broader social, political, and philosophical issues, often leading to a pragmatic, bottom-line mentality. The essay prompt was not intended to elicit definitive information about students' world-views (such views will be examined more closely in the following chapters, in the context of how students approached their coursework). Still, the pervasive, even exclusive concerns expressed about grades and classroom performance certainly suggest a strongly pragmatic, though also perhaps short-sighted, attitude toward writing instruction and toward college generally. Such a mind-set, reflected in most students' essays, is often expressed frankly and without equivocation, as in the following example from Randy, who bemoaned his unfortunate tendency in writing to "turn a good idea into a bad grade":

> To be totally honest, I would like to learn how to get an A on a paper. I want to find that special something that was missing in my B and C high school papers. I suppose there are ways I can do this. I just don't know how.

Many similar comments, while not always going so far as to mention aiming for a specific grade, emphasize the desire to learn how to write a paper that meets with the teacher's approval. At times, though, this desire is embedded in a broader rhetorical goal. A small group of students assert that they want to strengthen their writing generally for their audience, make it more interesting and memorable, not only for teachers but for whatever readers they might have. The notion of addressing and impressing an audience, of learning more effective ways to engage a reader's interest, is mentioned in almost a fifth of students' essays. This notion is often accompanied by an admission that readers, especially teachers but in some cases the students themselves, have in the past found their written efforts boring, confusing, or otherwise less than satisfactory.

A small number of students also assert the hope that, because they expect to write papers for other classes throughout college, the instruction they receive in first-year composition should help them more generally in their academic work. Such hopes are indeed an important part of the justification for a required composition sequence. Though a growing body of empirical research by psychologists such as Sternberg and Detterman (1993) suggests the extreme difficulty—some even say the near impossibility—of transferring knowledge from one domain to another, students anticipate using the knowledge gained from composition instruction in successfully carrying out writing assignments for other courses. One student who does so, Carl, earlier expressed positive attitudes about writing, describing previous successes and also indicating an interest in writing for personal reflection "when I'm upset, happy, or frustrated." This writer links the desire to write well for other classes with a sense of the importance, and shifting demands, of audience:

> By taking Freshman English I hope to gain a lot of writing skills. This is so very important in college because I will have to write papers for other classes this year and years to come. I hope to gain a better way of persuading my reader(s).
>
> I want for however long my reader is reading my paper, I want that person to feel like they're in my shoes for that time. I want

them to feel what I'm feeling and maybe affect them in some way. I do not want them to forget my paper.

An even smaller number of students cite the importance of writing beyond its role in college. Most such discussions center on the role of writing in the workplace, but a few mention the general importance in life of "good communication abilities," however variously phrased. The students whose essays look beyond college to career and later life are in almost every instance those who express generally positive attitudes about their own writing and present themselves as successful and enthusiastic writers. These students appear to have stepped back somewhat from their immediate situations in an attempt to look more broadly at a long-range trajectory of development. This inclination to discuss the "big picture" may be due in part to these students' apparently greater confidence and lower stress level. Those students feeling more anxious and intimidated might have found it very difficult, especially under the pressures of the timed writing, to look beyond the situation immediately at hand. A sense of perspective, or at least an attempt at perspective, comes through in these future-oriented essays; they seem aimed at conveying an attitude of mature reflection and calm deliberation, more so than the pieces which focus exclusively on performance in the class. Megan, who earlier said that she "loved" writing, particularly writing about herself (though she also said she enjoyed writing for school), takes such a broader view, and also links writing with speaking as key forms of communication:

> I need to be absolutely proficient in the language in order to be a good speaker and writer. Because, no matter what I do in the future, if I don't have the necessary skills to communicate, everything will be tougher for me.

Several other students, such as case-study student Josh, focus more on the demands of their particular major and future career:

> I am planning to major in civil engineering here at the University of Cincinnati. Due to the fact that my job will require me to communicate with a lot of different people, I need to learn how to effectively convey my ideas in writing.

Several of these career-minded students seem quite concerned about the image they will project. Like Marlon, below, they are eager to look good and avoid embarrassment:

> I hope to be able to write a paper and to look like I know what I'm talking about. I would like to look educated when I have to write a paper as an engineer instead of fitting in with the stereotype that engineers are not good at english or spelling.

However, a few students who express a "large" view make the kinds of sweeping, generalized, slightly pompous-sounding pronouncements that read like "Engfish" introductions to five paragraph themes, exuding a dubious authority. These essays seem to reflect how some students think academic writing should sound, the type of student prose parodied by Coles (1974), Macrorie(1970), and others, but still found in high school and college writing. Anne's is a prime example:

> As we all know, writing is a very important tool in the world we
> live in, because in order to be understood and effective, you must
> make your statements clear and clean cut to everybody. I believe
> that this class will help refine my skills as a writer so that I will be
> capable of giving my views in a strong and effective manner.

Again, it is important to keep in mind that students are writing at least in part for their teacher here, and have strong reasons to promote the importance of written communication in ways their teacher would presumably approve of and appreciate. Not surprisingly, the picture that emerges thus far of what students hope to learn about writing shows a group of students eager—and often quite anxious—to do well in the course. They have in the majority of cases not been satisfied by their past performance in writing, and want to make up for what they see as their deficiencies now. While a fair number of students express at least some confidence about themselves as writers, and a few even rather boldly offer their own views on what sort of material they think the teacher should emphasize in the course, none express the belief that they are already good enough writers and therefore should not be required to take composition at all. All seem to accept the writing requirement in this sense, at least overtly. However, the rhetorical situation (writing for a teacher's evaluation on the first day of class and wanting to make a good impression) may have something to do with the lack of such assertions. In my experience, this attitude that one should not have to take college composition is certainly prevalent, and does come out occasionally once the term has gotten under way and students have relaxed their defenses somewhat. Only a small proportion of the students express an awareness of the importance of writing as a communicative tool that will be useful, even necessary to them in their academic and professional lives. No students mention the kinds of intellectual and political goals that underlie the curriculum, goals with which they are unlikely to be familiar if they have come out of a traditional high school English curriculum. Most students appear to have focused their attentions on meeting the demands of the course at hand and developing the necessary skills. With this overall larger picture of their goals in mind, we will examine the more specific aspects of writing that students expressed a desire to learn about in the composition sequence.

In the previous section, we saw that many students attribute their difficulties with writing primarily to weaknesses in grammar, punctuation, and word choice. They feel this way even though the essays as a group do not seem especially problematic at the word- and sentence-levels, particularly for a timed writing at the start of the year. And they feel this way even though many of the difficulties students cite in their past writing appear to stem more from issues of motivation, organization and development of ideas, or coordination of the process than from problems of mechanics. In fact, some of the most error-ridden essays are those quoted earlier in which the writers express a guarded confidence about their writing. Still, for whatever reasons, this area is where students generally appear to feel most vulnerable. Thus, while it may seem rather incongruous, fully half of the essays express principally a desire for so-called "grammar therapy," "mechanics overhaul," or whatever one might call the quest for greater correctness in writing. This desire for greater correctness is by far the largest locus of concern mentioned. Some students target particular errors which have given them trouble in the past—and which apparently continue to trouble them. The following student, Nick, for example, earlier states that his previous teachers always praised his papers for their creativity and liveliness—they were never "dull, dry, and boring"—but that his mechanics were another matter entirely:

> In this class, I'd like to become more experienced with my punctuation. Sometimes I just write and don't stop, which leads to poor punctuation. I don't really think about putting commas in sentences when I write, or even periods sometimes. Since I do this I end up proof reading my papers at least twenty times. Putting in and taking out commas and shortening up my sentences.
>
> Sometimes when I write I do a lot of run-ons. I would like to know when to stop a sentence, when I have a good idea I like to keep writing so I don't lost my train of thought, so sometimes I think of putting punctuation in as I write a disturbance.

Thus, in describing his punctuation problems, this student also illustrates them clearly, though the illustration is presumably not intentional. This anxiety about issues of correctness appears traceable to past experiences with negative evaluations, as a number of students describe frequent run-ins with the "red pen" and the long-term consequences of such negative feedback. Here is a typical example from Ned's essay:

> What I really hope to learn about writing in this class is how to get my point across more clearly. Also, where to put all the commas

and semi-colons. I think my ideas start off great, but once I start getting it down on paper it all gets messed up. It seems every time I get a paper back that I think I did well on, it's always cluttered with rules from the Writer's Inc, or the teacher tells me that the main focus got lost. This is very frustrating, and I'd like to solve the problem.

Like other students, this writer conflates what a composition specialist would probably see as two distinct though not entirely unrelated problem areas, making sentence-level mistakes and losing the main focus of the paper. In fact, the essays as a group show a strong inclination to depict nearly all problems in writing as stemming from weaknesses in word and sentence-level skills. Yet the composition curriculum, while requiring students to edit and proofread carefully, does not give much emphasis to such pursuits. Issues of mechanics are only infrequently and briefly covered in class, with far greater priority placed upon the development of ideas and other rhetorical concerns. We cannot conclude from such comments that students' high school teachers focused exclusively on sentence- and word-level issues in responding to writing. It could be that teachers point out such errors more often than they focus on larger rhetorical or conceptual aspects of students' texts. However, it could also be that marking of errors is somehow more conspicuous and painful to students—that the dreaded red ink makes a particularly strong impression—and they therefore pay more attention and give greater weight to such comments than to comments about global aspects of discourse. Such overall comments may appear most often in a brief, disregarded note at the end of the paper rather than in a series of more visible marginal notes or corrections included in the text itself. Perhaps students simply pay more attention to the "marking up" of their texts. In any case, it appears that many students come into the composition sequence expecting, apparently even hoping or wishing to convey the hope, that the class will focus on issues of mechanics, an area of writing that they see as problematic in their own prose.

Besides improving their grammar and punctuation, a number of students also want to increase their vocabularies, reflecting the prevalent idea that use of "fancy" words is an important sign of intelligent writing, is indeed a necessary condition for good writing, at least good school writing. One student who wants to do so, Paula, relates past problems in writing to a limited vocabulary, expressing the belief that knowing and using more words is key to becoming a good writer:

> I feel that as a writer I am sometimes limited in my vocabulary. This limit is set by the fact that my spelling skills are not the greatest. The reason my skills are lacking is I did not put forth a great effort through the first year or two of high school. This lack of effort caused me to

be limited in my later writing classes. As a writer I feel that if I practice enough and get the help I need, I will be able to survive.

In this class I hope to learn how to sharpen my writing skills.
Accomplishing this task can be done if I keep on top of things in
this class. I feel that I will be at a great disadvantage if I let things
start to slide. The skill I want to strengthen is how to write with
more of an advanced vocabulary. This skill can help me when it
comes time to put my thoughts into words. In turn, I will be able to
write more meaningful papers.

This student's worries about "survival" in the class, and the concern
not to "slide," echo other students' fears about college writing, the
"doom" and "dread" expressed earlier. Some of that anxiety also comes
through in another goal many students emphasize: to write with greater
clarity in order to get their points across. Aside from wanting to improve
their sentence-level and vocabulary skills, students most frequently
mention a desire to learn how to write "more clearly," so that their readers can better understand what they are trying to say. Almost a third of
the students list achieving clarity as a key aim. The desire for clarity is
closely related to the feeling many students express that their good ideas
often fall apart in the transition from head to paper. The anxious writer
who earlier mentions not liking to "just stare at a piece of blank paper"
goes on to say:

> I would also like to be learn how to be more organized. I would like
> to learn how to take all of the thoughts floating in my head and put
> them into sequential order, so they make sense to everybody in-
> stead of just me.
> I would like to learn how to write intelligently, clear, concise,
> and to the point. But at the same time make my writing interesting.

Correctness, clarity, and conciseness thus emerge as something of a
holy trinity in the essays, those features of writing to which students most
aspire. They are certainly the three most frequently cited aspects of "good
writing" mentioned in the essays. These characteristics are of course
admirable features of much good writing. They have a long history of
importance in composition teaching and are closely associated with what
has by now long been called the current-traditional paradigm of writing instruction. Moreover, these aspects of writing may well have been
stressed in much of students' previous instruction. Yet, as far as the college writing course is concerned, the idea of basing a course around
notions of correctness, clarity, and conciseness has been strongly criticized by composition specialists for some years. Critiques of current-traditional approaches date back to the late 1960s with the advent of pro-
cess- and writer-oriented instruction and have long been items of faith
in the profession. To be sure, a look at the curriculum reveals a very dif-

ferent set of primary goals for the composition sequence, which are in important ways not consistent with the Strunkian emphasis on correctness, clarity, and conciseness. Reflectiveness, questioning, elaboration, revision, and other such features of critical literacy are not just different goals, but in important ways even run counter to students' desires to make their points clearly, concisely, and in sequential order. While not intended to produce students whose writing is unclear, rambling, or disorganized, the critical approach emphasized in the curriculum attempts to complicate initial plans for writing and to encourage students to re-see and move beyond their early ideas. The approach seeks to extend students' writing processes, in order to allow for more careful reflection, questioning, and elaboration on the topic. Surface correctness, clarity, and conciseness, if the content of the paper is superficial and has not been questioned, reflected upon, and examined from several different perspectives, are not in themselves greatly desired goals. Indeed, teachers may work hard to move students away from such an approach. The neat and tidy essay which does not show evidence of serious thought is only a pedagogical starting point, something to improve upon, in the critical literacy classroom.

In students' essays, this desire for correctness, clarity, and conciseness frequently goes along with a desire to learn "proper" form, often expressed as the right way to organize a paper, as if there were just one way. Many students here allude to structures such as the five-paragraph theme, which they describe as a "correct" format. Some express the belief that there must be other such rigid structures for use in college and professional writing. The official curriculum, however, stresses that there are a multitude of possible ways to organize an essay, depending on the logic of the particular points the writer wishes to make and on the rhetorical and cultural situation. The composition class therefore attempts to teach students not to rely on, indeed to move beyond, such formulaic ways of structuring their writing.

Some students do say they would like to learn how to write longer, more detailed papers, a desire more consistent with composition theory, which places considerable value on the ability to elaborate about one's subject and to develop one's ideas deeply and fully. But even here the focus is not a heuristic one but a largely pragmatic one. It is not that students state a desire to learn how to explore their ideas in greater depth and complexity. Rather, they hope to learn how to achieve a desired length. These students say they have had trouble in the past meeting a length requirement and therefore need to learn how to expand their prose, in order to fill in the blank space on the page. They want to get sufficient numbers of words down on paper as an end in itself, not, as would be more consistent with the curriculum, to explore their ideas as fully as possible. Getting words down on paper is, implicitly at least, a process issue. And nowhere are students' goals more greatly opposed to those of the curriculum than where writing processes are concerned. The program seeks to extend, enrich, and broaden students' writing processes, to build in greater opportunities for reflection, interpretation, and development. However, students appear to want the opposite: shorter, more streamlined, and more efficient writing processes. Rather than spending more time on their writing assignments and doing more and better planning, drafting, and revising, students want to do less. Very few students even allude to process concerns, focusing instead primarily on the structure and content of their texts. However, the few students who do mention going over a previously written draft, talk about wanting to develop their editing and tightening skills, rather than learning how better to extend and develop their drafts.

One can understand this desire for greater efficiency: students are busy people. Even at the start of college, they already appear concerned about the demands of other academic requirements, particularly those in the major area of study. Students are also perhaps not inclined to devote as much time, effort, and thought to their studies as instructors wish they would. Well over half of the beginning students at this university have jobs, often working close to forty hours a week or even more, and with other demands on students' time, academics often do not hold as central a place in students' lives as faculty might wish or expect. But for whatever reasons, greater speed and the development of a more compact and readily applicable set of writing strategies emerge as key features students wish to learn, though clearly in conflict with the goals of the curriculum.

If correctness, clarity, and conciseness (both in terms of having a concise product and employing a concise process) make up students' holy trinity of writing virtues, the fourth C would be creativity. One-sixth of the students say they want to learn how to be more creative in their writing, making creativity the fourth most frequently expressed goal. Students differ considerably, however, in what they appear to mean by the term *creative*. Some, like a writer quoted above, relate creativity to knowing "how to get things flowing so that I don't just stare at a blank piece of paper." They also connect it with being interesting, exciting, and unconventional in their writing, as a way of attracting and holding a reader's attention, a concern that the above student expressed. Others relate creativity to being uninhibited, expressive, and free in one's writing, not bound by repressive rules and requirements such as length and form. Some assert a desire to study those types of writing traditionally known as "creative." Several students hope that the composition course will be more of a creative writing course, providing opportunities to produce fiction and/or poetry. As Jay, a confident writer who describes himself as "good at writing thorough, informative research papers," puts it:

> One of my weak points in writing is poetry. I have never fully un-derstood difficult poetry and I have not done very well at writing it. I would like to improve my poetry writing skills, because it is a necessary part of any English class.
>   My basic problem with poetry is understanding it. I have always had trouble analyzing difficult poetry to find hidden messages and symbols. I have to understand poetry before I can write it well. I would like to become a more proficient poet this year. I think I should learn to put meaning and symbols in my poetry instead of just rhyming words.

Jay never actually says he likes to write poetry or is even particularly interested in writing it, but rather describes poetry writing as "a neces-sary part of any English class" which for that reason must be mastered. This description suggests no deep affinity for poetry, only the thought that students might well be required to compose and/or interpret some of it in the first-year writing class, and he had therefore better learn how to do it well. Thus, as with correctness, clarity, and conciseness, creativ-ity as defined by students is generally not an important goal for the com-position curriculum (except in the first two senses described: the ability to generate words and the ability to be interesting to one's audience).

Conclusion

On the whole, as the preceding discussion illustrates, the approaches to writing and even the types of writing that students hope to learn about in the composition sequence differ substantially from those that will soon confront them. We can see students as implicitly forming their own or-ganization, a counter-CCCC emphasizing correctness, clarity, concise-ness, and creativity. This CCCC stands very much in opposition to our own professional organization in terms of the students' philosophy of writing, their discussion of the uses and value of writing, and their ex-pressed curricular goals, however inchoate, unselfconscious, and below the surface these goals might be. Students report little interest in engag-ing in critical analysis, in extending their writing processes, or in enter-ing the sort of intellectual community that the composition class entails. The curriculum emphasizes writing as reflection, while students empha-size writing as practical action. The curriculum focuses on writing at a global level, emphasizing larger rhetorical aspects of argument and interpretation, while students focus more on the sentence and word levels. The curriculum seeks to extend and complicate the composing process, while students seek to streamline and simplify it. The curriculum regards text as situated, contingent, and open to a variety of interpretations, while students see it as fixed and straightforward. The curriculum pushes for questioning of the status quo, with hopes of encouraging social transformation, while students wish to find a comfortable place for themselves within the existing status quo. There is thus a serious discontinuity between what we expect students to learn in college composition and what they hope to learn, just as there is a discontinuity between the idea of writing as embodied in the curriculum and as understood by students. Compounding these discontinuities are the negative representations most students present of themselves as writers and the disaffection and outright fear many express for the course requirement that confronts them. Indeed, for many of the students the act of writing is itself an enigma. Not only do students find mysterious the process by which an idea or set of ideas becomes a finished text. They seem to think there exists a secret, preferably painless technique for achieving "that special something" that will finally allow their writing to find favor with their teachers, other readers, and even themselves.

Given this large gulf of understanding, expectation, and attitude, both students and teachers face difficult challenges in the composition sequence. On the one hand, teachers must hope that students can somehow be persuaded to adopt the values and attitudes, the habits of mind, that underlie the curriculum, and they must work hard to convince students of the advantages of critical literacy. It may be, after all, that students have simply never been exposed to such ideas before and once made aware will find this view of writing quite congenial. Failing such persuasion, teachers know that students want to do well, are generally cooperative and respectful, and in any case will more or less do what they need to do to succeed in the class. Of course, teachers have the power to require students to complete the assigned work, however disposed students may be, and perhaps through exposure and practice the intellectual dispositions of critical literacy may have a chance to take root. On the other hand, students face the challenge of having to take on a difficult course of study that appears to require a certain orientation that they themselves do not possess and that runs counter to their understandings and inclinations. To adopt critical literacy would involve for students a major shift in world view, attitude, and approach to schooling. Moreover, such a shift would be quite complicated and probably time-consuming as well, something more likely to happen gradually, over the span of an entire college education, than during the first quarter or two of college.

With all these problems, the situation would not appear to leave much room for optimism. And yet, as Tom Newkirk illustrates in his recent book on personal writing in first-year composition (1997), optimism is perhaps the one quality students and teachers have in common. A glimmer of optimism can often be seen beneath all the fears and doubts that students express, underlying what their teachers might see as a narrow concern with getting a good grade and preparing for a future career, a concern that threatens to shut out larger matters of social, political, and intellectual importance but does not always succeed. Despite their worries, students want to do well in college and feel they can do well, though it might take great effort on their part. At times in these essays, an energy and determination comes through that should inspire hope in the most despairing of teachers. The following student, Shawna, earlier critiques her own disorganization in writing, suggesting it sometimes feels as if she is writing in a foreign language. But she concludes her essay this way:

> Throughout my schooling writing has never been my strongest point. Being a musician I never really worried about it. That is until now. Now I'm in a whole new ballgame. In college they (Professors) don't care why you're there, just as long as you learn what they're teaching. So that's my attitude! When I walk into this classroom every Tuesday and Thursday I'm not going to even think about the fact that I'm a voice major. The minute I set foot in the classroom I'm going to imagine myself as a journalist or a novelist, that way I can really put my "all" into writing and learn the most I can.
>
> I hope to learn the basic skills I need to know for writing a good, no, a great essay or paper. I hope that when I'm finished with English 101 I will be more than prepared to move on to a higher level of learning. Either that or become a "Bestseller" novelist.

Students also suggest that, despite their sometimes single-minded careerism, they are by no means completely closed off to new possibilities. If one looks hard at the essays, one can find flickers of an openness, a willingness, even a desire to experiment with new ways of thinking and writing. Another student, Ted, who also began his essay with a slew of negative comments about his own writing, even critiquing his letters to his girlfriend, ends with this analysis of what he would like to learn:

> I hate researching! I hope to learn ways of motivation to research topics further than my present knowledge. Research is so time-consuming and seems to drag on forever to the point where I forget what I'm doing at the library in the first place. Is there some kind of technique that allows me to integrate with the information rather

than just writing fact after fact after fact? If there is someone who knows, where were they when I needed them in high school? The ironic part is, they probably were there; I just wasn't paying attention. I guess I need to work on that too. What was I writing about again?

I cannot say how other readers would read the above two comments, but their liveliness, humor, and insight, as well as their hopes, make me as a teacher feel encouraged about the prospect of working with these students in a composition course. I find similarly hopeful and engaging comments in the other essays as well, which make the possibility of teaching these students more appealing than it might on the surface appear. For as teachers, we too show great optimism. We must work closely with students, far more closely than our colleagues in other departments whose first-year courses are typically in large lecture formats and involve mainly multiple-choice evaluation. Our curriculum in composition is extremely and unabashedly ambitious. Our goals are not just to help students become more articulate, stronger communicators in writing, but to help them become more critical and intellectual, to deepen their interest in the workings of the world, and to encourage their active participation in the construction of that world. We may not often fully achieve these lofty goals, at least within the confines of the few quarters in which we can work with students, but they are nonetheless extremely worthwhile aims for which to struggle. In the chapter that follows, I will briefly discuss the two teachers whose classes the book analyzes, examining their own complicated relationships to the "official" curriculum of the writing program. The chapter investigates the work of these teachers and their students as they confront their differences and as they move, sometimes collaboratively and sometimes at odds with one another, through the first quarter of college writing instruction.

4 Ground Rules in College Composition

Fall Quarter. It is 9:00 a.m. on the first day of class in English 101. The early morning hour suggests that this is the first college class for many of the students. They file into the room a few at a time, not saying much to one another, and seat themselves in the prearranged circle. Dressed casually, the young men wear mainly tee-shirts with the names of colleges, sports teams, or bars, and blue jeans or shorts—it's late September but still warm in the Midwest (not that it has to be warm for college students to wear shorts). Some students look a little preppier, with Izod-style shirts and khakis. A number of the men and a few of the women as well wear baseball caps, generally pulled down low over the forehead, making it difficult to get a good look at their faces, especially those who stare down at their desktops. The young women also wear jeans and tee-shirts, some emblazoned with designer brand names or southern-vacation memories. A few of the students sport a more alternative look, with longish hair, ripped jeans, tie-dyed tee-shirts, and colorful bracelets. With the exception of one Asian woman, the students are all white. A woman with short red hair and large, expressive eyes looks to be a returning student in her thirties; the others all appear about eighteen years old and fresh out of high school. In an arrangement reminiscent of a junior high dance, the women sit mainly on one side of the room, the men on the other. The teacher, a graduate student with long, wavy blonde hair, not that many years older than her students and wearing a gold pantsuit, stands at the front of the room greeting students. I sit in my chair looking around, right on the dividing line between the men and the women as it turns out, an older observer, not the teacher but apparently not a peer either. The faces of the students are a little flushed with excitement, apprehension, and, it seems to me, some fear. College has begun.

The students' excitement is understandable: they are beginning a dramatic new phase in their lives, entering an institution highly valued by our culture. For this same reason, their worries are also understandable: today, they enter a new and unfamiliar setting, a large urban university with a reputation for impersonality. Many students have undoubtedly received warnings from family, friends, and teachers about the difficulties that lie ahead, not just the Byzantine registration system and inadequate parking facilities, but the increased demands of college assign-ments, the "weeding-out" process reputed to take place the first year, the need to be self-motivated and not fall behind, the necessity to change long-held habits and attitudes. How many beginning first-year students declare that, though they took it easy in high school, they are really go-ing to get serious about schoolwork now they are in college? Most of them, it seems.

As Michael Moffatt argues in his ethnographic study of Rutgers un-dergraduates, *Coming of Age in New Jersey* (1989), going to college in our society is an important part of the ritual move from childhood to adult-hood, and this transition, glorious though it may be in many ways, is also fraught with worries for students. Most of these worries, as Moffatt shows, concern social aspects of being at college, such as making friends, having relationships, and finding interesting leisure activities. But at least some of these concerns focus on academics and course work, if only as possible impediments to students' obtaining the freedom, independence from parents, and interconnectedness with new peers that are important goals in attending college. Given the pragmatic instrumentalism, the focus on developing skills and qualifications that the previous chapter suggests is a primary impetus in these students' approaches to school-ing, the stakes are high in attending college and may seem particularly so as students begin their first class.

Part of students' anxiety comes out of their need to learn to negotiate this complex new environment, not just the physical and social settings of the large campus and, for many, new city (around 40 percent are liv-ing in dormitories and about that number will be pledging fraternities or sororities), but the academic terrain as well. It is this making sense of the academic terrain, specifically in the first-year writing class, that the present chapter will examine. Students must grasp the wide array of new demands that make up their coursework as a whole. About three-quar-ters have already chosen a major in a pre-professional area and are be-ginning classes in that area as well as many others. Hence, students may well feel the need to organize their studies on a hierarchy of importance. Students must decide whether or not to devote particular attention to courses in their major, and if so, to decide which of their other courses should be seen as closely related to their major, therefore deserving of significant attention, and which as more peripheral, hence perhaps less important. Of course, students are also determining not just how valu-able, but how interesting and how difficult their courses are, and such decisions, as I will show in this chapter, affect how much time and ef-fort students devote to any particular class. The first-year writing course sits in an interesting position here: not part of the major, but probably close enough in an instrumental sense for many students to consider it important. But underlying students' questions and concerns is the need to become oriented in this new situation, to assess how different, and in what ways, their college courses will be from their previous instruction. Students must figure out the underlying ground rules operating in their classes. This idea of ground rules, with the term used in a specific, technical sense, takes on considerable importance in this chapter, as well as the following two chapters, and I will therefore discuss it in some detail below. Following that discussion, I will look in-depth at several important student-teacher conflicts in the first course of the composition sequence, using the notion of ground rules as a cultural frame for examining classroom interaction and student-teacher conflict. I will focus on the classrooms of Sherry and, to a lesser extent, Nan, looking in particular at the experiences of students in each class as they attempted to figure out and master the often implicit expectations in their respective courses.

The Idea of Ground Rules

I define ground rules here *not* as rules or requirements in the traditional, prescriptive sense of the term—due dates, length limits, homework assignments—but rather as teachers' more tacit or underlying expectations of what students need to know and do in order to successfully carry out an academic task. Such expectations may carry considerable weight in influencing how teachers interpret and evaluate students' attitudes, comments, and coursework. The notion of ground rules comes originally from speech-act theory and pragmatics, the study of language use in particular contexts, as developed by philosophers such as J. L. Austin, in his book, *How To Do Things with Words* (1962) and Paul Grice, in his essay, "Logic and Conversation" (1975). Discussing the exchanges of middle-class Britons, Grice suggests that participants in conversations rely heavily on implicit, shared expectations and mutually understood cultural knowledge that are needed for speakers to make sense of one another's comments. For example, typical conversations are governed by what Grice calls a jointly held "cooperative principle," which participants expect each other to follow. The principle states: "Make your contribution such as is required, at the stage at which it occurs, by the accepted purpose or direction of the talk exchange in which you are engaged" (p. 45). This principle breaks down into four subareas, which Grice calls "maxims," concerning the truth, informativeness, relevance, and intelligibility of the contribution. Essentially, these maxims state that we expect a speaker's contribution to be accurate, of an appropriate length, germane to the subject under discussion, and in a form that we can understand. The maxims take into consideration differences imposed by specific contexts and purposes, such as status roles allowing one person to hold the floor longer than another or change the subject, or situations such as sales transactions in which a speaker might be expected to withhold or even provide inaccurate information.

Of course, this description of principles underlying conversation may work well in the abstract, but actual conversations frequently violate aspects of the cooperative principle. Speakers are often inaccurate, rambling, off-topic, or obscure. People are often not so cooperative or may have conflicting purposes in a conversation. Yet by examining these very situations in which maxims seem to have been violated, the principle can actually be observed most clearly. For one's first response in a conversation when a maxim appears to have been breached is not to reject it as meaningless, but to attempt to understand the utterance as if it did indeed "make sense" and fit with our tacit knowledge of how conversation works. So, when I ask a student if he turned in his essay, and the student replies, "I was sick all weekend," the comment at first appears not to respond to my question. However, because I assume the cooperative principle to be in effect, I look for and easily find the missing propositions to make sense of the reply, and therefore can then ask when the paper will be ready. Because the principles underlying conversation may vary across cultures with limited amounts of shared knowledge and assumptions, cross-cultural misunderstandings are to be expected and frequently take place, but to a large extent can be explained using Grice's framework. Discourse analyst Stephen Levinson (1983) argues that Grice's maxims are not simply linguistic ground rules but govern forms of social interaction—including conversation—in a more general sense.

While some scholars attempt to adduce overarching principles governing conversation and social interaction generally, others focus more on contextual variations, the ways of using language and making sense of it that characterize particular groups or settings. Legal, medical, and business communication have been studied extensively, as has educational discourse. In Britain, the importance of tacit understandings, or ground rules, in communication has been applied to the study of classroom discourse and teacher ideology in elementary science classes by educational theorists Neil Mercer and Derek Edwards (1987), to whom the above discussion of Grice's work is indebted.

This notion of ground rules has also been applied to research on secondary school writing in English, science, and humanities by Yanina Sheeran and Douglas Barnes (1991), who studied working-class and middle-class children at several British schools. As this work is particularly important for the present study, I will discuss it in some detail. According to Sheeran and Barnes, some ground rules are general to schooling as a whole, such as the importance of punctuality, class participation, and an "interested" attitude. Some are particular to a subject or discipline, such as the conventions of a specific genre, for example a lab report in chemistry, which teachers may make explicit to varying degrees. And some are specific to a teacher or even a particular occasion, such as an individual instructor's preference for a literary as opposed to an expository style in composition. The existence of unstated ground rules, these authors suggest, is not in itself a terrible or unusual thing. As I suggested in the above discussion of Grice's analysis of conversation, people generally organize their behavior in familiar cultural situations through such unstated expectations. But schooling is so riddled with evaluations, both formal and informal, that teachers' tacit expectations often take on heightened importance: hence, the constant search by students for "what the teacher is really looking for." As teachers who want students to be more intrinsically motivated and genuinely interested in their education, we often find such concerns petty and irritating, but I would suggest that students' anxiety can indeed be well-founded.

In fact, both sets of scholars examining ground rules in schooling, Edwards and Mercer as well as Sheeran and Barnes, found strong evidence that what teachers left unsaid regarding their expectations of students was often just as significant as what they overtly communicated. Sheeran and Barnes argue that many of the ground rules governing school writing tasks are unspoken, simply assumed by teachers to be understood, while students may have quite a different understanding of what they are expected to do. The authors suggest that teachers are often not fully aware of many of the ground rules operating in their classes, though such expectations may reflect the underlying purposes of an activity. For example, school assignments often have as their underlying purpose to encourage and initiate students into particular ways of thinking, such as abstract reasoning or the understanding and application of theories or category systems, though these approaches may never be clearly described. And according to Sheeran and Barnes, students are far more likely to resist carrying out a school task, not only if they do not agree with its justification, but also if they do not understand why they are being asked to do it.

Sheeran and Barnes found a number of different types of ground rules concerning writing to be operating in British secondary school classrooms. While the educational contexts are obviously very different, I would argue that some of the ground rules the authors discuss are directly relevant to the present study of American college students. For example, Sheeran and Barnes talk about the importance for students of taking on forms of hypothetical thinking in assignments and activities across the school curriculum. Teachers frequently require students to suspend their usual ways of understanding the world and to try out alternative conceptual frameworks, an activity I would argue also takes place frequently in the first-year college writing class. A writing assignment they observed in a science class asked students to apply seven tests for determining whether something was a living organism. The teacher chose as a readily available model a set of keys, to which students had to subject the seven tests. While the majority of the class followed the teacher's directions and applied the tests, a small but vocal group of working-class students resisted the assignment, arguing that they knew the keys were not alive and that therefore the tests were unnecessary. These students were, of course, correct that the category system was not needed in this instance. However, the point here is that entering a "what if" realm in which one does things one would not do in ordinary life is an essential part of schooling. Yet, according to Sheeran and Barnes, some students, particularly those from less privileged backgrounds, often seem to be less willing to engage in such activities, to enter the "what if" realm, indeed often resist the activities, either because they do not understand the importance of such hypothetical thinking or because they expect a school activity to be more closely related to everyday life and to have more immediate application. Related sorts of conflict and resistance can be found in first-year writing in American colleges and universities.

Similarly, an area in which implicit ground rules were found by the authors to be operating and causing problems with regard to writing assignments in secondary English classes concerned the type of critical stance the teacher wanted students to adopt in writing essays about literature. Teachers frequently required students to adopt "new critical" analytic systems investigating such textual features as character, symbolism, theme, and setting in a particular work of literature. Yet many students resisted these demands, arguing that the category system detracted from their enjoyment in reading and also that it did not seem particularly revealing or relevant, a conclusion that has also been reached by many literary theorists today. Another example of an area of apparent ground-rule problems concerned the extent to which students were permitted to draw upon their own prior knowledge and experience in carrying out an assignment, as opposed to confining themselves strictly to course content. Teachers frequently did not specify this information, and students often assumed that an important ground rule in critical and argumentative writing was that they should only draw upon the actual subject matter as provided in the class, and that other knowledge they happened to possess was strictly off-limits for the assignment.

Ground Rules and Social Class

One key problem that makes the study of implicit expectations so important is that, for most of these areas in which tacit ground rules seemed to be operating, the authors found noticable differences in understanding and performance between students from different socio-economic class backgrounds. In particular, Sheeran and Barnes (1991) argue that privileged, middle-class students, because of their backgrounds and preparation, typically have a better grasp of the ground rules than working class and/or minority students, and that, therefore, the differential mastery of ground rules helps to perpetuate existing power relations through the schoools and into society as a whole. In this sense, the concept of ground rules is closely related to what Pierre Bourdieu, in discussing French university students, refers to as "cultural capital," knowledge of the kinds of knowlege, attitudes, and behavior required to be successful in schooling (1974). Bourdieu argues that middle-class students have far greater access than working-class and poor students to the sanctioned ways of interacting and interpreting teachers' words and actions in school, and that these differences contribute significantly to academic performance.

Sheeran and Barnes's findings support Bourdieu's analysis, with the more privileged students generally more in tune with teachers' implicit expectations, more comfortable engaging in alternative ways of thinking and writing, as well as more compliant about trying out concepts and category systems that differ from their previous experience. The authors argue, along with Bourdieu, that less privileged students are not intellectually inferior to those from more middle-class backgrounds, but that poor and working-class students often lack the savvy, the understanding of how to operate most effectively in a school context, and the willingness to cooperate with and trust teachers, that their more privileged peers possess and benefit from. Composition classes at the University of Cincinnati, as, I suspect, at many other large state universities include students from a fairly wide range of socioeconomic backgrounds, from upper-middle-class to poor, though the majority of students are in the mid-range of the middle class. Thus, one important purpose of Chapters 4 through 6 is to identify and look closely at ground rules operating in the composition class in order to examine their impact on students from different backgrounds. Such inquiry may ultimately serve to raise teachers' awareness of their taken-for-granted expectations and to help teachers find ways of clarifying ground rules and sensitizing students to their existence and importance.

I therefore have several reasons for making the concept of ground rules central to my analysis of the first quarter of college writing instruction. First, a close look at this issue of ground rules and how they affect students' understanding and classroom performance in first-year college writing helps to explain some of the important but generally obscured cultural and political forces behind key conflicts teachers and students experience in the class. Second, working-class and some minority students, that is, less privileged students, appear to be disproportionately affected by the problem of a lack of awareness of the implicit ground rules and therefore may have much to gain from an improved understanding of this issue on the part of educators. Third, I would argue that the first-year writing course, in that it serves as an introduction to discourse and thought at the university, is itself in large part a class about ground rules, that is, about making clear to students the ways of thinking and communicating that will be expected of them, and likely not made so explicit, throughout college and even beyond. Yet at the same time, the writing class has its own set of not fully stated ground rules for students to figure out, and which they comprehend with varying degrees of success. Therefore, the concept of ground rules takes on particular importance with regard to the first-year writing class and can serve as a powerful frame for examining the ways in which beginning college students and their teachers approach the course material in first-year college writing.

The complexities of classroom interaction, and of student and teacher interpretation of curriculum, raise a number of important questions about teaching and learning in the composition class. What takes place when we attempt to enact a highly sophisticated and ambitious curriculum with beginning college students whose understandings and expectations are so different from our own? How do students tend to make sense of the course? How do they go about their work? How do the teachers themselves understand and view the curriculum, and the theory which underlies it, and how do they enact it with the students? What sorts of conflicts emerge when students and teacher's orientations differ? What are the effects of these conflicts? How are they dealt with by students and teachers alike? Such questions have not been explored sufficiently in composition, a field replete with ambitious approaches to teaching but short of inquiry into classroom enactment and possible transformation of curriculum.

Chapters 4 through 6 address the above questions within the context of a particular first-year college writing program, as students attempt to figure out and master the implicit ground rules for the class. But rather than provide a comprehensive, chronological discussion of twenty weeks of instruction, the chapters will instead highlight key areas in which conflicts and misunderstandings frequently take place. In the present chapter, I discuss student responses to one of the primary underlying expectations governing the course. I refer specifically to the expectation that, in terms of their general behaviors and attitudes, students will begin the process of socialization into the academic community. Teachers gauge the level of socialization in part, I suggest, by examining the extent to which students seem to be taking their work seriously, doing it promptly, and spending a sufficient amount of out-of-class time on class assignments, as first-year writing is the closest course the university has to a general introduction to university study. I also refer to the not unrelated expectation that students will learn to extend and complicate their writing processes, which is an important goal of the writing sequence and is particularly stressed during the first quarter.

Teachers' Approaches and the Received Curriculum

A key aim of the first-year writing curriculum is to help students establish a high level of engagement with their course work, that is, to make a successful transition from high school to college not just in their writing and reading, but in their overall work habits, attitudes, and general approaches to academics. As is prominently stated near the beginning of the First Year Writing Program mission statement, the sequence

> is about textuality, how texts are produced and consumed; the sequence, therefore, is necessarily about critical thinking, critical reading, and critical writing. It seeks to give students access to the discourse of the university community, and it also seeks to preserve the student's critical relation to that discourse. We need to help students develop the oppositional, questioning ability that makes of them not just passive consumers, but thinkers who can hold new materials up to genuinely informed scrutiny.

Underlying this goal is the assumption that high school students typically have a more perfunctory attitude toward their coursework than is needed in college, are accustomed to spending too little time studying and completing assignments, and often lack the level of intellectual and critical engagement necessary for serious college academics. What's more, most students in first-year writing have been fairly successful in high school, maintaining at least a B average overall, whatever their past performance in English classes, and thus may desire if at all possible not to change their approaches while in college, despite whatever warnings they may have received about the greater difficulty of college. Of course, no first-year writing class could prepare students for the wide variety of prose formats and ways of writing that exist in college and that students might be required to undertake; from the various disciplines in the sciences and technical fields, to business, to social sciences, and to the arts and humanities, the range is enormous. However, the course can and does attempt to provide a kind of intellectual orientation to university academics and a set of strategies, or dispositions of mind, that will help prepare students for not just the writing but also the kinds of intensive, rigorous thinking, reading, speaking, and problem solving that make up a university education. I would argue that this goal of the course is particularly important for less advantaged students whose families and previous educational experience may not have fully prepared them for the nature of college work.

This idea that the first-year writing sequence functions in part as an introduction, not just to the ways of writing students will be expected to master in college, but also to the ways of thinking and learning, while highlighted in the Program's mission statement, is not necessarily shared, or shared to the same extent, by teachers in the Program as they enact curriculum in their own classes. Moreover, the focus of instruction is not necessarily the same for each of the courses in the writing sequence. The second course in the sequence, English 102, which involves critical reading and writing about cultural and political issues, as well as a research-writing component, may be seen by many instructors as the primary site for teaching careful engagement and critical reflection about one's subject matter. The first course in the sequence, 101, appears to be viewed by instructors as focusing more exclusively on preparing students to be effective college writers. In this course specifically, individual teachers seem much more likely to focus directly on issues of writing, rather than on questions of overall intellectual development, though clearly thought and intellect are key concerns of teachers in helping students improve their writing.

Both teachers, Sherry and Nan, when discussing their goals for 101, make this point clearly. As Nan describes her purpose in 101:

> I want [students] to move away from expressive or narrative writing to expository and analytical writing. I want to wean them away from bad high school or teenage writing habits (gushing, ranting) and encourage them to be more controlled and sophisticated writers. I think we help them be more effective by presenting them with a range of writing assignments and giving them the specialized tools in invention, organization, and self-editing. By the end of 101, they should have practiced these tools and be ready for any kind of college writing.

For Sherry, the goals of the course are wider but also more nuanced. Among other points, she states:

> It is important that 101 *invite* first-year students rather than bully them with a "You're in the academy now" kind of ethos; at the same time, the curriculum should lead them to take risks with their writing in an academic setting—and to become more aware of themselves as rhetors in rhetorical situations, making choices which would affect an audience's reading/response/action. I also want them to develop some awareness of the antecedent notions of genre influencing their relationship with assignments and to begin considering alternative definitions for writing in the academy.
>
> In 101, I want students to explore relationships with literacy, with their own reading and writing processes. While helping them develop a prewriting habit, I strongly emphasize invention. I have become increasingly convinced that this is a critical stage of literacy that most students have not been taught to value and explore. I also attempt to help students become aware of their own subjectivity, competing authorities, and some of the complexities involved in taking a "creative" approach in an assignment.

In addition, both teachers cite sentence-level skills as an important part of students' self-presentation in writing, but both also argue that superficial correctness is less of a priority than are larger concerns of process, rhetorical awareness, and discourse structure. As Sherry puts it:

> I want my students to leave 101 understanding correct (standard English) grammar as a tool which lends them authority with many audiences, especially academic audiences. . . . But, because I do not want students to fixate on surface "correctness" as the end-all of writing, I direct most of my emphases in grading and in class discussions, on content. Students in 101 are still experimenting with the amount of energy it takes to write an effective piece; if that energy is being distributed by writers in a limited-resource fashion, I want them to direct most of it toward critical thought and development of ideas.

While emphasizing that 101 should bring students comfortably and nonthreateningly into the academy by focusing on personal knowledge and experience, Sherry and Nan each assert that the course should be rigorous and demanding as well. There is, thus, a tension built into the 101 course which teachers themselves seem to wrestle with. On the one hand, drawing upon a philosophy that owes much to student-centered writing pedagogy, the teachers want to "meet students where they are" (Nan), and "to invite first- year students rather than bully them" (Sherry). On the other hand, they also have the goal of challenging students to be more reflective, engaged, and hard-working. Complicating this tension even more is the disparity in degree of preparation among students in first-year writing, with certain students who are writing at a fairly high level to begin with and others who have serious trouble even meeting minimal standards of development, organization, complexity of ideas, perceptiveness, and surface competence. If the teacher is at all concerned with maintaining consistent standards of evaluation, as the Program officially requires them to do, then this variation in levels of preparedness can make for a difficult moving back and forth between the nurturing and the challenging stance.

For example, teachers must walk a fine line in making the course doable for those students who come in with low-level writing skills and weak preparation, while at the same time making the course appropriately challenging for the students who enter the course already writing at a higher level of competence. The following section examines how the teachers themselves dealt with this potential conflict and how case-study students who entered the course at these different levels interpreted and responded to the teachers' conflicting desires, on the one hand, to create a comfortable setting in which students would be engaged with their writing and, on the other hand, to create a rigorous atmosphere in which students would be appropriately challenged.

Comfort Zone, Conflict Zone: Degrees of Difficulty in Composition

One idea behind the "greater engagement" approach is that students will push themselves harder if they are engaged in their writing, that is, if they enjoy their work and feel stimulated by it. Yet in examining how students went about their work in 101, we can see just how complicated and multifaceted this notion is, and how great the tension can be between the emphasis on comfort and the emphasis on rigor.

Indeed, as one way of stressing rigor, college teachers often advise students that, for every hour of class time, they are expected to spend two hours working on their own. Thus, students would be expected to spend about six hours working outside of class per week in a writing class that met for three hours per week. In my initial interviews with case-study students, I was therefore interested to find out approximately how much work students had done outside of class in high school, in order to see just how far from their experiences the college expectation proved to be. I assumed that students had spent much less time in high school working outside of class, nowhere near the two hours for every one hour of class that was being presented to them as standard for college. However, what students said in response to my query surprised me. As described earlier, I chose for case study a wide range of students, including some who had been successful or even very successful at strong suburban or private high schools, some with more average academic records from not particularly distinguished schools, and some who had been average or struggling students at average or academically weak schools. I am characterizing schools here according to their reputations, their placement of students in college, and standardized test scores. What particularly surprised me was that even the most academically successful case-study students from the strongest high schools enrolled in the most demanding undergraduate programs described doing extremely little course work outside of school.

A prime example would be Vince, an electrical engineering student in Nan's 101 class who had made his own computer out of component parts, had done well in advanced placement courses (testing out of much of the standard freshman math and science curriculum), and had achieved high honors at a suburban high school with a strong reputation across the state. A child of college-educated parents who had relocated to the Midwest from the East Coast due to a corporate job transfer when he was in junior high, Vince told me that, while he almost always completed his high school assignments, he generally did no academic work of any kind outside of school, completing all of his homework during a study hall period. He did review for tests and also write papers at home, on the infrequent occasions when asked to write papers, but very rarely did he spend even as long as an hour on such tasks, though finishing high school with very nearly a 4.0 grade point average (with extra points awarded for taking advanced classes). As he put it, "I did the slide-by routine, basically, and it worked." Vince was typical of the case-study students, for whom the prospect of spending many hours per week on school work outside of class appeared to be quite a novel idea.

Vince, however, was highly motivated—determined to do well in the writing course and in his other classes; at the beginning of the quarter, he expressed a desire to spend as much time as necessary on his 101 course work, in part because he saw writing as a potentially important part of an engineer's work but also because he saw his own writing skills in English class generally as

> okay but not particularly good. English was probably my worst subject. My mechanics are all right, but the content was never there in my English papers. The critical thinking part. I'm not sure if it's something I can develop. I've never put enough time into it to really try to develop it, but I've never had the ability to just take a poem and get much out of it. I feel like, whatever.

When I asked why he thought the content was weak in his essays, Vince replied that most of his essays had been analyses of literature, and that literary analysis was

> too time-consuming. I've never been very good at reading. It's my
> most difficult topic. First of all, I'm not a very fast reader, so it takes
> me a long time to do things. And then the problem is, not being a
> fast reader, I don't want to go back and read [the work] again to find
> things you're supposed to find. So interpreting literature was sure a
> pain in the neck. . . . I don't read. I've never been into that. Reading
> novels or anything fiction was always just boring. I read for infor-
> mation, I guess. That's when I do reading.

Still, as a successful student in honors classes, Vince had taken advanced placement English and gotten a grade of B, but had elected not
to take the AP test, out of a worry that he would not achieve a high
enough score to exempt first-year college English. "I started to get ready
for it, because I wanted to see what I'd get on it. Then, I didn't think it
was worth the $70.00, because I didn't think I'd pass it, to be honest with
you." Yet despite his profile as an engaged, highly motivated student
enrolled in the University's selective College of Engineering, and by his
own admission aiming for "the 4.0 grade average," Vince's idea of studying was far from the college ideal. As he described his approach to college course work early in the first quarter, "My general strategy is to figure out how much I can put off and still get a good grade."

And as he himself stated, Vince's strategies in first-year English 101
did not differ significantly from his somewhat casual approach to school
work in high school. He did the work that he needed to do, in fact occasionally completing drafts a day or so ahead of schedule. However, he
spent little more an hour or two on his drafts and subsequently did
extremely little revising. Yet once Vince found he could do basically "B"
work with such an approach, and realized at the same time that "A" work
would take considerably more effort, he was quite satisfied to do the
minimum. In addition, despite his relatively strong academic background, Vince almost never participated in class discussion throughout
the quarter. He preferred not to take part and even resented somewhat
those students who did talk in class, viewing them as "you know, always
the same old people, people that just like hearing themselves talk." On
the whole, while Vince was a very bright student, well-prepared for college especially in the technical areas, and while he did consistently B-
level work throughout the quarter, his attitude toward the first-year
writing could only be described as perfunctory; he did what he had to
do to get by in the class.

Moreover, it was not the case that Vince was working harder and
spending more time on subjects in Engineering, his major area of study;
he said that he was working no harder in his other classes, where he was

also doing B or A level work. All of the other case-study students, with two noteworthy exceptions who will be discussed later in the chapter, similarly reported spending considerably less than the suggested amount of time on their 101 coursework. Most of the students did, however, say they were working at least somewhat harder than they had for their high school courses.

Yet Vince and also Elizabeth, an architecture major, both upper-middle class students from Nan's class, did state that first-year college writing was actually a good deal *less* demanding than their twelfth grade English classes! Both had taken the AP course at strong suburban high schools, which had involved considerable difficult reading of literary works such as *The Iliad* and *The Odyssey*, plus works by Shakespeare, Dickens, Faulkner, and others, as well as regular essay assignments. The other students in the class were in their view extremely strong—among the best students in the grade. In the first-year writing class, however, there was a much greater spread of students, from very bright and well-prepared to much less so, and the general academic level, as well as the nature of the work, with the emphasis on writing from personal experience and knowledge, seemed to these students much less demanding than their previous English classes in strong suburban high schools. This sense that the coursework was not particularly demanding and some of the peers not particularly bright or articulate led to a somewhat contemptuous attitude on the part of these relatively high academic students toward the course and toward some of their peers in the class. Vince and Elizabeth each expressed a bit of disappointment about the degree of difficulty of the class, though it must also be said that neither student got an A in the course with their less than stellar efforts. Both were in Nan's opinion solid B students. Thus, at least looking at this one rather crude indicator of academic socialization, the amount of time spent on coursework outside of class, students seemed successfully to resist the teacher's desire that they become more fully engaged in their writing. Because they could do the required work to their own satisfaction without putting in significant amounts of time outside of class, they rejected Nan's implicit ground rule that they ratchet up the degree of seriousness with which they approach their academic work in English class.

Students' Ways of Interacting with Authority

An equally important indicator of the degree to which the students were being socialized into the academic community as part of first-year college writing concerns their classroom demeanor, level and manner of participation in class discussion and activity, and ways of interacting with the teacher both in and out of class. Regarding such issues, I was interested in (among other things) seeing whether the students from less privileged backgrounds, who had attended academically weaker high schools and whose parents had not gone to college, would indeed possess less cultural capital, and have more trouble adjusting to the expected norms of behavior, than did the students from more privileged backgrounds.

In Nan's 101 class, there was indeed a marked difference in the level of savvy, and in general preparation for college writing, between the two working-class students from inner-city high schools, Felicity and Cindy, and their more upper-middle class suburban counterparts, such as Elizabeth and Vince. In classroom demeanor, Felicity and Cindy seemed more like high school students than college students, a bit distracted and often not terribly involved in the activities of the course. They generally sat in a small cluster with two other young women. Shawn was a high school friend of Felicity's, and like Felicity was from a poor background, having been brought up by her mother, who had had serious health problems throughout Shawn's childhood. Chloe was a slightly older (early 20s) and more cosmopolitan woman who had lived in many cities and even traveled abroad quite a bit (her parents had been professional ballet dancers and then ballet teachers who toured and relocated frequently). She had just returned to school after several years of secretarial work and appeared to be at the center of this group, with the others at times competing for her attention. The foursome chatted almost nonstop during class, usually quietly, about matters of personal interest, though occasionally about the topic being officially discussed, throughout the class period. When Nan divided the class into groups, they tended to form their own circle. Privately quite annoyed by the chatting, several times during the quarter Nan talked individually to these students and asked them to be more considerate, but the discussions continued, though generally in a more circumspect manner, at least for awhile. They seemed less concerned that it was not "proper" classroom behavior to chat throughout class, or if aware, did not mind being mildly rebellious, while the more privileged case-study students, though no more engaged in the coursework, were more careful to avoid this kind of distracting, disrespectful, and potentially dangerous behavior.

The more classroom-savvy Vince, on the other hand, deeply resented the attendance policy requiring him to come to class regularly, believing that he would do just as well attending infrequently. Even though he generally sat next to Chris, a friend and a student in his major who was taking most of the same classes, he resisted the urge to chat during class. Of course, Vince also did not take part in sanctioned class discussion, saying toward the end of the quarter,

> To be honest, those class discussions are starting to get pretty old
> with me; it seems like the same thing over and over again. I was
> telling you before about how I don't say much at all, but now I have
> like no desire to say anything. It's just people with the same ideas,
> coming out with their little things. It's so predictable sometimes
> what's going to be said.

But despite his not participating in discussions, Vince made sure,
through his papers and his one-on-one interactions with Nan, that she
knew he was a serious student. He tended to write about academically
oriented topics, such as the principles of flight for his essay explaining a
concept, and two papers specifically discussing school situations, both
of which were concerned with problems of grading. The first was his
significant-event essay discussing an incident of perceived injustice in
his junior year of high school, in chemistry class when many students
in the class got the answers to a take-home test from students a year older
and therefore got higher grades than Vince and several others, who had
done the work without outside help. The second was his problem-solution essay about his college computer programming class, in which the
tests included material not covered in class and points seemed to him to
be deducted rather unfairly by the teaching assistant in charge of grading. Certainly in these papers discussing school assignments in considerable detail, Vince came across as a serious student, if perhaps in Nan's
view an overly grade-conscious one.

Felicity, however, gave a somewhat different impression. She was a
working-class student of Puerto Rican descent from a very disrupted
family and an urban high school that sent few students on to college.
Enrolled in a special program for underprepared students that allowed
her to take below the minimum number of course credits, she had managed to bypass the required composition placement exam, which most
likely would have placed her in a remedial section. Felicity quickly became dependent on Nan, went to see her during office hours, called her
regularly at home (a practice Nan encouraged, particularly with struggling students), and would look to Nan for what began to seem like more
than a healthy amount of guidance. Felicity's dependence began to feel
excessive even to Nan, who had a nurturing, maternal quality in her
teaching and was especially concerned that students like Felicity, from
weak schools, poor homes, and difficult backgrounds, and with fairly
weak writing skills, get the help necessary to pass the class. In fact, Nan
was so concerned about students like Felicity, and to a somewhat lesser
extent Cindy, whose writing was also marginal in many ways and who,
Nan feared, might not pass the class, that she acknowledged lowering
her expectations for those students coming in with relatively stronger
writing skills and academic backgrounds. Thus, she now worried that

the course was too undemanding for those more accomplished students. Indeed, bright students coming in as competent writers, including Elizabeth and Vince, found the course surprisingly easy, put in only minimal time, and were still able to come out with the B grade which they were fairly satisfied to get. As Nan put it, "These students and others like them probably don't even need the course; they could probably pass it in the first week." These students were thus able to focus the greater part of their efforts on coursework in their majors, and did not need to alter significantly their high school approaches to writing.

Students' Approaches to the Writing Process

But what, then, were students doing with the time that they did spend working on their assignments for first-year writing? For the most part, they were writing and, to a lesser extent, revising their papers. Students had other assignments for the class, which mainly involved reading sample essays and keeping a journal, but they reported spending minimal time on these activities, largely because such work accounted for only a small proportion of the course grade. To examine more closely how students spent their time on coursework outside of class, I will look at their responses to a second underlying ground rule concern, the requirement that students extend and develop their writing processes, making greater use of prewriting and revising. This goal of the course appears prominently and in several different guises in the mission statement. English 101 is intended

> to encourage students to reflect on their own writing processes and to recognize those patterns or habits that have or have not served them well; to teach students to try a wide range of invention strategies, emphasizing the importance of what Donald Murray calls "writing from abundance," and of writing multiple drafts before the deadline draft; and to persuade students that revision means more than recopying a paper or correcting superficial errors; to teach students how to revise their drafts, moving them ever closer to being reader-ready.

These goals were stressed in both Sherry and Nan's classes, with considerable class time given over to learning and practicing invention techniques, working on revision, and providing peer and teacher feedback on drafts.

A decade or so ago, most students seemed to enter first-year college writing with an extremely limited understanding of the intricacies of the writing process, having had little experience in prewriting or revising. Indeed, for all but a few students, revising appeared to mean "doing it over in ink" and correcting a few surface errors. These days, however, increasing numbers of students, trained by teachers with Writing Project experience, enter the first-year writing course with some background in process-oriented pedagogy. These students have some experience with such aspects of process pedagogy as prewriting in its various forms, including not just outlining but also cubing, looping, freewriting, and brainstorming; journal-keeping; peer feedback; and revision. These students have learned that writing is a time-consuming activity that can involve considerable thought and effort and can even require rethinking. The students from suburban high schools all expressed familiarity with the "writing workshop" approach. Elizabeth, for example, who said rather disdainfully that the composition class was considerably easier than her twelfth-grade English course, was also faintly contemptuous of attempts by her teacher, Nan, to have students do more prewriting: "Cubing? Oh, we did that in junior high," she remarked. Even Felicity, from an urban high school with a weak academic reputation, which sent only a small percentage of its graduates onto postsecondary education, said that rough drafts and required revision were a normal part of her routine for writing papers in English classes. More students these days also have experience writing their essays on word processors, which make revision considerably more do-able. Yet despite more students using computers and having been exposed to invention and prewriting strategies and to the greater advantages of writing more than one draft, there was in both Nan's and Sherry's classes considerable resistance on the part of students to the teachers' desire that they extend their writing processes.

The 101 course, particularly in the beginning weeks, emphasizes invention and provides numerous opportunities for students to practice prewriting strategies both in and out of class as they prepare the first essay assignment. Moreover, for every essay, students are required to write a rough draft and bring it to class for peer feedback several days before the actual paper is due. It would seem, therefore, that an extended writing process is almost built into or required by the first-year writing class. However, an examination of the case-study students' approaches to the essay assignments reveals a different, more complex, and, one might say, more depressing picture. Students were particularly resistant to the idea of prewriting. They much preferred, and were more accustomed to, simply coming up with the kernel of an idea fairly quickly, along with a general plan which was never written down, and then writing the essay, conceived as an essay rather than as a rough draft, without spending much time exploring various possibilities or considering different directions their writing could take. The one area where students would take some time, often days, in fact, was in choosing a topic. This tendency seemed to stem most often from a mixture of indecision and procrastination. Many students had a difficult time either thinking of a subject that fit the assignment and that they were interested in or knew enough about, or of choosing between a range of potential topics.

This inability to decide fairly quickly upon a topic had unfortunate consequences in the ten-week quarter, in part because it limited the amount of time students could take in conceptualizing and writing their papers, but also because prewriting activities nearly always took place right around the time when the paper had been assigned. Especially in Nan's class, where structured invention activities were particularly stressed, students would typically spend a good deal of class time generating ideas about their topic, and in this time prewriting approaches would be modeled and practiced. However, as I learned from my case-study interviews, often students would not yet be committed to a topic when the prewriting exercises were going on. And so in many cases the students could not really take advantage of the prewriting exercise. Vince would often simply stare off into space or rack his brain trying to decide upon a topic during the twenty or thirty minutes of class time when his teacher, Nan, was leading the class step by step through a cubing, questioning, or brainstorming activity designed to help students generate and organize material for writing about their chosen topic. As Cris put it, when discussing how she wrote an argumentative essay on date rape, a subject very important to her, "I really don't understand the planning process. I just wrote it. That's how I feel, and that's how I do it." Or in the words of Elizabeth, "I don't prewrite. I just write." To a surprising extent, then, students in first-year writing seem to resist teachers' efforts to have them take greater advantage of the composing process, particularly when it comes to invention, generating, conceptualizing, and organizing their ideas for a piece of writing. They do not understand it, seem rather mystified by it, and also do not believe in it. It could be that students are simply continuing to use strategies which, as Janet Emig (1971) suggests, have been effective in their high school writing assignments, where the predominant aim is the kind of knowledge-telling that does not require much planning. Moreover, many students in the first-year college course seem to feel they do not need to do more and find evidence supporting this belief, as they are able to write at least competent papers and earn B grades without engaging in significant amounts of prewriting.

Students were similarly resistant to the idea of revising their written work, though perhaps more willing to revise than to prewrite—and they were also more or less required to do some revision. For each essay assignment, students had to bring to class a rough draft which would be reviewed by other students in the class, and possibly by the teacher as well. Sherry occasionally organized peer feedback as a "read around" format in which she and the students read a variety of drafts, as many as they could get through in a class period, and wrote written comments on the drafts, giving no oral feedback. She believed that students' comments were often more candid and useful when given in writing because students were too often unwilling to go beyond a very superficial approval of the draft when speaking face-to-face. Nan organized her peer feedback sessions as "editor's days" in which students worked in pairs providing one another with detailed feedback. After the initial papers, students were not required to attend these sessions unless they were doing poorly in the course, though many did take part, usually more than half the class. Each student was asked to read one or two drafts thoroughly and carefully and to provide extensive written comments on it. And students were required to show that they had carefully considered the comments of their editor.

The emphasis in both classes was to ensure that students wrote a draft, received constructive feedback on the draft, and took advantage of the revising process. Yet what often happened was that most students were extremely reluctant to revise in any kind of substantive way, and did so only if they were very insecure about the quality of their draft. More often, students would make a few small changes based upon the comments of their peers, but make the changes primarily because they felt they were required to. Both Vince and Elizabeth, on the first writing assignment, went against their best instincts and made a change based on their editors' feedback because they wanted to show Nan they were being responsive to peer suggestions, but each later regretted the decision, feeling they had actually weakened their essays. As Vince puts it, "Dr. Reitz said I probably should not have agreed with the editor in this case. She liked the original ending. You know, we turn in both the first copy and the second copy. I was kicking myself. I had it better the first time." Such incidents raise the issue of the nature and quality of peer feedback, which will be discussed in the next chapter in examining the development of students' analytic stance.

Exceptions to the Rule: Joshua and Rachel

The two case-study students who departed most significantly from this pattern of what amounts to one-draft writing with minimal invention or revision, both from Sherry's class, were Joshua and Rachel. They appeared to have very different motivations from one another for carrying out the assigned coursework, with Josh consumed by a deep interest in his topic and a desire to communicate in writing, and with Rachel impelled by a fear of failure and a willingness to do what her teacher asked of her, in addition to a strong work ethic and what she termed "a desire to learn as much as possible." These two students stood out among the others for their willingness to put considerably more than a minimal amount of time into their essay writing and to devote much of that time to generating ideas, writing several different versions of their papers, and making a number of substantial changes in their drafts. Unlike the other case-study students, they appeared to grasp most fully and act upon their teacher's ground rule that they engage in a complex and extended writing process.

As mentioned in Chapter 2, Joshua was a successful Civil Engineering student in Sherry's class who had recently moved to this midwestern city from a nearby southern state with his family, as his father had taken a position with a large corporation in the area. He was something of a study in contrasts.

Josh had not taken school writing very seriously in the past, though receiving good grades for his work. He described revision in his high school writing assignments as a "joke," explaining that when his eleventh-grade teacher began requiring students to turn in a rough draft with their essays, he and his friends would deliberately write the draft *after* completing the essay, much the way students sometimes describe doing a required outline after writing. "Everybody, what they did was write their essay, and then in homeroom or something they would write a rough draft real quick." Indeed, Josh and his friends began competing to see who could make up the worst, sloppiest, most incoherent, problem-ridden rough draft, a competition he finally appeared to win, with his victory having a surprising effect upon the teacher's process emphasis. After printing out his essay, he would go back to the computer and "take out sentences and mess things up and make it look like I wrote crap. I was typing stuff in there and just playing around." After doing this sort of whimsical post-rough draft for several essays, Josh turned in a draft that was as bizarre and incomprehensible as he could make it, mainly as a joke, thinking that his teacher probably did not even bother to read the drafts, and somewhat curious to see whether or not she did. But it turned out that she did read the drafts, and his obviously doctored draft upset her so much that she read it aloud in class, to Josh's considerable embarrassment. However, the teacher subsequently dropped the requirement that students hand in a rough draft, a change that Josh attributed largely to his own semidefiance of her policy.

And yet, despite his previous scorn for the idea of doing more than one draft, Joshua got very involved in his 101 essays, said that he was beginning to see the rationale for substantial revision, and for some of his papers did make fairly major changes. His involvement in the writing was closely related to the fact that he was able to more or less choose his own topics within the overall parameters of the assignments. A serious mountain biking afficianado who not only rode frequently but had strong opinions about issues and laws relating to his hobby, had worked in a bike shop, and subscribed to several biking publications, Joshua found a way to write about different aspects of mountain biking for every paper except the first assignment. For the "explain a concept" paper, he prepared an overall description of mountain biking, organized chronologically around a single trip from the planning stages through to the postride soak in the bath. For the problem/solution paper, he considered the issue of trail maintenance, and what mountain bikers could do to help. For the argument essay, he discussed the importance of wearing helmets. And for the profile, he wrote about a colorful bike shop he had worked at in his hometown. As he explained, "What made the class go so well for me was that I was able to link every essay to a subject I liked and was interested in."

Largely, as Joshua suggested, because it gave him a kind of nostalgic pleasure to write about his favorite subject and old stomping grounds, often bringing in anecdotes and situations and people from his hometown and earlier life, he got deeply engaged in his essay writing. He typically spent most of a day in writing an essay, reading drafts aloud to his family at dinner time and revising based in part on their suggestions. In preparing his final portfolio, Josh even provided photos of aspects of mountain biking related to his essay topics, inserted between the essays, creating a kind of theme unifying his written work for the quarter. Moreover, he was a serious student with a strong work ethic, a curiosity about life, and a love of language. For example, he enjoyed learning about a variety of subjects from Egyptian history to British romantic poetry, and he liked to pepper both his spoken and written language with occasional use of archaisms. Yet even Joshua rarely spent more than a day on his essays, typically on either Tuesday or Thursday when he did not have classes, made few changes in response to comments by his peers, and like his classmates spent very little time on the other parts of his coursework for 101, such as the journal or the reading assignments, which counted for only a small part of the grade and which he therefore saw as less central to the course. I would argue that it was largely Josh's greater subject matter knowledge and interest in the topic of mountain biking that accounted for his seemingly more serious investment in the course. Other students appeared not to have topics about which they considered themselves to have some expertise. Or if they did, as in the case of Vince and his computer background, they seemed to feel either that there was not much to say about the topic, it was not appropriate for English class papers, or the teacher would not be interested in reading about it.

Josh's experience raises the question of whether he may have achieved too high a comfort level, and whether he might have been better off in some ways, more challenged, for example, if he had been encouraged, or required, to write about topics other than mountain biking. Certainly he did not explore a very wide range of material for his 101 papers, staying within areas where he himself was the expert, writing about topics he well understood. Sherry, his teacher, wrestled with this issue, deciding not to push him into other areas largely because he seemed so much more engaged in his writing than did most of the other students, but also because within the overall topic of mountain biking he was able to explore a number of different possibilities and types of topics, including several kinds of argument, explanation, and narrative, even reflection. As Sherry put it,

> There was a temptation to insist that he stay completely away from bicycles after the concept essay; obviously, one goal in FE 101 is to expose students to varied writing experiences and topics. Yet, I was impressed with his attempts to look differently at one general topic, at his efforts to explore relationships between a personal fascination (mountain bikes) and various rhetorical approaches. He never led me to believe he was being intellectually lazy, and I decided to let him explore.

Josh seemingly found a motivation to engage his writing at a deeper level than that of most of the other case-study students. And he was rewarded for his interest, and his output, with consistently very positive evaluations from his teacher. By end of quarter, he was seriously considering submitting some of his work to a trade publication and was beginning to think of himself as a "real writer" and a budding expert on mountain biking. By focusing upon a topic which he was both interested in and knowledgeable about, Joshua was able to achieve a mastery of the course ground rules which to a large extent set him apart from his classmates, giving him a distinction as a strong writer in the class which he clearly enjoyed. In Chapter 6, which discusses English 102, it will be interesting to see how Joshua responded to a situation in which he could not always rely on comfortable and familiar topics of his own choosing.

In contrast to Joshua, Rachel was one of those students who felt she knew little that was of value about anything and that nothing much of interest had happened to her. Her significant-event essay was a light-hearted piece about the time she thought a small snake had crawled into her sleeping bag on a family camping trip. A student in the College of Nursing with a parochial school and working-class background, partial to math and science courses, she considered English her least favorite subject and one of her weakest, though she did enjoy writing poetry of the rhyming sort, mainly for herself as a cathartic way of working through personal issues, rarely shared with others. Yet Rachel was a "good" student in the sense that she was conscientious, followed directions, and had a very strong work ethic. The previous year, her sister had been a first-year nursing student at the University and had very nearly failed her composition class during the fall quarter. As a result, Rachel was very worried that she herself would have problems, and was thus doubly inclined to work as hard as she could.

About her efforts in 101, she said, "I'm working in English because I have to get a good grade on this paper if I want to pass, basically. I mean, I'm working on it and putting time into my essays, rather than writing them at the last minute, which I tended to do in high school." She was also noteworthy in being one of two students to volunteer for an interesting and challenging class activity for the third essay of the quarter, in which students were to discuss a problem and propose a potential solution to it. Sherry asked for students to bring multiple copies of a rough draft to class for the rest of the class to work on as a way of practicing giving peer feedback in small groups. Rachel (along with another student, Chuck, who liked to write about boating-related issues and did so on almost every paper, though with less success than Joshua had writing about mountain biking) agreed to do so, saying she wanted the additional feedback but also wanted to find out "what people really think of me as a writer."

Rachel's problem/solution paper was on the issue of procrastination, focusing primarily on her own tendency to delay school work but considering her habit of procrastination to be fairly typical among students. She specifically dealt with the tendency of busy students with nearly full-time jobs to put assignments off until too close to the due date, then have to hurry to complete the work. The paper was addressed to a teacher audience, asking for some understanding on the part of teachers who always seem to think their class is the only one students are taking, but also suggesting ways teachers could break assignments into parts to discourage students from procrastinating and find other incentives to encourage students to make better use of their time. As it turned out, during the class activity students spent so much time working on Rachel's paper that they were only able to spend a few minutes on Chuck's draft.

Despite feeling rather nervous that her classmates "were going to destroy the essay," afterwards she said she found the experience quite helpful in getting her to work hard on her draft earlier than she otherwise would have, as well as in providing her with considerable feedback with which to sharpen her ideas and improve her draft.

As another illustration of the extent to which Rachel was a cooperative and engaged student, she was also willing to take part in class discussion, and did so with evident sincerity and satisfaction, taking the ideas under discussion seriously, despite appearing to be nervous as she spoke. Her face would get a bit red and she would gesticulate as she tried to make her points in a way that she didn't in one-on-one conversation. Indeed, she felt a responsibility to participate in discussion, saying, "It bugs me when the teacher tries to get discussion going and everybody just sits there. I'd always be willing to say what was on my mind." For one class session when students were preparing to write the problem/solution essay, Sherry arranged a group discussion about the issue of teen pregnancy that was to take the form of a PTA meeting, with students taking certain roles, such as sex education advocate, concerned parent, unmarried teen father, and student council president, as the rest of the class observed, almost as a talk show audience. The idea behind this activity was that students could practice defining problems, proposing solutions, and addressing varied audiences, while discussing a topic of interest and importance to students. The discussion proved to be a tense and awkward activity, and something of a disappointment to Sherry, with some of the students treating the subject matter very lightly and playing to the crowd, a few other students arguing rather heatedly, and one student, herself an unmarried teen mother, leaving the class in tears. The primary joker was Bart, a former high school wrestler who liked to draw attention to himself by making flamboyant and often flippant comments. For example, he told students during the beginning of the quarter introductions that he had been arrested twice for assault, wrote his first paper about having his jaw broken during a Golden Gloves boxing match against a well-known opponent, and his second paper about a supposed aphrodisiac he and his girlfriend had used. He did his "author of the day" piece about a fatal car crash involving his brother, only to state laughingly after students expressed hushed condolences that the piece was fiction rather than autobiography. Cast as a conservative father for the roleplay exercise, Bart generated nervous laughter by declaring in a "redneck" accent, "I want mah son to wear a 'jimmy head' when he does it!" and making other such lighthearted comments. Yet despite the atmosphere of levity, Rachel tried hard to inject a note of seriousness into the proceedings, arguing as forcefully and straightforwardly as she could that high school students needed more sex education and more access to birth control.

The case of Rachel is paradoxical in two different ways. First, in a class emphasizing critical thinking and with a teacher intent upon developing in students a more intrinsic interest in and motivation for learning and communicating ideas, it was Rachel, one of the most cooperative, if not compliant of the case-study students, who was practically the only one to do the kinds of critical thinking and employ the extended writing process suggested by her teacher, Sherry. But she did so more out of a sense that she was following directions, doing what she was told would benefit her, than out of a critical spirit of inquiry. Hers appeared to be an almost uncritical acceptance of the requirement to think and write critically as an approach which, while difficult and time-consuming, would help her achieve her desired level of success in the classroom. The more independent thinkers such as Elizabeth, who took a critical and often negative attitude toward the class and the subject matter, were far more likely to reject the teachers' advice about taking a critical, interpretive approach to their coursework and about spending time planning, generating ideas, and revising early drafts. Susan Jarratt, in her essay, "Feminism and Composition: The Case for Conflict," illustrates ways in which traditional, process-oriented, decentered composition classes that discourage disagreement while privileging personal expression can actually mask inequities and oppression. Conversely, the case of Rachel suggests that a student stance of questioning and critique, when that is the teacher-sanctioned classroom approach, can itself be a form of cooperation and compliance.

A second paradox in the case of Rachel is that, in a course designed to help students become more self-motivated and intellectually engaged in their own education, it was in part a fear of failure, along with the coercive power of the grade, that motivated her to work as she did in the course. She was not particularly interested in the kinds of writing she was being asked to do, but was worried about not passing the course and wanted to achieve a high grade if she could. Combined with her general ambition, conscientiousness and a professed "desire to learn as much as possible," she ended up doing solid B work. More important, from a teacher's perspective, she ended up taking Sherry's suggestions and pedagogy very much to heart. Toward the close of the quarter, Rachel commented: "I've learned [through this course] that planning helps keep me from going off on tangents and that revision helps me explain my ideas better." She also proved to be a successful student generally in her first quarter of college, earning A's in all of her other classes. Yet it is somewhat ironic that the student to enter most fully into the critical, analytic ways of writing stressed by the 101 curriculum was the student who most carefully followed directions and did little questioning of the curriculum. Because most students' primary goal seemed to be to get through the class with a minimum of effort and as much as possible maintain their accustomed approaches, while still doing as well as they could, and because students were able to do fairly well without significantly altering their approaches to writing, the course apparently did not succeed to the extent desired by the curriculum developers in getting students to employ a more fully developed writing process.

Lad Tobin, in his book, *Writing Relationships: What Really Happens in the Composition Class* (1993), argues that composition pedagogy's emphasis on student-teacher and student-student cooperation tends to obscure the competitive, achievement-oriented attitudes which often motivate students even in classes of teachers who attempt to de-emphasize competition. He also suggests that competitive attitudes, in moderation, while probably close to impossible to do away with, are also not necessarily unhealthy or destructive but can help provide students with the motivation needed to learn. Rachel's experience in the 101 course supports Tobin's claim about potentially beneficial effects of competition. Motivated not so much by a desire to do better than others as by an eagerness to do well in order to achieve personal success, and by a concomitant fear of doing poorly, Rachel adopted the critical literacy strategies advocated by her teacher and ended up feeling that, as a writer, she had benefited substantially from this approach.

In the following chapter, I turn to a related consideration, the development of the analytic stance, focusing on two "flashpoint" areas in which interesting and complex conflicts took place regarding the type of critical approach students were expected to adopt. These flashpoint areas involved problems in explaining a concept, and conceptualizing and addressing opposing points of view in an argument, two particularly difficult interpretive tasks in which students and teacher often had conflicting agendas.

5 Flashpoints: Developing an Analytic Stance

This chapter focuses on places in the first-year writing curriculum that the class found particularly difficult and Sherry found most demanding, as she encouraged and pushed students to move beyond their initial ideas and plans for an essay to a more extended, in-depth consideration of subject matter. I will examine two "flashpoints" during the quarter in which conflicts between Sherry and her students over approaches to writing appeared greatest: the second assigned essay, asking students to explain a concept, and the third, asking students to describe a problem and propose a solution to it. Both assignments asked students to choose subject matter they were interested in and were familiar with from their own previous experience. Of all the essays students wrote in 101, these assignments stood out for the class as a whole as the most difficult to understand, plan, and carry out. Here is where students had the most trouble learning what they saw as new approaches to writing, approaches that required unfamiliar and challenging ways of thinking.

While examining in general terms how students approached these assignments, I will look most closely at the experiences of case-study student Cris. I choose to focus on Cris and her specific difficulties because she represents, in many ways, a best-case scenario. A bright, enthusiastic writer with a book in progress detailing her experiences with men, as well as an avid reader of contemporary fiction and science fiction, Cris approached her essays with a good deal of energy, a strong desire to be creative and provocative, and an unusual willingness to receive what she termed "harsh, picky criticism and suggestions" on drafts from her classmates and from Sherry. Despite these characteristics that made her a very willing and lively student, Cris had considerable difficulty with the concept and problem-solution essays, specifically in thinking through and conceptualizing her topic and approach. An examination of Cris's experience may be helpful in shedding light on the complexities involved in students' development of an analytic stance in first-year college writing.

Ground Rules, Critical Thinking, and the Composition Class

This composition class, with its emphasis on critical literacy, is intended by the architects of the curriculum to be rigorous and challenging on an intellectual level, in terms of the kinds of thinking required of students. As we saw in the previous chapters, students have come to English 101 mainly hoping to get a good grade, but also wanting to learn how to make their writing better by making it clearer, more concise, more correct, and more creative. They also wanted to make their writing processes more efficient and streamlined. In other words, they have come expecting a writing course of a very traditional kind, perhaps modelled on the previous instruction they have received. And, of course, English 101 is a writing course. But the focus of the class will be different from what students expect, for 101 is not just a writing course. Equally important, it is a thinking course, and this is where the most difficult and hidden ground rules lie.

The curriculum is designed to require students to adopt very particular ways of thinking as an integral part of their writing, ways of thinking that many students may be unfamiliar with, resistant to, or even not fully aware that they are being asked to engage in them. For the course focuses as much on students' intellectual orientation and development as on the improvement of their writing skills. This dual focus exists because of the close connection many composition scholars have come to see between writing and intellect, and the priority they assign to working with students on the latter in order to help develop the former. That is, composition specialists with a critical literacy orientation define writing—and structure courses in it—in such a way as to focus primarily on types of analytic, interpretive writing, with considerable emphasis placed on helping students develop their analytic faculties. In composition, this deep interest in students' intellectual development as a fundamental feature of our work can be seen, for example, in the longtime fascination of the field with scholars investigating development, including Perry (1970), Piaget (1959), Vygotsky(1934/1988), and more recently, from a feminist perspective, Gilligan (1982) as well as Belenky et al.(1995).

Chief among the ground rules, or the teachers' tacit expectations in this first-year writing program, is the requirement that students adopt an analytic stance toward their material, whether focusing on themselves and their own experiences and acquaintances, or on texts they have read, including their own, their classmates', and those of published authors, or on some combination of text and personal experience. This expecta-

tion that students will learn to take an analytic stance is manifest throughout the curriculum in a variety of ways. Teachers wish to help students
develop the critical, reflective tools needed to question the commonplaces
and go beyond the received wisdom, as David Bartholomae (1985) suggests in his essay, "Inventing the University." Many students are indeed
quite comfortable with the commonplaces, finding strength and security in received wisdom, but the composition class attempts to push students toward more complex ways of looking at the world.

Specifically, the course asks students to lay an interpretive framework
onto their subject matter, to critique the ideas of others as well as their
own ideas, to develop their own understandings and opinions, and to
support these with carefully considered and appropriate arguments and
evidence of different kinds. The composition course thus has a much
more ambitious agenda than simply to help students improve the surface aspects of their prose. The student's intellectual development is indeed a key, though, I would argue, often not clearly stated focus of the
course. This intellectual development can take many forms in the composition classroom, as reflected in the course content: greater political
sophistication, deeper understanding of the significance of popular culture in our lives, awareness of the meanings of the symbols and signs
that make up our world, analysis of gender roles and other forms of
cultural difference, explorations of literary response, awareness of the
many uses of language, rhetorical understanding, self-realization. What
all these subjects have in common is an emphasis on helping students
develop ways of thinking about and making sense of the world and their
place in it, and their understanding of the role of language as an integral part of this process. Critical thinking advocates and researchers, such
as Robert Marzano, author of *Cultivating Thinking in English and the Language Arts* (1991), argue that this kind of higher-order thought requires
certain intellectual dispositions or stances, habits or patterns of mind,
all of which demand intense engagement with one's subject matter. These
dispositions include a metacognitive inclination to monitor and reflect
on one's own thinking and problem-solving approaches; a tendency to
think critically about subject matter, asking questions, exploring different positions, considering others' ideas, and generally going beyond the
information given; and a propensity to think creatively, looking at ideas
and events in new, uncommon ways. Encouraging such ways of thinking has become a central purpose of the composition sequence. As a result, what was once commonly known as "Bonehead English" and still
lacks the respect of many academics with little understanding of what
composition is about, has now, perhaps partly in response to this historical lack of prestige, become a complex, intellectually rigorous, and

theoretically sophisticated course, at least at the level of curriculum.

But theories are one thing; what takes place in class can be quite another. The dynamics of teaching and learning, and the complexities of classroom interaction, may cause a curriculum as originally conceptualized to undergo changes, perhaps substantial ones, when a teacher and a group of students meet to enact it in class. Curriculum in the first-year writing program exists for the composition program as a whole, but each individual teacher must take that curriculum and make sense of it, adapt it to his or her own preferences and ways of seeing, ground it in a particular, though, at least in part, implicit view of writing, reading, thinking, and learning. This structure adds an additional layer of interpretation to the process than if the teacher were simply developing his or her own curriculum. The teacher must put the curriculum into action in the classroom, at which point individual students then interpret it in their own way, variously influenced by cultural and political forces. And teachers may well reconfigure aspects of the curriculum based upon how they perceive students to be doing with it, which could itself trigger changes in students' understandings and actions. Throughout this complex process, a variety of important—and implicit—ground rules are in effect, stemming from the major underlying requirement that students adopt a critical stance toward their subject matter. To a large extent, this requirement to develop a critical stance, which pervades the composition curriculum, is quite implicit, though enormously difficult to achieve and of great importance in the class. The ground rules stemming from this requirement must be figured out and responded to by students.

Explaining Concepts

First-year writing begins with the drama of self-presentation and self-realization. The first writing assignment of the quarter, the personal narrative, is intended to ease students more or less gently into the course. It involves writing about an important event in one's life, both narrating the experience and discussing its significance. Students' motivation level is generally high at this beginning point. Distraction has not set in, disillusionment is not yet in the air, pressure from other classes is still manageable, and most students seem to feel that they can do well in the course while possibly even enjoying themselves. Most students reported enjoying this assignment, telling about an important event from the past. But many also described having difficulty with the second part of the essay, in which they were asked to reflect on the significance of their experience. They were also somewhat shaken by Sherry's seemingly high standards. They were shocked by the sheer amount of written feedback she provided, and were alarmed to find that she was suggesting—and in a number of cases requiring—substantial revision.

If students found this first writing assignment disconcerting, and were particularly confused by the analytic aspect of it, they were even more jarred by the second assignment, which required greater movement away from the world of events to the world of ideas and abstractions. This essay asked students to explain a concept, not only by presenting factual information but by doing so in an interesting, critical, and creative manner that would appeal to an audience. Many students found this assignment extremely difficult, and said so in class discussion, in cover letters, and in interviews with me; they had a hard time not only in choosing topics but also in figuring out how to turn their topics into strong essays. This section of the chapter examines how Sherry presented the assignment and helped students develop their essays, focusing on how Cris managed the essay. The section looks in particular at the complexities of exposition, definition, and audience analysis, and at how students attempted to organize their work in order to make the topic manageable while at the same time making it interesting for their readers, that is, their teacher, primarily, and other students, secondarily. One intended challenge in this assignment was to ask students to move away from a reliance on narrative, with which most seemed relatively comfortable and which came with a built-in chronological structure, toward a more openended form of writing in which they would need to think seriously about such important issues as how to structure their essay, how to manage and narrow down a large topic, and how to make their essay appealing to their audience. The purpose of this assignment was, again, to have students explain a concept by providing a definition, illustrations, comparisons, and whatever other textual strategies they thought appropriate, including embedded narrative if it helped explain the concept.

After handing out, reading aloud, and briefly explaining the writing assignment, Sherry—typically imaginative and with her usual political edge—opened discussion of the explanatory essay by having students listen to part of a tape she had made for a study of family dinner-table conversations. The tape consisted of a family—parents and two college-aged children, one male and one female—talking about and trying to explain to one another sexism in the 90s. After Sherry discussed this tape at the composition program workshop held at the beginning of the year, many other teachers had also been interested and had made copies to use in their own classes. To introduce the tape, Sherry told the class, "We'll listen to some people talking about sexism in the 90s. Think about the tone, how people are defining something, how they do or don't use specific details, and how you react personally."

After playing the tape, which took about ten minutes, during which time students seemed to pay close attention, with some taking notes, Sherry asked for reactions, and students were eager to talk. Discussion centered more around the opinions expressed by the speakers than around their approaches to explaining the concept of sexism in the 90s. The tape engendered a good deal of discussion, close to fifteen minutes' worth, divided along gender lines just as the speakers on the tape appeared to be. Joshua said, "The second lady was nit-picky. It's right to be concerned with real discrimination, but she was concerned about just regular words like 'man-made.' It's not the same thing as actual discrimination. A word's just a word." Other students murmered their assent, and another male student, Billy, added rather defensively, "Yeah, and all the criticism was pointing at guys." Cris, the artsy case-study student who had introduced herself to the rest of the class as a feminist, responded that maybe guys *deserved* a lot of that criticism, and several other women students echoed this view. Finally, Rachel, ever the "good" student, tried to bring the discussion back on task by focusing more on the writer's explanatory strategies, though even she managed to retain a bit of a polemical edge by saying that the third speaker on the tape, a male, "took the know-nothing approach." Sherry let students talk freely about the tape for several minutes, not wanting to interrupt the spirited discussion. Then she said, "This tape is to open our minds to the idea that we all have different approaches to explaining ideas and defining concepts. The key question is how to attract and engage your readers, how to keep them interested. That's something I want you to think a lot about as you prepare for this paper, how to keep it interesting."

Next, Sherry broke the class into groups of four, giving each group a concept and asking them to "generate thoughts, define and explain the concept to your classmates." The topics, which she had decided upon, included bulimia, vegetarianism, the American family, and several others. She said the goal of this activity was "to share ideas, create an explanation to share with classmates, and to be interesting," thus reiterating the importance of going beyond encyclopedia-like exposition to create a text that others would want to read. She also asked that each group select a speaker "to report on findings." Students worked in groups for about fifteen minutes, with Sherry circulating around the room, asking and answering questions and making sure the groups stayed on task. Upon completing group work, Sherry asked speakers to talk briefly about what their group had found. She responded to each speaker with praise and encouragement, occasionally pressing for some extra clarification or detail. After one speaker had finished, she said pointedly to the class, "These people didn't just define. They discussed their topic as a problem and also proposed some solutions. They went way beyond just a boring, pointless listing of information."

As class finished, Sherry referred students to the homework assignment on the board. The assignment involved reading an explanatory essay from the textbook by a journalist on asexual reproduction in animals, analyzing the essay for its interest value and also considering how the concept of asexual reproduction might be made more interesting. She also asked students to brainstorm possible topics for their essays and, moreover, to practice both explanation and audience analysis by writing about the concept of "death" for two distinct groups, such as 10-year-olds and senior citizens, first listing what they knew about the two groups. Thus, to prepare students for the second essay, the ground rules stressed most strongly on this first day of the unit, reflecting the specific challenges of this writing assignment, included trying to turn potentially boring content into an interesting essay and considering carefully the demands of different audiences.

During the next class, students had an opportunity to share what they had written about death for two differing audiences. Sherry wanted students to first read the lists they had written characterizing the two groups and then the descriptions themselves. Most seemed shy about reading their work aloud before the rest of the class, with only a handful of students volunteering. Louise, confident and eager to speak, and Rachel, ever willing to help out, were two of the volunteers, both of whom had chosen the two groups Sherry had listed, young children and senior citizens. They each read, following which Sherry pointed to and reinforced the audience analysis and explanatory strategies of the two students, saying of Rachel's entry, "Hmm . . . so old people ,knowing more about death than young people, won't need as much background information, whereas young people will need more specifics," and continuing in this vein to model the kinds of thinking she wanted students to engage in for this essay. After Louise and Rachel presented their entries, Sherry asked for more volunteers, and Bart, the wisecracking student whose comments nearly always suggested a desire to get attention, offered to read his. Bart had chosen to write about death for auto racers and golfers, and his comments characteristically poked fun at the assignment while taking it at least semi-seriously; he drew some laughter from the class for his attempts at morbid humor. Sherry, seeing the sarcastic Bart's intelligence and eager to mold him into a constructive citizen of the class, praised his use of humor as an appropriate strategy for the essay, if done thoughtfully. She also pointed out with approval that he had "gotten into the psyche of his two audiences, thinking about how those people think," adding, "This is a very good strategy for figuring out your audience."

Analysis of the essay on asexual reproduction followed, with Sherry listing on the board a set of textual strategies including transitions, developing topic sentences, description, specific explanation, voice/tone, and thesis. After giving students a few minutes to look the essay over again, she briefly explained each of these concepts and why writers use them, suggested a section in the textbook where students could learn more about them, and broke students into small groups. Each group was given specific paragraphs from the essay and asked to identify examples of the above-mentioned strategies in the paragraphs. Following ten minutes of group work, Sherry pulled the class together to discuss the essay's use of textual strategies. Somewhat confused about the specific meanings of the terms but working together with help from Sherry, students were able to point to examples of each strategy. However, the class quickly tired of talking about structural issues and moved eagerly into a discussion of their overall reactions toward the essay. One after another, students criticized the essay as "boring," "dry," and "too technical." One dissenting voice, case-study student Joshua, who was interested in science and nature, said he had not found the essay particularly technical or "jargony." But most students appeared to have been quite frustrated with what they perceived as a dull essay, with several commenting that they had been quickly put off by it and given up, while others nodded in agreement. Clearly, students were not accustomed to this sort of technical and rather complex reading, particularly in English class, though the essay was actually a journalistic effort intended to engage a nonspecialist audience, and was considered elementary enough to be included in a first-year college composition textbook.

In response to students' rejection of the essay, Sherry took a hard line, saying, "We'll talk about this notion of boring. If you think something is boring, that's your privilege, but I challenge you to at least say what specifically is boring and why it's boring, point to something. Or what's interesting and why. That'll be more helpful to your classmates as you read their work. Don't just use 'boring' as an excuse not to engage with a reading." Students responded to her challenge by pointing to some difficult vocabulary and extended descriptions and by stating a general lack of interest in the technical topic. Several admitted they had simply found the essay hard to understand in its level of technical detail. Marty, a somewhat independent voice, said that, while he too had found much of the essay dull, "the part about baby aphids eating their mothers was pretty interesting."

Unwilling to accept the dismissive attitude of most students toward a challenging but to her mind not overly complex text, and sensing that such rejection of complexity was likely to be general rather than limited to just this one essay, Sherry was trying here to encourage greater intellectual engagement on the part of the students. Her inveighing against this tendency to draw back from complexity was part of Sherry's larger project of attempting to instill in students a constructively critical approach to subject matter. Yet with many of the students Sherry was clearly fighting an uphill battle. Case-study students Cris, Louise, and Rachel complained about having to work with difficult texts on subjects they were not particularly interested in nor knowledgeable about. Much of the class, however, seemed downright offended by its complexity.

Somewhat discouraged and at an impasse with students over the issue of reading, Sherry moved the class into a discussion of possible topics for their own explanatory essays. Over half the students indicated they had no idea what to write about, with more than one student complaining that there was no topic of sufficient interest about which he or she knew enough to write an essay. The students with topics who seemed most confident about the essay at this point tended to be those who, like Joshua, an avid mountain biker, indicated having a strong interest in a particular subject. Though even here, others with such an interest may for various reasons not have felt comfortable writing about it. One student said, tongue only partly in cheek, that his main interest was watching television sports but that this did not seem like an appropriate topic for a college essay.

Concern and confusion regarding this assignment carried over into the next week's classes. Sherry had planned to spend much of a class period working on sentence-level issues of grammar, punctuation, and style, using sentences she had pulled from students' significant-event essays. She had a handout ready and a full set of activities planned. However, just as she was passing out the handout, Cris, raised her hand, asking if she could ask a question about the current writing assignment. Without waiting for an answer, she went on. "We're supposed to write an essay explaining a concept, right? Well, I'm not sure what you mean by *concept*." Sherry had another student read the prompt aloud, then asked the class, "How would this assignment be different than the first one?" Carla, one of the small group of students who regularly spoke up, the daughter of a school principal, responded, "We were telling a story, and now we're explaining a concept." Leslie, another regular participant, asked, "Do we explain briefly, then give examples, or what?" At this point, Sherry turned to Cris, who had asked the original question, and said, "Cris wants to write about tattooing. How might she explain tattooing?" Marty said, "She could tell about a time she got one, then [readers] could learn about the process that way." Sherry then asked the class, "What would readers need besides a story?" and went on to answer her own question: "Readers need to understand the subject in a different way. This shouldn't be a do-it-yourself manual here. You have to bring it to life, like in the aphid sex essay. Have the steps in there, but also be creative, elaborate the details, try to make it interesting and make the reader want to learn more about the subject."

Students still appeared confused and vexed about the assignment. Someone asked, "How do we not get bogged down in the details? Should we just not bring in many details?" Another student replied, "We should avoid the boring or obvious stuff." And Sherry asked Louise, who had so far remained rather uncharacteristically silent, "In writing about, say, alcoholism, how could you get bogged down?" Louise considered the question but did not reply, seeming not sure how to answer, but another student said, "Too much statistics." Sherry added, "You could also try to cover too many aspects of the topic, be too exhaustive, especially if it's a really broad topic. So you'll probably want to think of a way to narrow your topic down to a manageable size for a three-page essay." Then Sherry came back to Cris's paper on tattooing, asking Cris what her main point was that she wanted to get across in the paper. Cris said, "I want to show people that tattooing is an art, it's not what other people think. Even the procedure is very different than people think. I know because my roommates have tattoos and we live across the street from a tattoo artist. I'm thinking of getting one." Still confused, Marty then asked, "Could you tell a story to explain your concept?" to which Sherry replied, in essence, "Yes, but don't get so caught up in telling the story that you don't explain the concept."

Shifting gears, Sherry asked, "What will make this a better paper? You might want to write this down: Creative narrowing of the topic." (She wrote this phrase on the board.) Then she asked for an example topic. Louise gave her own topic, "Halloween." For the next ten minutes the class discussed how this subject could be narrowed into a do-able three-page essay. Clearly, Sherry was thinking on her feet as she spent the last five minutes of class outlining a possible essay on Halloween, including in her tentative list sections such as an engaging introduction, a definition, some history, discussion of current customs. Yet she emphasized that the essay should be focused around a thesis or main point that the writer wanted to make about Halloween, and she gave several examples of such a point. Still, despite spending the full class period helping the class gain a basic understanding of what they were expected to do, many students still seemed puzzled.

At the root of their insecurity about the paper appeared to be two key factors: the difficulty of finding an acceptable topic and the fact that this essay had no built-in structure. More than one student harked back longingly in class discussion to the good old days of high school when the content of writing assignments was generally given to them and did not have to be thought up out of thin air as it were. And regarding the structural issue, the paper did not seem to lend itself to a fully narrative treatment; nor did the standard five-paragraph theme many had learned in high school seem appropriate. What's more, the three sample essays in the book, on asexual reproduction, schizophrenia, and American individualism, seemed both much more intellectual and more carefully researched than students' own papers would be, and since this quarter was the first time the essay had been assigned, there were no sample essays written by previous students in the program to help guide them. And too, Sherry had just given back students' first essays, requiring many to revise their papers even to a passing level. Indeed, as the clock ticked away,with only two days left until the rough draft was due, and another two days until the final draft had to be in, with many still without topics, students were understandably quite anxious about this assignment. To an extent that seemed to frighten much of the class, they would need to figure out largely for themselves how to organize and develop their essays. There was no ready-made format for students to apply, and time was getting extremely short.

However, as Dr. Johnson said in regard to a convicted murderer's eleventh-hour letter-writing campaign, "Depend upon it, when a man is to be hanged in three weeks time, it concentrates the mind wonderfully." And so the students, under the pressure of being required to come to class with a complete rough draft in only two days, all managed to do so. They chose a wide variety of topics reflecting their different areas of interest, knowledge, and experience. Nine essays focused on medical or psychological phenomena, including stress, impotence, AIDS, Alzheimer's, drug addiction, multiple personalities, dreams, narcissism, and homophobia. Seven essays examined activities such as mountain biking, color guard, jazzercise, kneeboarding, scuba diving, baseball pitching, and participating in contests. Five essays discussed cultural phenomena such as Christmas, Halloween, tattooing, and country music. Two essays centered on particular groups in society, the elderly and police officers. And finally, two essays mainly narrated an event, though each did at least mention a concept. The attention-seeking Bart described an experience in which he and his girlfriend experimented with a supposed aphrodisiac called "Flaming Love," while Gideon, from a small town in Kentucky, told about a time he had gotten arrested for underage drinking as a way of illustrating the importance of telling the truth. Of Sherry's case-study students, Joshua wrote about his favorite pastime of mountain biking, Louise profiled Halloween, Rachel discussed multiple personalities, and Cris, as mentioned above, wrote about tattooing. Cris was one of the most anxious—and most vocal—students throughout this unit of the course, with her question about what a concept was and how one might write about it sparking a full fifty-minute class discussion. I will therefore look more closely at how she approached her subject of tattooing; how Sherry's feedback and the assigned preparatory activities influenced her; and how she had particular difficulties with what she perceived as the greater freedom and open-endedness of college writing represented by this assignment.

Cris was in many ways an ideal student for Sherry's 101 class. Besides her active interest in writing and her regular participation in class discussion, she was politically aware in a radical, questioning way, and considered herself a staunch feminist, in marked contrast to the conservatism of most of the other students. She also had a lively sense of humor and an uninhibited, unpredictable, slightly off-the-wall quality that added spice to the class. Sherry told me she looked forward to hearing what Cris had to say in class and to what she wrote in her papers. And so did I. Unlike Bart, whose comments, though often provocative, seemed designed mainly to draw attention to himself, Cris appeared genuinely interested in and serious about the course. She viewed herself as a good writer, and had been successful in the past, but saw lots of room for improvement and wanted classmates to, as she put it, "rip her drafts to shreds" so that their criticism would help make her papers that much stronger. Cris said that success in writing had always come relatively easily to her, particularly writing of a certain type—funny, sarcastic, colorful, slightly shocking narrative. That is exactly what she produced for the first paper, describing how her best friend, during a trip to the mall, had confided that she was bisexual and how Cris had reacted to the news. Entitled "Confessions," the essay concludes by accepting and defending her friend's decision, but consists mainly of tongue-in-cheek observations:

> Martine only wanted good-looking girls and she didn't want me. In all honesty I didn't know whether to be relieved or offended. On the one hand, did this mean I was ugly? On the other hand, I don't know how I'd have handled, "Hey Cris, let's go to the mall and pick up some motion lotion to lick off of each other."

A rambling, humorous, provocative personal experience piece was no challenge for Cris; that was exactly the kind of paper she liked to write. The idea of a concept paper, on the other hand, intimidated her; it seemed too abstract and academic, too dry-sounding, and she was not sure how to bring her powers of narrative and humor to the assignment. Also, the matter of organization stumped her completely. She said she had never done prewriting before or any planning at all, for that matter, had written her papers spontaneously and then edited for style and mechanics but generally not for content. Now here was a paper that seemed to require a much more self-conscious and involved planning process, and Cris was shaken. Her insecurity is evident in the cover letter she attached to her essay:

> This assignment was both difficult and easy. I knew a lot about tattooing, but I didn't know how to put everything together. I had a problem understanding the term concept. I was also hoping to get better feedback from my classmates, but I got the same old "I liked it, it was well written." Thanks, but I'd like to know what wasn't written well. I'm not enough of an egoist to actually believe that it was perfect. I had difficulty developing my concept, which was "tattoos as artwork." I couldn't really prove it any other way, other than discussing the artists themselves. Actually I couldn't think of another way to do it. The paper really challenged me because it was a totally different problem than any I'd been confronted with. I'm still not used to college writing, which is, "Here's your problem, Fix it." No how to's, just do it how you think it needs to be done. Which I can do except that I know I do some things wrong and no one will ever tell me what they are until after I've turned the assignment in.

Sherry had viewed Cris's first paper, excerpted above, as witty and clever but, for a writer with obvious talent, rather underdeveloped and with much room for growth. Cris willingly accepted this evaluation, stating that she had written the paper "cold, without any real preparation, just sat down and did it and didn't really change anything except for some little style things and corrections." This method had served Cris well in high school, in which she said she had been an A and B student in English, had participated in a writing workshop, and had written for the school literary magazine. But for college writing, Cris felt she was going to need to be more disciplined, especially after receiving Sherry's comments about her first paper. Yet Cris was unclear about just what this discipline would involve. Prewriting, in particular, was a new activity for her. She preferred simply to sit down and let the inspiration come. While the assignment to write an essay explaining a concept was frightening, Cris had no trouble choosing a topic. Tattoos and tattooing had become frequent topics of discussion among some of the 101 students in the moments before and after class, particularly among the women students. Cris was one of them, and as soon as the essay was assigned she decided to write about tattooing.

What Cris wanted to write was not an explanation of a concept, but a story about how a friend had gotten a tattoo. She had not yet taken the big step herself but was planning to, and writing the essay seemed to be part of her process of "psyching herself up" to get a tattoo. The idea of writing a story seemed straightforward and fun to Cris. She worried that an explanatory essay about tattooing would be little more than a dull listing of procedures, and wanted to write something interesting and exciting that did justice to the topic. The prewriting exercises Sherry had students do both at home and in class were not particularly helpful for Cris, because she still had no idea what information to focus on or how to organize it. She had talked to her boyfriend about how a tattoo is applied, and she had also talked to her neighbor, a professional tattoo artist whose body was covered with tattoos. Yet she had not actually observed him at work, which he did not want her to do and she was not sure she wanted to do either.

Cris was stumped right up until the class session before the rough draft was due. This was the day she opened class by interrupting Sherry's planned activity with her basic question about the assignment. In the ensuing discussion, when Sherry asked Cris how she was planning to focus the paper, she realized she wanted to write about tattooing as art, and the seeds of her organization started to grow. Rather than write a general description, Cris decided, she would try to persuade readers that yes, tattooing was an art and should be respected as such. She would attempt to counter the negative attitudes that many people had about tattooing. This way of focusing the topic allowed Cris to take advantage of what she perceived to be one of her strengths, the ability to argue passionately and effectively about an issue she believed in. She also felt that, with this approach, she could bring in enough narrative and humor to make the essay worth reading. When I asked Cris after she had turned the paper in to describe her plan for writing, she said she wanted to give her own point of view and thus persuade her readers, but also to define tattooing, tell how a tattoo is given, and make the paper funny. Yet this plan was purely in Cris's head; she had no preliminary notes, no outline or plan sketched out, and did not even refer to the prewriting she had done for class, though she told me that work had "helped subconsciously" as she wrote about the topic. She wrote the first draft fairly quickly the night before editor's day, as she was accustomed to doing, taking about an hour, then worked on it some more early the next morning before printing it out for class. Receiving minimal comments from her classmates, beyond positive feedback which she did not fully trust, viewing her classmates as insufficiently critical, she waited until the night before the final draft was due, then spent another hour or so revising, making mainly small changes in sentence structure and style.

Cris titled the essay, "Blood, Ink, and Sweat." She tried hard to convey why she believed that tattooing was art. Her enthusiasm for the topic and her developing knowledge are evident throughout, as is her desire to hook the reader into her subject and make sure the essay is lively and interesting. For example, she begins with a question and an anecdote, and sprinkles the essay with humorous asides and personal information. The argumentative nature of the essay also keeps it from bogging down. There is doubtless much more that she could say to support her view of tattooing as art, and some parts of the essay, though enjoyable, do little to advance her argument; certain statements and images in the essay even seem to undermine it. Yet the piece as a whole is quite engaging, and Cris's personal style comes through strongly, as shown in the following excerpt:

Blood, Ink, and Sweat

Did you ever notice how there is a tattoo horror story in every family? In my family it's my cousin Annie. One day when she was young and slightly intoxicated, she decided that the cool thing to do was to get a tattoo. She happened to find a guy who said he could give her a perfect tattoo for about five bucks.

When she woke up the next day, low and behold her beautiful tattoo had turned into a crooked, uncolored rose. Well, the only thing left for her to do was to get it covered up by a bigger tattoo. Thus was born the awful tiger lily that now resides on Kathy's chest. The bigger she gets the bigger it gets.

Despite the fact that my entire family has warned me against tattoos, using Kathy as an example of course, I still think tattoos are wonderful. Tattoos are more than a craft; they're artwork. Everyone has seen the awful blue faded anchors that sailors proudly display and they have thought to themselves, "God, that's awful. Why would he want something like that for the rest of his life?" But, take a minute to open a tattoo magazine and view the wonderful things needle and ink can do. Tattoo artists do more than tattoo roses on people; they create emotions. A tattoo is more than a picture; it's an extension of oneself. Take for example the creepy tattoo guy who lives across the street from me. His entire body is enveloped in traditional Japanese designs. In all honesty, I can't say as I've ever seen anything as beautiful as his tattoos on paper.

Tattoo artists have to be both artistic and skilled in the craft of tattooing. The craft of tattooing, which is very difficult, has to do with the mechanics of giving a tattoo. The tattoo artist first draws your design on a piece of parchment paper with a hectograph pencil and presses it to your skin. This creates the outline for the artist to trace. Then, he takes his tattoo gun and inserts a needle into the tip. He then dips the needle into a capful of ink and begins your design. The needle creates a minor abrasion while injecting the ink under your skin at the same time. Yes, it does hurt. However, after a few minutes you get an adreniline rush, or a tattoo high. After that you barely feel the pain. There are several reasons why tattooing is difficult. Think of it this way, when you draw on a piece of paper it always has the same consistency. The paper doesn't move, shake, or jump. It doesn't get up and walk away half-way through because it decides you are hurting it too much. No, your paper pretty much lies there and takes it. Every skin type is different. Some people sweat more than others, some bleed more than others. To be able to create similar images on people with any degree of success is not only hard, it's impossible; tattoo artists do it day after day . . .

She goes on in the final two short paragraphs to show how tattoo artists must be artistic, disciplined, and creative. And here she rather seems to run out of steam, devoting only a relatively short space, about a fourth of the essay, to what is supposed to be its main thrust. But in adding an explicitly persuasive stance to her paper, Cris was going against the grain of the class. Few other students approached the assignment that way, choosing instead to emphasize the informational aspects of their topics. Sherry had encouraged students to engage in such "creative narrowing," and one way she suggested doing so was by having a main point or thesis to support and develop. Cris therefore took Sherry's advice and was apparently much better off for it. Given Cris's interest in writing and her determination to improve, it is perhaps not surprising that she took Sherry's advice seriously and produced a lively paper buttressed by a critical viewpoint.

However, her resistance to the planning process still threatens to limit her ability to progress significantly as a writer. And as the course and her own interests move Cris away from her areas of strength into topics that can not so easily be handled by a lighthearted, colorful treatment—to be detailed in the following pages—serious problems arise to confront her written work. Yet at this point, guided and to an extent pushed by Sherry, she found herself working harder than ever at her writing, enjoying the work, and beginning to develop new skills in response to the challenges of the course. Cris was not engaging in the sort of political and cultural analysis described and advocated by James Berlin in his posthumous 1996 book *Rhetorics, Poetics, and Cultures*, in which social practices are examined in a larger political context for their root causes, relationship to the economic system, and effects on different social groups. However, such analysis as she carried out in the essay on tattooing did lay the groundwork for deeper cultural critique. Such critique would be an important part of the curriculum in English 102 the following quarter.

Problems and Solutions

This section of the chapter looks closely at the approaches Sherry employed to help students learn how to do argumentative writing, at strategies students employed in dealing with counter-arguments, and at the specific difficulties both teacher and students encountered. I examine how the class as a whole and Cris in particular dealt with the challenges posed by the role of considering counter-arguments in such writing.

Argumentative writing can have much of the immediacy and power of narrative; it can lead to deep engagement for student writers. At the same time, I have found, along with many others (e.g., Fulkerson, 1996), that argument poses especially difficult problems for student writers. Indeed, much of the struggle between teachers and students in composition revolves around the particular demands of argumentative writing, especially, but not only, when such writing also involves critical reading. As teachers and curriculum developers, we strive to create classroom conditions in which students will care about their topics and will be immersed enough to write with both passion and thoughtfulness. But often, these qualities—not to mention the presence of both at the same time—can be hard to achieve. The level of engagement may be high. As Joshua said, "There's nothing like a good argument, in conversation or in writing." Yet he added that, while interested in politics, he liked to avoid political arguments and discussions in class, especially with feminists, because such arguments could be a little too highly charged for his tastes: "I hate talking about political issues. A lot of times my views are so different from others. And if you know you're right, why waste time talking and arguing?"

Written argument, to be effective, not only involves passion and enthusiasm. It also requires complexity of thought, preparation, and sustained attention. Such writing must be built systematically, conflicting positions examined, one's own developing views related to those of others, evidence generated and then sifted through, generalizations critiqued, audience taken into account, questions of essay structure considered. Stuart Greene (1995) details such difficulties, and examines student and teacher strategies for overcoming them, in his article, "Making Sense of My Own Ideas: Problems of Authorship in a Beginning Writing Classroom." Above all, he suggests, a degree of abstraction, an examination of relationships between generalization and detail, and an ongoing attention to the overall shape and direction of the discourse are required in argumentative writing. It is this abstract thinking and rhetorical focus that many students appear to find uncomfortable, confusing, boring, even alienating. Yet these requirements are exactly what make argumentative writing such a crucial intellectual project in the first-year writing class. If one of our most important purposes is to help develop students' analytic and reflective abilities, a focus on argument, while difficult, seems invaluable and unavoidable. As much as possible, the composition curriculum struggles to retain the personal element, and the high level of engagement that typically goes along with it, even when moving toward argumentative writing.

One of the major challenges facing teachers in working with students on argument is how to get students to take their subject matter seriously enough, and engage with it thoroughly enough, to write strong arguments. This difficulty in creating an atmosphere of student engagement is one reason for encouraging students to write about issues that are important to them and that they choose. Yet in my experience as a teacher and administrator in the composition program, whether topics are assigned or self-chosen, students often prefer to take a less rigorous and more superficial approach to the issue they are writing about than is generally needed for an effective argument. Of course, a resourceful teacher strives to find ways of getting students more involved. As usual, Sherry tried a combination of carefully designed group activities, critical reading and discussion, and invention. In addition, she wanted a certain amount of drama. Therefore, directly after assigning the problem-solution essay, Sherry set in motion a fishbowl project that required the direct participation of only six students, while the rest of the class was to look on and take notes. This activity consisted of a roundtable discussion about issues surrounding teen pregnancy, a matter of real concern to students, as I had gleaned from previous class discussions, and the topic of one of the sample essays in this unit. To prepare, the class was asked to read an essay from their textbook that argued in favor of putting birth control clinics in the schools.

For the activity, students were assigned in advance to roles, including conservative mother, liberal father, school board administrator, teenage father, and student government president. Interested students, in all cases people who had been fairly regular participants in class discussion, volunteered or were asked to take the roles, and Sherry asked them to think before the next class about what their positions would be and what they would like to say. She asked other students, not directly involved in the role-play, to think about the issues themselves and, when the time came, to observe the role-play closely in order to examine and evaluate the participants' ways of arguing. Preceding the role-play would be small group discussion to get students comfortable speaking about the issues. And following the role-play, there would be whole class discussion, both about the issues and about the argumentative strategies students employed. Sherry introduced this role-play as a good activity to help students prepare to write the two essays involving argument, focusing as it did on an important and interesting topic that was particularly relevant to the students. In general she tried to motivate students to take the activity seriously and to view it as part of a larger unit on argument, in part because I had mentioned to her that the case-study students told me that in many cases they were not seeing the connections between classroom activities and writing assignments, obvious as these connections may seem to teachers and curriculum developers. Thus, a good deal of planning preceded the role-play, which should have provided an excellent opportunity for students to practice many aspects of reflective argument, including making, understanding, and responding to arguments. However, an analysis of the activity suggests that it was less than successful, pointing out some of the specific problems surrounding argumentative thinking and writing in the composition class.

The activity began amid a flurry of excitement at the start of the next class period. On the board, Sherry had written people's roles, such as Mr. Bart Mandler, a liberal dad, and she had also listed questions for the group, and the class as a whole, to keep in mind, such as the causes of teen pregnancy, the people affected, and potential solutions along with their benefits and drawbacks. We quickly broke into groups of five or six for some introductory discussion of the issues. In my group, students had a difficult time focusing on the discussion, quite possibly out of embarrassment. Instead, they joked around, laughed nervously, and tried not to meet one another's eyes, with no one taking the initiative to start discussion. After a few minutes, I tried to open discussion by asking what students thought were some of the main causes of teen pregnancy. When no one responded, I asked specific students until finally they were beginning to discuss their views. One student, Clarissa, sat a bit away from the circle and looked to me as if she was about to cry. I remembered that she had written her first paper of the quarter about getting pregnant and having a baby when she was only fifteen. The paper had been a kind of success story about overcoming fear and adversity, how she had gone on to graduate from high school with honors, taking part in activities like cheerleading and student government, and was now in college. She and the father of her child were still involved , though living with their respective families, and were planning to get married. Yet she had also expressed feelings that others looked down on her because of her situation. Not sure whether I should leave her alone, try to comfort her in some way, or attempt to bring her into the discussion, I simply asked if she were all right. She replied, fighting back tears, "I don't feel like saying much today," and did not take part in the discussion. Other students

in the group seemed to sense her discomfort, and the discussion remained bogged down. I felt relieved when Sherry finally announced the
beginning of the fishbowl activity.

The six participants moved their chairs into a circle in the middle of
the room, surrounded by the rest of the class. Sherry re-read the questions and gave the fishbowl participants their charge to discuss them and
try to reach some conclusions. When the class had quieted down enough
for the group to begin discussing these issues, the participants were
noticeably anxious. No one spoke at first, and there was nervous gig-
gling. Then the irrepressible Bart began joking in a mock "redneck" accent, drawing some nervous laughter from the class. He continued in a
semi-humorous vein until interrupted by Linda, who was cast as a conservative mom, but the discussion was uncomfortably stiff, with half the
participants saying little or nothing, Bart going on in a joking vein, and
Linda basically asking him not to be such a jerk. Rachel, portraying a
school guidance counselor, eventually worked up the nerve to have her
say. She tried to be a serious advocate of sex education, availability of
condoms in the schools, and accessible clinics for high school students,
but her earnestness and enthusiastic participation were not matched by
any of the other participants, who, except for Bart, seemed too embar-
rassed and self-conscious to speak freely.

When Sherry asked the fishbowl participants to wrap it up, both they
and the rest of the class seemed relieved. We then began a whole class
discussion, but again students had little to say. Not too far into this discussion, Clarissa gathered her books together and walked out of class,
crying noticeably, and Sherry went out to see if she was all right, asking
students to continue the discussion in her absence. A few students attempted to do so, notably Rachel, but most of the class appeared distracted and uncomfortable, and when Sherry returned, she concluded
class without any discussion about the ways of arguing students had
employed, and the mood of the class was rather unsettled as students gathered their books and filed through the door, saying little to one another.

In retrospective analysis, this class activity took on a Rashomon-like
quality, with participants interpreting and even remembering the events
in very different ways. From my vantage point as both researcher and
Program Director, I left class feeling the activity had been undermined
largely by some of the students, not in any way intentionally, but in part
due to immaturity, self-consciousness, and the unwillingness of most
students to go out on a limb and speak seriously about a topic of some
delicacy. Perhaps they felt manipulated by the activity and were resisting partly because they felt they were being forced to perform. I suggest
this because in many other sections that I have observed or taught, stu-

dents have had a great deal to say about the issue of teen pregnancy, but normally in a less heavily structured activity, simply as part of a class discussion of a reading. In contrast to my impression, case-study student Louise believed the class had broken down in large part because of students' concern for their classmate Clarissa. Seeing her distress, they became "uncomfortable and didn't feel like talking anymore." Alternatively, Joshua suggested that, rather than breaking down because of a too-casual atmosphere, the activity faltered because of *too much* intensity, causing him and other students to opt out: "It was too heated. Some people took the whole thing too seriously, and that opened things up for argument instead of discussion. I didn't want any part of it." University of Virginia English professor Mark Edmundson, in a 1997 *Harper's Magazine* critique of contemporary college students, argues that Josh's view is a pervasive—and unfortunate—one among today's college students. Talking of students on his own campus, Edmundson states, "There's little fire, little passion to be found . . . . Strong emotional display is forbidden. When conflicts arise, it's generally understood that one of the parties will say something sarcastically propitiating ('whatever' often does it) and slouch away " (p. 41). Similarly, most of Sherry's students showed little inclination to discuss the issue of teen pregnancy in class with passionate intensity. Overall, whatever causal analysis one might propose, the rather dismal outcome of this discussion reflects the extent to which many students had serious trouble accepting the responsibilities that Sherry was attempting to place upon them, and as a result, were not engaging in the kinds of arguing, and reflecting about arguing, that she was trying so hard to immerse them in.

Another small-group activity, a week later, revealed a different set of problems. By this point, students' rough drafts for the problem-solution essay were due in four days. They had already had more than a week to come up with a topic, research it, and generate ideas for writing. Sherry had asked students to come into class this day having thought carefully about the nature of their problem, defining it and considering it from different perspectives, so that they could begin to consider possible solutions and not do so before gaining a solid understanding of the problem itself. Their journal assignment for the preceding weekend had been to discuss in some detail the problem about which they were going to write. In the small group, students were to read their journal entries explaining their problems and to get some feedback from other students about the problem and possible solutions to it.

I was in a small group with two other students, Larry and Chuck. Larry was writing about the problem of guns in schools and Chuck was tackling the issue of removing toxic waste from Fernald, a closed-down nuclear power plant near his home. These are both extremely complex problems, yet neither student appeared to have given much thought to them. Chuck said he had done his journal entry, but had forgotten to bring it to class. He had only the sketchiest idea of specific instances of students bringing guns to schools, though there had been some highly publicized incidents in the previous year. The only case he could discuss at all was a high-profile one concerning a lone student at a rural high school, yet he argued that the problem of guns in school "seems to be caused by gangs," even though there was no apparent gang connection with this particular incident. Larry was also from a rural high school and had never encountered gangs or guns in school, but he thought he would urge the use of metal detectors in all schools as his solution, apparently without considering how expensive and how necessary they would be.

Chuck was only slightly better informed than Larry, but then, he had taken a high school class in technical and scientific writing that had focused on the Fernald issue. His class even went to Washington, D.C. to a student conference on toxic waste. For the conference-competition, they had written a collaborative, twenty-page summary which had been judged the best of all the schools represented. He therefore had some understanding of the problems inherent in cleaning up toxic waste sites. But he had little specific information to draw upon in discussing his problem; his journal entry was short and vague. As a result, at least these two students were not really at a point in their research to begin thinking in depth about solutions to their problems, though they fully believed they were ready. The problem was that they did not yet understand the complexity of the issue they were supposed to be dealing with. What's worse, they seemed not to comprehend their own lack of comprehension, appearing satisfied with a superficial level of analysis and understanding, and quite put out by my suggestion that their knowledge did not yet appear close to what was needed if they were to write strong essays in only a few days time.

Of course, these two students, neither of whom was doing particularly well in the class, do not necessarily reflect the level of preparation undertaken by the rest of the students, but my class observations and case-study interviews suggest that most were similarly underprepared and, what is more, only dimly aware of their lack of preparation. Students appeared not to view thinking and learning about their issues as a particularly important part of their writing process. Sitting down to write the paper, even with minimal preparation not really going beyond classroom invention exercises, appeared the norm for most students. The journal, the activities such as the fishbowl, and the small-group and whole-class discussions made up only a fraction of students' grade for the course, and hence were not taken seriously or engaged in fully by many. This approach resulted in a largely unimpressive set of essays that by every indication had not been very extensively thought out. For the most part, students seemed to think they could simply sit down and write successful essays without spending time—beyond class activities— thinking and planning in advance.

However, not all students turned in mediocre or weak essays; some students did very good work on this paper. They tended to be the students who excelled on just about every paper. I also suspect, with some evidence to back me up from the case-study students, that these were also the students who for one reason or another got very interested in their topics and were thus highly motivated to write. That is, these students were really trying to discuss a problem that affected them and to propose a solution to it. Other students, for whom the assignment was just another paper topic, did perfunctory work unless they were the type of student who always put forward a serious effort. So, Larry and Chuck, for example, knew they were not going to solve the problems of guns in schools and toxic waste at Fernald, respectively. The problem they actually attempted to solve was that of writing a paper for their English class.

The class as a whole focused their essays on a fairly wide range of problems. The single biggest group of students, ten in all, wrote about social or political issues affecting large numbers of people. These include teenage sex, pollution, stress, infertility, rape, traffic jams, the stereotyping of teen parents by others, censorship, and stalking. Several of these essays discuss problems experienced by the writers themselves, including the papers on stalking, rape, and teen-parent stereotyping. Almost as many students—nine—chose school-related topics. Seven of these focused on nonacademic aspects of education such as dorm life, drugs and guns in school, bikes on campus, and time management for working students. The academically oriented essays included a complaint about foreign professors who spoke poor English (by Bart, who admitted he himself had not encountered any such professors, though he still managed a high level of indignation on the subject) and a proposal for teachers to take more responsibility ensuring that students kept up with their coursework, for example by assigning more quizzes and regularly checking homework. Four additional essays focused on sports and leisure, including two on drinking alcohol, one on boating safety, and one on trail access for mountain bikers. Finally, one essay, also concerning a problem experienced by the student himself, discussed the effects of worker absenteeism on the job. The case-study students spanned the entire range of topics here, with Cris discussing rape, Louise writing about out-of-control bicyclists on campus, Rachel examining the issue of student procrastination, and Joshua arguing for greater trail access for mountain bikers. The following section will look more closely at Cris's experience in writing her essay. I will depict how, as an engaged, successful student writer with a topic she was passionately concerned about and a problem she actually wanted to solve, she approached the assignment with a high degree of motivation and care but still ran into serious problems in producing a well thought-out argument essay.

Break the Silence

"Nobody knows I was raped, the rapist stole my voice." As I stared at the words I could feel them burning into my brain. It was true, my rapist stole my voice. I never really thought about it until I saw those words underneath the rape awareness banner at school. Few people know I was raped because I am ashamed. I am ashamed of how it happened, where it happened, and who did it to me. I am ashamed of the fact that I trusted the person who raped me. I'm also afraid of the look that people give me whenever they find out that I was raped. As soon as I say what happened, the person usually gets really quiet and stares at me with disbelief, shock, and pity.

I used to think that I could deal with what had happened to me. I used to think that I was over the fact that I had been raped. I thought that I was strong, but I was wrong; I was weak. I never prosecuted my rapist. He got off scott-free, and I got a life sentence of pain and humiliation. I could have told the police who raped me, but I didn't want to believe it myself. Although my family knew I was raped, I couldn't bring myself to tell them who did it.

Sadly enough, I know that I am not alone. This is how most victims of date rape feel, ashamed and afraid. I knew I wouldn't prosecute the minute I stepped into the hospital and told the nurse what had happened. She called the doctor and told him my story. Then, they both stared at me with disbelief, and then they treated me as if I was lying. The doctor said he only wanted to make sure I was telling the truth. He wanted to make sure I wasn't some oversexed teenager with a pregnancy scare. I was treated like I was the criminal; I knew right then and there that if I prosecuted I would be raped again on the witness stand. Most rape victims are persecuted more than the criminals. Everything is done to protect the rapist's rights, while they tear apart every piece of the victim's soul and body trying to prove that she somehow wanted it. Instead of trying to prove that a crime was committed against the victim, the lawyers want to prove that she somehow deserved it. She deserved to be raped? How can you consciously or subconsciously want to be degraded to the point of self-loathing? I hated myself for what happened. I even thought it was my own fault for awhile. The doctors made it seem like the rape was somehow my fault. I told my friends that I was raped, and they asked if I was sure that's what had happened. It got to the point that I wanted to break the mirror every time I looked into it just so I wouldn't have to see the ashamed, degraded look on my face. It was so difficult to talk about it, until now, because nobody believed me.

I was afraid and ashamed before, but I am not now. I will never be ashamed and afraid again. The sick, pathetic individual who did this to me should be ashamed, and he should feel degraded for what he did to me. I wish that I could enforce this message to all rape victims. I wish that I could make them understand that this crime was not their fault. However, as long as there are people who refuse to believe that rape exists; people will still suffer the same.

What this city needs is rape awareness. There shouldn't be just rape awareness week, rape awareness should be year round. Rape is a crime, not a special cause. People would laugh if there was murder awareness week, or a burglary awareness week. Both of these are recognized as crimes; just as rape should be recognized as a crime. Rapists steal your innocence and murder your trust, and yet people refuse to believe it until it happens to them. There needs to be more education about rape in schools, on campus, and in the workplace. There should be support groups readily available to whoever needs them. Free counseling with good, reliable doctors also needs to be available. People need to be educated on why rape is a crime and how often it happens. Courtrooms and lawyers need to realize that once a rapist rapes, he has no rights. The only way to do this is through education. Start teaching rape awareness in the schools; teach the children that no means no. In high schools and on campus teach students that they have a right to what happens to their body. Teach students and faculty that anyone can be a rapist. A rapist is not just a big ugly man; a rapist can be the boy next door too.

My voice was stolen, but I will never be silenced again. Everyday, thousands of women and men are silenced by their rapists. The silence must stop now! Educate your family and friends on rape awareness and rape prevention.

Cris was generally, in Sherry's view as well as my own, one of the stronger writers in the class and one of the most enthusiastic and articulate participants in discussions and activities. Yet perhaps one reason she seemed so comfortable in the class, and such a strong writer, was that she had found a way to write about what interested her most. She differed from other students who struggled to find an acceptable focus for the essay partly, it may be, because she had such definite areas of interest. Many other students I talked with told me they did not really have a hobby or pastime that seemed respectable enough to be the subject of college essays. Shopping, playing cards, watching sports, fixing cars, and listening to heavy metal music could all make for interesting reading, yet there was a tendency for students, especially those who viewed themselves as not particularly strong writers, to avoid writing about issues related to such topics, even if the student had a solid understanding of it and considerable experience with it. These students, despite Sherry's urging that they write from a position of knowledge, often did not do so, and usually with very negative consequences for their writing. A prime example would be Larry, with his problem-solution essay on guns in school. He knew nothing about this subject and was only vaguely interested in it, but rather than choose a topic closer to home he went with what he believed would be a more respectable choice, and ended up writing a very poor essay. Joshua, on the other hand, was confident enough to write about what really interested him, and a good enough writer, knowledgeable enough about many aspects of mountain biking, including social, political, and environmental issues surrounding the topic, to produce papers that held the interest of his teacher and his peers. Thus, it seems that an important site of student-teacher conflict and disagreement is in the area of choosing what to write about. Students often simply do not see that their own interests can serve as excellent choices for essay topics or can help them find important issues to discuss. The student who believes the teacher when she urges the class to write about ideas and issues of genuine interest, is thus at a considerable advantange, while the less savvy student who does not, and I observed a number of them, appears to make the course even more difficult than it needs to be.

However, it would be too easy to say that if all students wrote about material of deep personal interest, then all students would write with greater engagement and that, therefore, the quality of their work would be much improved. For it seems that, in many cases, the better student writers tend to be the ones who are deeply engaged in some interest or another, while the less successful ones are often those who appear more detached both from the demands of the writing class and from issues, problems, and potential areas of interest in their own lives. That is, those students who seem rather passive, without strong interests or opinions, were generally among the less successful writers in the composition class, particularly when the class emphasized engagement and the writer's highlighting his or her own perspective as opposed to a more detached discussion of a topic. The pedagogy underlying the composition curriculum greatly favors those students who have or are able to simulate a strong interest in their subject matter, while the more detached, seemingly less passionate students, find their writing, while it may be competent or even skillful, less highly valued. Therefore, students in one of the demanding professional colleges (architecture, engineering, drama) who are, understandably, primarily concerned with the classes in their major, though they may be quite successful students, often tend not to be among the top students in the composition classes. Josh, however, found himself very interested in his writing, and this engagement was a major factor in his success in composition.

And yet, of course, engagement in the subject matter alone could not guarantee successful performance. For example, Cris wrote two papers on the issue of rape, about which she was extremely concerned as well as painfully knowledgeable. Cris was perhaps too close to her issue to write a strong essay. Ironically, given the advice she gave to Josh to tone down his language, Cris wrote such a dogmatic, strident essay that only those who already agreed with her position could find it convincing. She could not get the necessary distance from her subject to write convincingly about it. In addition, she was most comfortable with humorous, personal-experience writing, an approach she felt could not work with this essay, and so was experimenting with a new format and having real difficulties with argumentative writing, not yet having learned how to use her existing talents to serve this different rhetorical purpose.

And like Cris, two other case-study students in Sherry's course, Rachel and Louise, also felt considerably less comfortable as the course moved away from personal-experience writing. Rachel in particular seemed, in Sherry's words, "nostalgic for the joy she experienced in the first essay," in which she described a family camping trip when she (mistakenly) thought a snake had crawled into her sleeping bag, after she had frightened her little sister about the dangers of snakes in order to keep her quiet. As Rae Rosenthal (1995) suggests in her essay, "Feminists in Action: How to Practice What We Teach," many women writers (and male writers as well) seem to prefer non-agonistic ways of writing that are "less combative, definitive, and formulaic and more anecdotal and questioning than is academic discourse generally "(p. 145). Indeed, all of the case-study students, including Joshua, expressed a preference for writing whose primary purpose was not argumentative, writing that told a story, evoked a humorous response, laid out information, or discursively explored a topic of personal interest. In moving into argument, even while writing about issues students themselves had chosen, students had ventured into uncomfortable territory. As Cris's experience shows, even with the many supports Sherry tried to provide, and even when writing about self-chosen topics, students had a very difficult time figuring out and managing the demands of written argument.

Conclusion

The idea of engagement, its relationship to success in the first-year writing course, and its usefulness in explaining the performance of Sherry's students, can be understood in the context of the notion of ground rules discussed earlier. An important part of the work of English 101 for Sherry, and perhaps the most difficult part of the course for students, involved helping—and in many cases pushing—students to be more analytic in the ways they approached their course work. She wanted students to critically review their drafts, to question and extend their ideas, to consider multiple points of view regarding their topics, and to examine and reflect upon the nature of their own work. Most students, including the case-study students discussed in this chapter, found this work not only challenging but also quite different from most of what they had previously been asked to do in school. In Cris's case, though she was deeply engaged in the course, highly motivated about her writing, and intensely interested in the subject she was writing about, she may have been so close to the difficult subject-matter that the kind of calm, deliberate self-reflection and critical thinking Sherry wanted students to engage in were not possible.

Sadly, due to financial problems, Cris was forced to drop out of school following her first quarter of college, despite earning a 3.5 average for the term and doing fine in the composition class. She resolved at this time to get a full-time job, save money, gain residency in the state, and return to college as soon as she could afford to, this time paying the less expensive, in-state tuition. Rather predictably, perhaps, out of the eight case-study students I worked with in both Sherry's and Nan's classes, the only other student to drop out during the study was Felicity, the only student of color in my sample, who came from a very low-income background. Though not as successful in the classroom as Cris, she too dropped out of college not primarily for academic reasons but rather to work full-time, planning to transfer to a smaller state college about an hour's drive from the city. The case of both Cris and Felicity offers the clearest illustration possible of the marginalization of low-income students. The following chapter takes up further this issue of marginalization, but in the context of the second quarter of the composition sequence, which involved reading and writing about political and cultural issues.

6 Persuasion, Politics, and Writing Instruction

Where English 101 kicks off with excitement and anticipation, 102 more often begins with a touch of wariness and irritation. This change of mood is understandable given the course's sensitive subject matter—argument about issues of race, economic equality, and the family—and its timing in the college schedule. Back to school still smarting a bit from the academic and social adjustments of their first quarter in college, students seem from their tired expressions to have lost some of the expectation of novelty and possibility that characterized the beginning of 101 just three months earlier. In interviews, case-study students Joshua and Louise confirm this relative lack of enthusiasm, in comparison with their excitement at the beginning of the previous quarter. In Louise's words: "I hated 102 from the start, though it wasn't necessarily 102. It was winter. January and February are depressing months for me anyway after the holidays, getting back to the grind. And then all those things we talked about from the textbook, the political stuff. I thought there was no point to it all. It was irrelevant to what I needed to be in college for, so I lost patience right away."

By the beginning of winter quarter, students have experienced the grind, become a little more disillusioned and cynical. High-rise dorm dwellers have suffered the cold showers, bad food, broken elevators, and midnight fire alarms. Commuters have agonized over traffic jams, road construction, and the lack of parking. Students have heard from their 101 teachers or from peers that 102 will be a demanding course filled with abstract readings from a political textbook, *Rereading America* (Colombo, Cullen, & Lisle, 1992) and with complicated writing assignments. Sherry's students, about a third of whom were in her section the previous quarter, do not seem to be especially looking forward to the class. And so, after passing out her course description, Sherry begins the quarter by emphasizing the first paragraph, which she reads aloud:

> *Your Course Objective:* To explore, with a challenging eye, the cultural forces which have shaped your life . . . to analyze, argue and ponder perspectives regarding the individual, the family, progress and opportunity, race, gender, education, media and democracy . . . to discover your own writing authority by pushing yourself to take

some risks. Last quarter, you wrote essays drawn from personal knowledge and experience. This quarter will involve critical thinking, research, and closer, more complex reading. There are no rules stating that you have to agree with what you read in a text or with what you hear from a teacher or peer. But before rising to the challenge, you'll want to thoughtfully examine "other" ideas. If you keep an open mind, you'll be better equipped to search for words that will lend power and impact to your own ways of seeing. Success in 102 includes (1) finding your own creative ways to make topics and assignments personally interesting—especially if your first instinct is to label them "boring" or "too hard"; (2) believing that you have something worthwhile to say about the world around you; (3) saying it—after you've debated/pondered/listened/read/explored beyond the surface.

In underscoring this first paragraph, Sherry addresses the potential problems of complexity, level of difficulty, lack of motivation, alienation, and ennui. Aware that much of teaching is persuasion, she enthusiastically invites students to find ways to make the course, and its subject matter, their own, and not to fall back on convenient excuses that the work is just too hard or not interesting enough for them. Pointing to the last line of the paragraph, she foregrounds the importance of critical examination of complex issues. She tries her best to generate excitement about the topics to be covered, saying, "We're going to discuss issues that affect us," and describes the course as requiring a "questioning attitude." She makes it clear that the class will deal with socially important issues; that students owe it to themselves to be interested in these issues. She emphasizes that, for a democracy to work, citizens have to be not just knowledgeable and politically aware, but able to express their ideas and opinions to one another. Later in the class, to get students into an arguing frame of mind, she asks them to take out a piece of paper and "develop an opinion about something, anything, whatever you like, and write about it for around five minutes. Then we'll talk some about what you wrote." The results reflect the gulf that exists between students' interests and the curriculum. The following pieces offer a fairly representative sampling.

Amy

My favorite topic to discuss has to be the idea of a "well-rounded" student. I can not stand the emphasis put on this educational flaw. I feel that a person should only be required to take classes that pertain to them and their future, not a worthless elective soon to be forgotten.

I'm sure for some people taking electives is a good idea, but if you've chosen a major and are sure of the direction you'd like to head towards, then electives just waste time. A good example would be history classes. Why should anyone have to take a history class if they don't plan on going into teaching or something. They may be wanting to become an accountant yet can't pass their history class to achieve this goal. That's stupid!

I think a well-rounded person should be defined as someone who chooses what they become.

———————

Bev

I believe it is better for me and everyone else in this class not to have to climb three flights of stairs at nine o'clock Monday morning or any morning for that matter. Last quarter was hellish because of the penthouse classroom that was assigned. I think being able to walk in a door and right into class without being out of breath will make me more relaxed and alert, making me more eager to learn. Getting up early in the morning for class is bad enough without having to look forward to the marathon journey you will have to undertake to get there. I say either make all buildings one level or get elevators that always work and that you don't have to wait forever to catch.

———————

Joshua

I hate "women's libbers"! I believe in equal rights of men and women. But I still think w.l.'s take things a little too far. I'm the type that opens doors, stands up when ladies enter the room, throw my coat over the puddles (well, maybe not that). It makes me mad when women don't appreciate these things or feel it is degrading. Men and women should have equal rights, but I still believe in the stronger and weaker sexes and the abilities and responsibilities of each.

———————

Wendy

I hate coming up with things to voice my opinion on. Don't get me wrong. I love to talk and I especially love to voice my opinions, but I hate starting an argument.

Seriously, what really makes me mad is the issue of racism. For example, if a black person is excluded from something, it's racism and discrimination, but if a white person is excluded from something, it's ok. A prime example, Miss Black USA Pageant. Don't you think if there were a Miss White USA Pageant, all hell would break loose?

Other students covered a wide range of topics, including two anti-abortion pieces, several other statements opposing required courses outside the major, a comment against bombing abortion clinics, as well as pieces on the importance of seat belts, lowering the drinking age, the importance of alcohol in our culture, the greed of doctors, the difficulty of having to find one's own essay topic, and the unfair standards of a biology professor from the previous quarter. Many students' choice of topics seemed to be influenced by the timing of the assignment. Activities related to New Year's Day, such as parties, football bowl games, and car accidents figure prominently, as do important recent news stories, first day of term concerns about course selection and grades, and even the time of day, as with the complaint about having to walk stairs early in the morning.

Of course, it hardly needs saying that these pieces do not represent students' best or most carefully thought out work. They were writing a brief, impromptu opinion with very little preparation time and no opportunity to revise, on the first day back after Christmas break. Also, students knew their opinions would be shared with their classmates and quite possibly seen by their teacher (not to mention this researcher) as well, and therefore may have focused their attention more on issues of style, mechanics, and word choice, as opposed to substance, than would have been the case if they had had more time. For such reasons, these pieces are not indicative of the kind of argument and consideration of ideas students are capable of, given adequate time and instruction. Yet I would argue that these free writes do suggest, the way free writes often do, in a general sense where students are coming from intellectually and emotionally—their moods, their inclinations, their interests, their frames of mind, in sum, the ways of considering issues and of arguing which they have cultivated over time and brought with them to English 102.

With only a few exceptions, such as a piece calling for increased AIDS research and another condemning prejudice toward minorities, students' opinions that were explicitly political tended to be conservative. Many were also rather anti-intellectual, as in the pieces depicting college as a place that should be for career preparation only (see Hofstadter, 1963, for a discussion of the prominent role of anti-intellectualism in American culture). Students' pieces were often self-absorbed in focusing solely on the students' personal situation without considering larger implications; and they frequently seemed a little petulant that things should be as they were. Few students considered their issue from more than one perspective, offered any counter-arguments, or engaged in what might be considered exploring an idea. As a group, the opinions had the flavor of comments that callers might make on radio talk shows. Though some of the pieces were quite intriguing, the act of reading these opinions was, on the whole, somewhat deflating for Sherry—and for me—

because so many seemed rather reactionary, whiny, and solipsistic. On the other hand, the pieces also underlined the importance of a course such as English 102. Reading them, Sherry and I both felt strongly that students needed to learn more about critical analysis, argument, and political and cultural issues.

These opinions set the stage for the conflicts that would ensue throughout the quarter of writing instruction. The course would strenuously test students' developing reading and writing abilities, their intellectual abilities more generally, and their political beliefs and understandings, with a resulting classroom atmosphere that was often fraught with anger, incomprehension, and disagreement. Given students' many difficulties, the course would also test Sherry's abilities as a teacher. The remainder of this chapter will examine, first, theoretical and pedagogical issues underlying the politically focused subject matter of English 102, and second, attempts of Sherry to teach argumentative writing in response to critical readings. The chapter focuses on the efforts of Sherry's students, in particular, case-study student Louise, to learn how to satisfy the requirements of the course while at the same time resisting the interpretive stances Sherry was promoting.

Theoretical and Pedagogical Considerations

While it has a long history dating back to the "great idea" and current event courses of the early part of the century (Berlin, 1987, 1996), this politically oriented 102 course has been most influenced by contemporary composition theory. In what has come to be known as "the social turn" in composition studies (Trimbur, 1994), theorists have increasingly focused their attention on issues of equality, social justice, group differences, and oppression, and this interest has also found its way into many classrooms. Politically focused textbooks, teaching methods, and curricula have become common, at least among teachers who keep up with the literature. These approaches include, among others, multicultural analyses; critical examinations of American society and government; studies of race, gender, class, and sexual orientation; investigations of popular culture and media; semiotic analyses of prominent cultural symbols; and more. Such approaches have been popular since at least the early 1990s. But I would argue that this political stance in composition should not be seen as a new or even a recent phenomenon. Composition has long been a highly political field. I do not mean political only in the sense that, unlike most academic disciplines, composition focuses a good deal of its attention on teaching, and teaching can always be said to be political, in supporting, questioning, or even ignoring aspects of the status quo. Rather, I would suggest that, since the late 1960s, there has been a significant, explicitly political component to composition theory, and, accordingly, since instruction has been in large part theory-driven, to the teaching of writing at the college level. The field has been characterized by pedagogies of political progressivism that have placed great value on working with beginning students, including so-called underprepared or nontraditional students, and that have questioned elitist notions so prevalent in academia generally.

The modern discipline of composition studies was formed in a highly charged political atmosphere, coming on the heels of the college activism of the 1960s, and benefiting from the ideas, participation, and enthusiasm of some of those activists who turned their political energies to the cause of liberating students through writing pedagogy. Macrorie (1970), Elbow (1973), and Murray (1968) were making explicitly political statements in advocating turning over a good deal of classroom authority to their students and in challenging traditional adherence to academic conventions and genres. Shaughnessy and other basic writing specialists were arguing—and demonstrating—that students often viewed as incapable of college-level work could succeed if their teachers would take the time to understand and encourage them, and to work with them in an atmosphere of respect. Bartholomae (1985), Bizzell (1992), Bruffee (1984), and others, in their work on academic conventions and discourse communities, were aiming for greater inclusiveness in the normally restrictive academy. From an opposing direction, Britton and his British colleagues (1975), and American adherents such as Knoblauch and Brannon (1984) argued *against* the imposition of traditional academic discourse conventions and in favor of students using their own informal language and pursuing their own interests to explore academic subject matter. But they too were involved in the same quest for greater inclusiveness. Terms saturated with political meaning, such as *democratization, empowerment, autonomy, ownership, community*, and *liberation*, have been common in the field for some time.

The emerging discipline of composition itself openly challenged the more established and conservative field of literary study for a share of academic power and respectability. The focus of this early pedagogical work, and much of the developing theory, was directed toward opening up previously closed doors, helping individual students to find voice and disadvantaged groups to gain access, and turning the composition classroom into a more egalitarian site that emphasized collaboration and mutual growth rather than assessment, conformity, and gatekeeping. This joining of political, scholarly, and pedagogical interests drew budding academics like me to the field, lending a sense of excitement and relevance lacking in many other disciplines, including, at that time, most literary and linguistic studies. Beyond the academic interest, it was in part this sense of political progressivism, the idea that teaching writing was in key ways an anti-establishment activity, that drew me, and many others as well, to the field of composition. Initially a graduate student in theoretical linguistics, I found the subject matter fascinating but the discipline too remote from the struggles of everyday people. Prior to coming to graduate school, I had been teaching and counseling juvenile offenders. I saw teaching composition as academic work with a social conscience, work that would allow me to continue helping people improve their lives. Due to pressures for open admissions policies, higher education was beginning to provide access for increasing numbers of nontraditional students, and composition stood at the forefront of these efforts. Composition studies was a new field that could at the same time fight for academic respectability, help disadvantaged students, allow increased contact with and respect for students generally, and promote change in educational practice from within the system.

Now, more than two decades after these early manifestations—and manifestos—of radical writing instruction, with the infusion of several mini-generations of new texts and new theories, and with years to reflect on our goals as an academic community, the political landscape in composition has shifted from its prior focus on making the academy more inclusive and providing a student-centered pedagogy to a more ambitious focus on taking an active role in politics. One would expect and even welcome such changes of approach in a field characterized by a willingness to consider outside ideas, by an often generous inclusiveness of a variety of positions and approaches, by lively debate and inquiry, and by a longstanding interest in the politics of teaching and learning. Largely quiescent for so many years, literary study has itself been radicalized by the rise of critical theory and cultural studies, much of this work coming from continental Europe and Great Britain. Composition specialists have brought the new, politically oriented work into our thinking about the teaching of writing, moving closer to literary study after years of hostility and tense coexistence, in the process destabilizing and calling into question many of our most comfortable assumptions about our students and ourselves.

Critical theory in its various manifestations has caused many of us to examine the possibility of our own complicity as writing teachers and administrators in institutions that may help to perpetuate existing inequities. Foucault (1982) in particular has been effective in depicting ways in which even institutions designed to help individuals, such as education, can be subtly responsible for oppression of the disadvantaged and suppression of dissent. Work in critical theory, such as Derrida's theory of deconstruction (1981) and other postmodernist approaches, has also called into question many of our fundamental concepts in the teaching of writing, such as the idea of voice and the existence of a unified self that can be represented in texts, an independent subject outside of discourse, culture, and politics. Critical pedagogy, a set of theories of teaching identified with Freire (1970) and Giroux (1988) and much influenced by Frankfurt School Marxism, has raised the possibility of teaching more directly for social change, not only to empower individual students or provide access for underrepresented minorities, but to address explicitly in the composition class questions of political conviction and activity and to work against inequities in society. Feminist composition scholars such as Flynn (1988), Jarratt (1991), and Kirsch (1993) have also helped lead the way here, arguing for the legitimacy of moving beyond narrow issues of writing skill or even personal empowerment in the composition class into larger areas of belief, ideology, and action. Proponents of cultural studies, such as Bennett (1990) and Hall (1980), representatives of the Birmingham school, have influenced the development of curricula designed to help students uncover oppression and bias in their own society (e.g., Fitts and France, 1995).

Leading composition scholars, convinced of the need to go beyond simply providing access to education and effective writing instruction for traditionally discriminated against groups, draw on these academic traditions to argue for a pedagogy that attempts to persuade students to adopt political positions that foreground social justice concerns. In a self-critique of her own years of work advocating teaching academic discourse to basic writers, Bizzell cites Rorty's and Fish's anti-foundationalist position for the rhetorical basis of all knowledge and truth, and quotes sophistic philosophy to argue that as teachers we are responsible for "education of the whole person in culturally endorsed values" (1992, p. 281), not just for teaching writing as a "value-neutral" component or skill. She suggests that instructors therefore have the right, if not the obligation, to use rhetoric to persuade students to work for justice. In a 1994 *CCC* review essay, Trimbur applauds Bizzell for her emphasis on working for political action and social change. He criticizes two other progressive, theoretically oriented books on composition teaching, one by Spellmeyer (1993) and the other by Knoblauch and Brannon (1993), specifically for not going far enough in their attempts to use the classroom as a vehicle for radical politics. Trimbur notes that, while both books offer pedagogies influenced by a commitment to political change, they fall short, in his estimation, because of their unwillingness to advocate directly a social agenda. For Trimbur and others who share his views, the composition class is a political space in which teachers need to find the courage to advance their progressive views, and Bizzell is to be praised for her efforts "not to liberate her students from a false consciousness, but to hold them to their best visions of themselves and of a democratic commonwealth devoted to the interests of all its members" (p. 118).

Not surprisingly, perhaps, students often do not take so kindly to English 102. They tend to hark back frequently to the halcyon days of the previous quarter when the subject matter seemed so much more manageable—though at the time, students complained regularly about 101 as well. But in the politically oriented 102 class, which as I have argued has the twin purposes of teaching writing and teaching political concern and understanding, students frequently offer what I think of as "twin resistance" to these goals. First of all, even when teachers make it clear that they are free to develop and express their own views, students often complain that they are being force-fed "a liberal ideology." That is, they resist *politically*. They worry that the deck is unfairly stacked against them, that they lack the expertise and eloquence to argue effectively against the intellectuals, academics, and professional writers whose work, whose arguments they must respond to. And at the same time, they resist *intellectually* the work they are being asked to do in reading what seem to them unnecessarily abstruse essays and taking on the difficult task of forming and supporting interpretations of what they are finding out are surprisingly complex issues.

Of course, these two forms of resistance are not unrelated, and are frequently hard to disentangle, but I suggest they still need to be distinguished in efforts to make sense of the kinds of teaching and learning issues that characterize the politically oriented composition class. For even when the subject matter is treated far less politically, say as aesthetic analysis of literature, students may well offer similar resistance to efforts at requiring them to read difficult texts, consider varying positions, and formulate and expand upon their own ideas. In other words, they would still resist intellectually. But when the subject matter under scrutiny in the class concerns such issues as ethnicity, economic inequality, the changing role of family in our society, and materialism, then this intellectual resistance tends to be conflated with the political resistance that many students also feel pulling upon them. I will look now at how and why students experienced this "twin resistance," at ways in which such conflicts manifested themselves in the classroom, and at the effects of these conflicts on Sherry and her students as they worked their way through English 102.

"This Is Retarded!" Politics, Writing, and Classroom Practice

In teaching a writing course organized around social and political issues, and in using a textbook that directly confronted many students'
beliefs and assumptions, Sherry was following the official syllabus. But
she was also to a large extent following her own inclinations as a politically concerned, civic-minded graduate student influenced by current
composition theory, postmodernism, and feminist theory. She sincerely
believed that students would be well served by immersing themselves
in critical analysis of important social and political issues; not making
up their minds too quickly about the issues under scrutiny; and listening, reading, and writing carefully, thoughtfully, generously, even passionately. She strongly hoped that, by immersing themselves in their
coursework, students would develop not only improved reading and
writing abilities, but also more thoughtful, sensitive, sophisticated, and
genuinely critical (as opposed to merely dismissive or knee-jerk) political understandings. All of these beliefs and desires she tried hard to convey to students that first day of the quarter as she described what they
would be required to do over the next ten weeks. With her energy, her
sincerity, her confidence, and her ability to generate enthusiasm, she set
out to bring students on board. Knowing that their resistance would have
to be dealt with, she wanted to ensure that she could make that resistance constructive for the class in generating an exchange of ideas, rather
than debilitatingly negative and rejectionist. But given the unexpected
strength of that resistance, her goal of incorporating it into the class
would prove difficult to achieve. Moreover, the related problem of dealing with complex questions for which no easy answers exist would prove
perhaps even more debilitating to students' work than the accompany-
ing political differences.

Louise, a returning student who was politically conservative and
Christian, was by her own description determined but academically not
so confident. She was the mother of three school-aged children and a
housewife in her mid-thirties who had taken a vocational curriculum in
high school and who was coming to college—and into a demanding
academic setting for the first time—with the ambition of completing a
nursing degree. She was the type of open admissions student Mina
Shaughnessy (1977) and others had worked to provide access to college
for. But Louise objected to the content and arguments of the vast majority of the liberally oriented readings. She was also extremely resistant to
and confused by the demands of the critical analysis required in the assignments, not to mention suspicious of her teacher and impatient to

complete this required sequence and get on with what was to her the important part of her college education—her nursing studies. She worked hard but had serious trouble developing her own arguments and interpretations in relation to the readings, and was not skilled at incorporating parts of other texts into her own. Yet her struggles were not that different from those almost every student in the class was experiencing, struggles that became evident from the very start of the quarter.

The required textbook, *Rereading America*,(Colombo, Cullen, & Lisle, 1989) immediately set many students' teeth on edge by calling into question a number of their basic beliefs. One student even grumbled about the book's cover design, which showed sixteen different-colored American flags, while others said they disliked the title itself, professing no need or desire to "reread" their country. One of the assignments for the second class session was to read the book's introduction, entitled "Thinking Critically, Challenging Cultural Myths," which lays out the book's critical thinking agenda of looking afresh at aspects of U.S. culture, such as democracy, economic opportunity, education, the media, the family, gender, and group differences, from perspectives that students may not yet have considered, including alternative, critical, and radical views. The book is thus intended to help students develop better informed and more carefully thought out views and become more active learners, "with the ability to shape, not merely absorb, knowledge" (p. 2).

The introduction defines cultural myths as ways of thinking and being that bind people together and provide a shared understanding of their place in the world. But according to the introduction, these myths also "selectively blind us" (p. 3) to negative features of our own culture. Rightly or wrongly, a number of students, including Louise, found the book, and the introduction in particular, presumptuous in telling them both what they thought and what they should think. Moreover, students were uncomfortable about having to state and support their views on topics of cultural importance. Like many, Louise assumed, rightly, that doing so would involve hard work, that it could lead to unpleasant disagreements with the teacher that she would rather avoid, and that she preferred to summarize the views of others or to write about less controversial, safer topics as they had the previous quarter. As she put it, "I always felt English was so subjective, and if you didn't take the same exact point of view as the teacher, then you were wrong." Despite Sherry's oft-stated support for diverse perspectives and encouragement of students to develop their own views, the class clearly feared the possibility of disagreeing with Sherry, and wondered if she would be as fair as she said she would.

College students in the United States have been primarily conservative and career-oriented for some years now, as the student activism of the 1960s and early 1970s has waned (Horowitz, 1987). Despite some exceptions, a surprisingly large proportion of UC students seem very resistant to questioning established views. Soon after I arrived, a colleague told me about her experience using Shirley Jackson's short story "The Lottery" (Guth & Rico, 1993), in a first-year writing class. The story, first published in 1948, is about a New England community in which, as the reader becomes gradually and chillingly aware, one person is chosen randomly each year to be stoned to death by the others. In discussing the story, one student argued that it was about the importance of maintaining tradition. To my colleague's surprise, no one in the class attempted to contradict her.

I soon realized that many of our students clung tenaciously to the belief that authority was to be respected and accepted, not rejected or even called into question. Feeling pushed for time by the ambitious syllabus, Sherry was eager to get into the first unit of the course—the topic of family—so she did not spend much time discussing the book's introduction with her students. However, several expressed strong concern that the book, in part simply by terming their basic beliefs "myths," was saying, in effect, that the United States was not really a democracy and that the nuclear family was an outmoded institution. Some students argued quite strongly that the book, and therefore the course as a whole, were pushing them, not simply to examine their familiar cultural and political structures anew in a critical light, but to reject strongly held beliefs.

Virtually from the beginning of the quarter, an "us versus them" mentality appeared to be developing among at least some of the students, with "us" being the students themselves and the cultural traditions they represented and believed in, and "them" being Sherry, the textbook, and the curriculum as a whole (and, by extension, me). While not every student adopted this stance toward the class, a number of the most vocal students clearly did, including both Joshua and Louise. This oppositional stance came through clearly in the first unit of the quarter, the section of the text entitled "Harmony at Home: The Myth of the Model Family," which contained essays looking at the nature of family structure in the United States, including essays on family breakdown, African American families, a Hispanic family, gay families, an American Indian family, and friends as a replacement for family. Like most units in the book, this one was anchored by a theoretical piece, in this case Arlene Skolnick's sweeping survey of American family life, "The Paradox of Perfection," (1992) which suggests a host of problems, past and present, in the nuclear family, and with the remaining essays examining or exemplifying subsets of the larger topic of family. The unit is intended to help students develop a critical perspective on families in American society, to look beyond the stereotype of the happy, secure, comfortably middle-class family as the norm. As the authors' introduction to the unit states, after going through a litany of challenges to today's family (including divorce, domestic violence, and teen suicide), "In our world it is no longer clear whether the family is a blessing to be cherished or an ordeal to be survived" (p. 401). The class quickly and strongly reacted against this critical analysis of what was, to most of them, indeed a most cherished institution. As Joshua put it, "I've read this stuff about family, like that Skolnick essay, that goes completely against what I believe. It undermines what a lot of people think their family is, what their family really is. Typical college, liberal stuff." In Louise's words, "I put a lot of value on family and home life. I think it's the foundation for success in everything. The book seems to be making the family out to be less important or even a bad thing." While several students proved willing in discussions to question traditional views of the nuclear family, these students too seemed to be engaging in intellectual resistance and having difficulty reading the assigned essays.

Very early in the quarter, as students were being asked to think critically about the family, Sherry modeled ways of reflecting about the topic which she wanted to encourage, such as asking questions, considering familiar issues from a new perspective, and speculating about the ethical and philosophical issues embedded in the topic under scrutiny. She therefore read to the class a journal entry she herself had written some years earlier as a college freshman studying the concept of cultural relativism in an anthropology course. Focusing on footbinding in pre-revolutionary China, Sherry read her entry questioning whether absolute standards could be applied and footbinding categorically condemned or whether the individual culture should decide on a particular tradition's appropriateness. In the entry, though expressing distaste for the practice, she did not so much attempt to answer this question as to reflect on it and present a case for both possibilities.

After reading the entry, Sherry asked students to consider the ways of thinking she had attempted in the journal entry. But as so often happens in the composition class when the teacher attempts a discussion of "method," students wanted to talk about "content." In the ensuing discussion, somewhat to my surprise, I found that students would not even openly critique the tradition of footbinding, though it was not one of their own cultural traditions and was indeed quite different from anything they might have experienced. Instead, Louise stated that, if footbinding were an important tradition in her culture, she would probably go along with it. Several other students murmured their assent. Not one person suggested that they would, or even could, break with tradition, even after

I, unwilling to let this viewpoint go unchallenged, joined the discussion by suggesting that traditions often do change, after all, and that our own country was marked by sharp breaks with authority, such as the abolition of slavery and the granting of voting rights to women.

I found this apparent unwillingness to question authority, or at least certain kinds of authority, rather frightening yet consistent with what I had observed in other classes. It seems to me that this attitude was not actually an unwillingness to challenge authority, particularly since, as we will see, students did show themselves more than willing to challenge the teacher's authority when it seemed to conflict with their traditional notions of what was appropriate. Nor was this resistance to questioning authority an example of students' unwillingness to think critically, since students clearly were thinking critically in rejecting arguments put forward by their teacher and their textbook. Rather, I believe that such moments may represent a kind of solidarity in which students resisted the curriculum and subtly defied the teacher in taking positions they knew differed from her preferred view. Already in conflict with the instructor over the demands of the course, and what they believed was the excessively negative perspective offered by the textbook, these students took every available opportunity to depart from the script. Defensive, resentful, and resistant, they rejected efforts by the teacher or textbook to get them to adopt ways of thinking, beliefs, or critical attitudes which were uncomfortable. Such was the context in which students began their writing instruction embedded in a critical investigation of American culture in English 102.

According to the First-Year Writing Program's Mission Statement, the official goals of 102 revolve around the idea of critical reading and writing. With the assumption that students have read little argumentative and interpretive writing, and that such work is an important part of a university education, the course emphasizes reading of argument in a way that the other courses in the first-year sequence do not. But, as important, the class is designed to provide opportunities for students not just to read such texts but to write their own analyses and arguments concerning issues raised in the readings. Sherry believed that her own goals for the course did not depart significantly from those of the "official" curriculum, except for one possible area. She used the terminology of classical rhetoric to discuss this perceived difference:

> I worry that the accepted way to teach 102 is to emphasize the type of argument typically labeled "logos," or logically oriented, intellectual. I find that pathos- and ethos-oriented activity seems to lead students to make an all-important initial investment in their learning and their writing. I'm not saying that I think 102 should be a

> touchyfeely kind of course saturated in expressivist pedagogy.
> Rather, I'm just beginning to articulate to myself (as a developing
> teacher) the critical place that activity labeled as "personal" can take
> in complicated learning situations . . . how so-called personal writ-
> ing and discussion activities can become a bridge for exploring com-
> plexities that extend beyond one's experiences.

Thus, Sherry was particularly concerned with finding ways to convince
and encourage her students to care deeply about what they were writing, believing that such an investment, crucial if students were to go
beyond simply fulfilling an assignment, was needed if students were to
produce writing worth reading, given the difficult nature of the assignments. The issue of engagement, so important to Sherry in 101 the previous quarter, was, if anything, even more important to her here in 102,
where students would of necessity be bringing more "outside ideas" into
their own texts and would have less individual choice about the content of their papers. The first essay prompt of the quarter asked students
to consider their own experiences and attitudes in relation to the essays
they were reading and discussing in class, rather than aiming for a kind
of unobtainable objectivity or definitive "proof." The assignment, which,
to provide practice in timed writing would be the only paper students
would write during the class hour, rather than on their own time, read
as follows:

> You have just read a series of essays from the unit *Harmony at Home:
> The Myth of the Model Family*. For this assignment, you'll be asked to
> consider these five essays in relation to your own complex experi-
> ence of family life, both that of your own family and that of people
> close to you whose family experiences you are familiar with.
>   For your first essay in 102, **please write about your own defini-
> tion of family**. Relate your ideas about the family to those of the
> authors in the textbook. You can focus most closely on one of the
> textbook essays if you like, but be sure to bring in several of the
> others as points of comparison or contrast.
>   Whatever you choose to say about families (and the way we view
> them in America at this time), use both your own experience, your
> own attitudes, and the evidence provided in these texts to shape
> your discussion.

This unit of the course was intended to provide a comfortable, familiar
starting point for students' critical analysis of their own experiences of
American culture—beginning with their notions of family. The readings
would expose students to analyses of the nature of family, which they
may well not have considered, such as the role of families as economic
units, the influence of mass media on our attitudes toward family, the
different types of family that exist in our society, the history of American family life, and the influences of family on individuals' development.

In short, this unit would help students take a more interpretive look at a key social institution which most of us tend to take for granted, an institution deriving much of its power from cultural myths we rarely call into question. To get students started thinking about the nature of family and the role of family in their own lives, in the second class session of the quarter Sherry began the unit on family. After briefly previewing the above-mentioned readings and giving out and explaining the essay assignment, she asked each student in the class circle first to write for five minutes about whatever comes to mind when they hear the word *family*. Then she said, "To break the ice, let's talk about one thing that occurred to you about *family*," and she began by reading her own free-write, a rather cynical analysis of a family gathering, the predictable roles taken by everybody there, and her own feelings of distance. One by one, each student talked about his or her own views of the family, with students holding the floor for approximately half a minute each. Some students mentioned divorce or feeling greater closeness toward friends than toward relations. However, the vast majority of students discussed the topic of family, and portrayed their own families, in almost reverential terms, as a kind of sacred unit. The activity loosened up considerable emotion, with several students getting choked up and barely holding back tears as they described their families and the importance of family in their lives. One student, Wendy, who had written her first-day opinion about what she considered reverse racism by blacks against whites, was overcome with emotion just as she began to speak and had to leave the room briefly. On the whole, this activity may have succeeded in engaging students with the topic of family. I was surprised and impressed by people's willingness to share sensitive details of obvious personal importance, and on only the second day of class. However, at the same time, I was concerned that this atmosphere of reverence that was beginning to surround the topic of family would make it even more difficult for students to adopt a critical, analytic approach to the topic.

My fears were immediately put to the test following this emotional discussion when, with only a few minutes left in class (the earlier discussion having spilled over), Sherry asked students for their reactions to the essay, "The Paradox of Perfection" by Arlene Skolnick, on changes in the American family over time. Skolnick's main point is that the image of the so-called ideal, happy, problem-free family of two parents, a few children, a comfortable income, and a house in the suburbs, has never been as common in the United States as people typically think it has; but its pervasiveness as a media image makes the vast majority of us who are from less-than-ideal families feel bad about our own situations. Skolnick argues that the family, contrary to its idealized representation, has been as much a site of conflict, disagreement, and pain, as it has been "a haven in a heartless world" (p. 406). Predictably, perhaps, students' comments about the essay were almost entirely disparaging.

First of all, a number of students seemed to misunderstand the essay in an almost fundamental sense. Given the piece's complexity and level of abstraction, and given students' lack of familiarity with reading texts that are meant to convey an argument, such a lack of comprehension is perhaps to be anticipated. In fact, it *had* been anticipated. As mentioned above, the Skolnick essay was the theoretical anchor for the book's unit on family. Knowing that it offered an unfamiliarly critical perspective as well as a difficult academic style, Sherry had previewed the Skolnick essay for students during the previous class and, moreover, the editors of the book summarize the essay not once but twice in the preceding pages of the chapter. For whatever reasons—comprehension, motivation, familiarity, preparation, lack of experience in reading argumentative texts, or some combination of these—there appeared to be a serious breakdown in the ability of the class to read for argument.

Students' misunderstandings mainly entailed their thinking that the author was herself taking the positions that she was actually attempting to characterize and, in some cases, to critique. For example, many students seemed to think she was arguing that the family was a pure, perfect institution, the very view she was attempting strongly to critique. These students tended to complain about "all the big words she used" in making what was for them a rather simple point. Other students believed she was "making fun" of the family. Wendy, for example, quoted a concept Skolnick discussed, which Sherry had asked students to pay particular attention to in their journal entry on the essay, the concept of "pluralism" or multiple-family systems. Flushed with anger, Wendy launched into a critique: "She says, 'What was once labeled *deviant* is now merely *variant*.' This is retarded!" Wendy objected both to the relativistic argument Skolnick was making and to the abstract language used. No student rose to defend this view of the family, despite Sherry's exhortations. To cap things off, after discussion of the Skolnick essay, when Sherry asked if there was anything else students wanted to say before class ended, Louise raised her hand. She calmly said that she had read the essay "The Gay Family" by Richard Goldstein—an essay that offers a positive view of such families—and wanted to voice her opinion about it. In her view, gays could not be families, and that was that. Sherry asked if anyone wished to comment on Louise's comment, hoping, she told me later, that students would speak out against this intolerant view, but no one did.

Thus, as class finished, it seemed that a combination of anger and confusion regarding the Skolnick essay, and a feeling of defensiveness about the traditional family structure, still reigned. The unit on family, though it was the fourth chapter in the textbook, was placed first in the curriculum because it seemed to be a bridge between the personal topics that dominated 101 the previous quarter and the larger cultural and political concerns that would dominate 102. Yet there was proving to be considerable resistance on the part of students to the idea of reexamining their own assumptions about the nature of family.

Interestingly, at the start of the next class, Sherry began a discussion of the remaining textbook essays by asking if any students would be willing to read aloud a journal entry concerning the essays. Two women volunteered, Diane and Traci, each reading a response to the Goldstein essay about the gay family, which Louise had critiqued so strongly the previous session and to which no one had been willing in class to respond. Howev⸳⸳⸳ ʰhis time each student's journal entry argued that gay couples could indeed constitute a family unit as long as the relationships were based on love, trust, and the other emotional criteria that characterized traditional family units. Diane even said that she had a very good gay friend who was married to his boyfriend, and that they were as close as any married couple she knew. Thus, while students were unwilling or unable to respond immediately and directly to the conservative views of Louise and some of the other students, some seemed more willing to present their own views in a less confrontational way through journal writing. But when given the opportunity to present their views to the rest of the class, these students probably felt more comfortable reading what they had written, as opposed to arguing spontaneously and extemporaneously. Equally interesting, neither Louise nor any of the other conservative students attempted to counter the sentiments expressed in favor of the possibility of gay families by two of their classmates. When I asked Louise about the lack of exchange, she suggested that students did not like to argue with one another, preferring a less threatening group solidarity to the idea of intra-class conflict and disagreement, although Sherry wanted and gently encouraged them to take sides as a crucial part of their serious consideration of the subject matter from different perspectives.

To prepare students to write the essay, Sherry worked with them on incorporating the written sources into their own essays in various ways as they developed their own arguments. The Writing Program's Mission Statement discusses the need "to foreground for students that the work of [academic writing] is to learn how to surround another text (or texts), to incorporate, assimilate, and critique the positions of others. This, of course, is not an easy thing for students to do, but we think it useful to set out the problem and the challenge at the very beginning of the course." Sherry advised students to "work in those other voices," not through plagiarism and unacknowledged inclusion but more effectively and strategically to develop their own views. And as an illustration she had them turn back to the Skolnick essay, which, as it originally had appeared as an article in an academic journal, is rich in its use of other writers' ideas, to examine some of the ways that this author employs secondary materials in her own writing. Focusing specifically on one page of the essay, she asked students to read it over, note for themselves other sources that appear, and consider exactly how and why Skolnick includes them. Like many of her classmates, Louise found this activity very difficult to understand and put into practice, but it did at least introduce to her the idea, which would be developed throughout the quarter, that other written sources can be brought into one's own essay not only as support but also as points of contrast or to explore a particular idea.

In their essays, most students strongly defended the traditional nuclear family structure that they felt was under attack in the textbook and in the class as a whole. While students may have resisted being critical of the institution of family, as they felt the book was pushing them to be, a number were indeed critical of the negative perspective they felt was being foisted upon them. Even Traci, who earlier read her journal entry in favor of gay families, wrote,

> Arlene Skolnick believes family is a "media event." She thinks the view of a "normal" family comes from biased television shows. Skolnick also believes that "Americans tend to project the ideal back into the past," and I agree.
>
> However, I do not see a problem with this projection. What is wrong about trying to keep a family together as a mom, dad, and a few kids? As long as there is still love and support, the traditional family should be idealized.
>
> I don't think we will see another "Cleaver" family, but why not try to imitate their actions? We never saw abuse, pain, or problems with their family and maybe it was because of their love and concern for one another.

Louise also disagreed strongly with the politics of the assigned essays. In addition, she was unaccustomed to reading for argument, and was also put off by the complicated, scholarly style of some of the pieces. She believed that the textbook, while extremely critical of traditional aspects of American culture such as the nuclear family, was not critical enough of alternative institutions such as the gay family. But, unlike Traci, she found it difficult to counter, in writing, the perspectives of liberal, learned academics and professional writers. However, she enjoyed very much writing on the topic of family, one of the main areas of concern in her life and a subject she had thought considerably about. Her main problem in the assignment, as she saw it, was "how to bring in the readings." This incorporating of other voices in her own texts was something almost completely new to Louise; she could barely remember doing so even back in her high school days when she mainly studied business English. Moreover, the ideas she wanted to express, the paper she wanted to write, seemed to her to have little to do with the points expressed in the assigned essays. At the very least, she was having trouble figuring out how her own views were related to those of the essays, in part because she was not sure just what views were being expressed. Especially in the Skolnick essay, the theoretical anchor around which all the other readings of the unit were based, Louise did not feel she adequately understood the author's view despite reading the piece over several times. The additional problem of how to apply readings to her own writing nearly overwhelmed her.

Add to these concerns the fact that this was to be an in-class essay, the only timed writing of the quarter. Students had received the topic in advance, were permitted to all but write the essay in advance, and could bring in up to a page of detailed notes. Still, Louise was always worried about her grammar, punctuation, and mechanics, and was used to working with a Writing Center tutor on all her papers. Her frustration was apparent. Her solution was to virtually ignore the readings in her own essay, saying what she had to say about family as best she could and making only token mention of the Skolnick essay. As might be expected, Louise's essay makes a strong, and for a timed essay, at times even eloquent statement about the importance of family, especially in the development of children. And in her own way, she does examine critically the way families function and occasionally do not function, though she couches her argument not in the abstractions of the readings but in a candid analysis of her own upbringing, which she contrasts with the way she has tried to bring up her own children. Louise consciously attempts to counter what she feels are the liberal, anything goes, anti-traditional family sentiments confronting her in the class, and she draws on what she believes are her strongest, most effective rhetorical strategies to do so.

"A Strong Pillar—Families"

My second child was only a few hours old when the nurse brought her into my hospital room. She was wrapped tightly inside a soft, warm baby blanket. She had just been given a bath and had a scent of Safeguard soap about her. My mom and grandmother were standing around my bed admiring the new addition to my family. My grandmother was stroking the baby's cheek with her wrinkled hand and said, "Lu, you now have the perfect family—a boy and now a little girl!" At that particular moment, I felt like we were the perfect family. I was June Cleaver and my husband was Ward Cleaver. But reality soon set in and I realized I wasn't June, nor was my husband Ward.

I knew long before I had children that I wanted to raise my children differently than I had been raised. I want to raise my children in a home filled with love and honesty. When I was growing up love was one thing me, my brothers and sister rarely felt or saw. We knew first-hand all about yelling, hitting, and screaming. When we did something wrong we paid the price for it. My mom would stay mad at us for days, and nothing that we did during that time was ever good enough to calm her down. I want to show my children that I love them for who they are. I want them to know that I love them all the same. When me and my siblings were growing up it was always clear to us who was our mom's favorite. We were in competition all the time against each other for her approval. Now that we are adults and have families of our own, I try to show all members of my family that I love them equally. I want them to know it's things of the heart that is what is important to me.

In Arlene Skolnick's Paradox of Perfection, she says feelings of love, warmth, and fun is the invisible glue that holds the family together. The family should be a haven where members can grow in love, be encouraged, and work through their problems as a team. They should have one common goal that they all work toward acheiving. In our fast paced, stress filled society that we live in, this is a difficult task.

I once read in a magazine that the greatest gift parents could give to their children is love and support for each other. Children need to feel secure and loved. Parents need to guide and direct their children to be able to function as well adjusted adults later in life. They must be firm in their discipline and open in their love. It's important to make the child feel loved even though his deed or behavior is not approved of. Teenagers are scared and insecure. They are too old to be children and too young to be adults. They need a place where they feel like they fit in and belong. That place of refuge should be the family.

In a 1990's world of shifting social realities it's more difficult to have a strong, successful family. Divorce is on the rise, they are more blended families, mom and dad both work, children spend more time at the babysitter, and teenagers are pressured by sex, drugs, and aids. All these factors confirm my belief that the family is more important than ever. It takes dedication and commitment by each member, from each member to make the family a pillar against a society that has diminishing morals and values.

There are only two references to other texts in this essay, one to the Skolnick essay about feelings of love, warmth, and fun being the invisible glue that holds families together and one to an unnamed magazine article describing love and support as the greatest gifts parents can give their children. In incorporating the Skolnick essay, Louise virtually transforms it to fit her own argument, selectively taking a particular view of the family expressed in the essay and presenting this view as if it were the specific notion of family that the author wants to recommend to readers. Louise seemed to think this was the case, having had trouble comprehending the way Skolnick weaves a variety of interpretations of the family into her text, comments on all of these, and uses them to create her own metanalysis. Louise's essay has a dogmatic quality particularly common in student writing when students are asked to take on a kind of authority they do not know how to assume, that of an academic and intellectual. The essay contains numerous assertions—generally unsupported, from an academic point of view—about the declining state of society's morals and about the role of the family, as well as directives about what people should be doing. These were the kinds of extended argumentative texts, church sermons, and the kinds of authoritative discourse, homilies and stories with a moral, with which she was most familiar, and it seems understandable that she would emulate these comfortable models.

However, it is clear to me—as it was to Sherry as well—that, whatever its failings, this essay is the result of serious contemplation, strong feeling, and genuine concern for the topic. As a first attempt, it shows considerable potential for further development, while Louise learns to examine her own views in a more self-critical way, to bring in more comfortably and fully the views expressed in the readings, views that have more connection to her own than she thinks, and to formulate her ideas in a more self-reflective manner. Louise would not revise this essay, choosing instead to concentrate on the subsequent assignments, particularly as Sherry gave the essay a fairly positive evaluation. Sherry noted that the essay did not adequately consider and interact with the perspectives on family offered in the required readings—and did not bring the readings into her own discourse sufficiently. But she also recognized that the piece makes a strong argument, attempts to support it in a variety of ways, and brings in other texts, if minimally. Moreover, Sherry noted the obvious improvement in Louise's writing and the hard work that had gone into it since the beginning of the previous quarter. Given the difficulty and the long-term nature of helping students interact intellectually with the words of others as they learn to formulate their own interpretations, Sherry saw Louise's current set of strategies as, in many ways, a solid place to begin the work that lay ahead.

The Affirmative Action Director's Visit

Following this first writing assignment, the course focus moved from the family to the larger society. Students wrote the next paper on distribution of economic opportunity, and the following one on ethnicity and group differences. As course subject matter began to focus more on political issues, the conflict between many students' views and those of the textbook became more pronounced, as did students' frustration over the critical thinking requirements of the class. Part of the conflict seemed to stem from students' fears about their own futures. Nowhere do students' concerns about their futures, and the relationship of those concerns to political policies, come out more sharply than in their attitudes toward affirmative action, the preferential hiring of underrepresented minorities. Several times in class discussion, when issues of careers, equality, or diversity came up, a handful of students would raise the issue of affirmative action. Candace, a history major whose father was a police officer, complained that he had been denied promotion several times in favor of minority candidates even though he had scored higher on the promotion test than those candidates. Other students, including the most vocal in the class, such as Wendy, Louise, Randy, and Joshua, also spoke out strongly against such programs. They argued that preferential hirings were unfair, that all applicants should be treated equally, that minorities were given an unfair advantage based on discrimination that took place in the distant past. Why, they asked, should people like themselves who never discriminated against anybody, suffer because of mistakes others had made long ago. There were laws against discrimination, and that was enough. Not one student, even the small group of African Americans in the class, who tended to sit together in a cluster, would publicly challenge what appeared to be the dominant view on this issue in class.

Not wishing to impose her own views upon students, and hoping that a discussion could take place on the issue with some students in favor and some against, Sherry did not explicitly argue that affirmative action was fair or necessary. However, she did take a rather bold step in that direction: she wrote a letter to the University's Acting Director of Affirmative Action. In this letter, Sherry listed some of the "opinions" students expressed in writing very early in the quarter (including several I listed at the beginning of this chapter) and discussed her worry, saying "I'm convinced that these responses to 'diversity' represent an overwhelming number of students. As their instructor, I do not want to silence them—I want to expand them . . . invite them to think past their familiar boundaries." About her reason for inviting him to her class, she said, "My primary goal here is that all of my students become more aware of the difficult questions and problems your department faces every day on this campus, so that they might begin to complicate their personal readings of a world which includes, yet paradoxically excludes, 'others.'" James Wilder, the acting director, agreed to come to the class and give a 15-minute presentation about his job and the reasons for it, followed by a question-and-answer session and class discussion in which students could speak their minds on the issues. Sherry had invited James Wilder very early in the quarter, but after negative discussion of affirmative action issues persisted, she became more and more convinced that such a visit would be very helpful indeed. The day before he was supposed to come, she told students about the visit and asked them to prepare questions and be ready to discuss the issues. He came to class the day students handed in their papers on economic opportunity. His visit, and the issues it raised, are relevant in considering students' attitudes toward their place in American society, the opportunities open or closed to them, and the nature of "official authority" as they perceived it. The visit would also prove extremely relevant to the following unit of the course, which students began the next class session. This unit would examine what the textbook called "the myth of the melting pot," looking at the nature of prejudice and discrimination, and at relations among the diverse groups that make up the United States.

I was very interested to see what would happen on the day when James Wilder came to class. I had listened to and read students' anti-affirmative action comments, and had noticed that no students ever spoke out with a more supportive view. Yet I strongly suspected there were such students in the class who, for whatever reason, were unwilling to speak against the apparent conservative consensus, perhaps made stronger by Candy's bitter comment that her own father, a police officer, had lost promotion to less qualified (based on their test scores) minority candidates. I had read Helen Rothschild Ewald and David Wallace's 1994 *CCC* article, "Exploring Agency in Classroom Discourse," which depicts a rather heated disagreement in a midwestern university composition class over the issue of affirmative action. For all of these reasons, I had a feeling the class would be tense and students hostile. Such was indeed the case. James Wilder entered the room at the beginning of class, a large, bespectacled, professional-looking African American man with salt-and-pepper hair, wearing a suit and tie. He appeared to be in his mid- to late-50s. Sherry briefly introduced him as the Acting Director of Affirmative Action for the University, mentioning that she felt what he would talk about was closely related to the subject matter students were reading and writing about in the course, and then she turned the floor over to him.

Leaning on the table at the front of the room, he began talking in a soft-spoken, modest, reassuring, disarming manner about the nature of his job and about his own background, responsibilities, and attitudes. His manner was extremely mild and conciliatory, exuding a calm reasonableness, as if he sensed students' opposition, which must have been the case, considering Sherry had referred to it in her letter requesting that he come to her class. He described himself as a native Cincinnatian, a longtime business person, a former personnel manager with a major corporation based in Cincinnati and surely familiar to students. He characterized his primary job as helping to ensure fairness in hiring and to aid the University in its efforts to increase the percentage of women and minority employees. He stressed at the outset that his job was not, as some may have believed, to support preferential treatment for any groups. Indeed, he pointed out, it was in response to such preferential treatment up until very recently that positions like his had been created, and he gave examples of hiring policies discriminating against minorities that he could recall from his own experience, as well as some statistics on such discrimination. Nor, he said, was it his job, or anyone else's, to establish hiring quotas or to support the hiring of anyone who was not qualified for a particular position. Such hiring, he stated, would be problematic not only for the University but for the individual hired under such circumstances and for the group he or she represented. As if to reassure students that their own interests were not being threatened by the kind of work he did, he pointed out that a very large percentage of the new positions at the University were still being filled by non-minorities, though the numbers of women and minorities were slowly increasing. It seemed to me that Wilder took pains to present a benign, nonthreatening picture of affirmative action as it existed at the University of Cincinnati, and, by extension, at other institutions. Warm, articulate, and avuncular, he was clearly no radical, and the picture he presented of his job made it seem more bureaucratic and matter-of-fact than controversial or dictatorial. After about fifteen minutes of speaking to students, he closed by asking if the class had any questions for him.

There was a long, nervous silence after Wilder's invitation to the students. I generally like such breaks in the discussion for the tension they create—productive silences—and for the unpredictability of where the silence might lead. But this one went on to the point where even I was becoming uncomfortable. Finally, one hand went up and then another. Rather than ask questions, students wanted to make comments. Candy told the story of her father being denied promotion in the Police Department even though he had scored higher than minority and women candidates, and said that as a result she was against affirmative action be-. cause everyone should have an equal chance at a job; the most qualified person should be the one hired. Wilder replied that conditions here at the University were very different from what she was describing. Joshua followed up with a similar complaint about reverse discrimination, and before Wilder could respond, Louise reiterated the same point. Several other students eventually joined in with views very opposed to the entire idea of affirmative action, insisting that a fairer policy would be simply to hire the best qualified person for any open position, which they saw as a straightforward matter of assessment.

Wilder tried calmly, reasonably, but, it seemed, vainly, to reassure students that affirmative action was, in the long run, in their interests as well as the interests of minorities, and that students had no reason to fear the policy. However, it was clear that students did fear it, and considerably. I was annoyed at the students for being so unwilling to consider what James Wilder was trying to say to them, for taking such a dismissive view of the long history of discrimination in this country, and for assuming that such discrimination was a thing of the distant past. At the same time, I appreciated the bravery of those students who had spoken up against what they perceived as the voice of authority. Rather than listen in deferential but aggrieved silence, some of them at least had spoken their minds, and though in large measure I disagreed with their views, I was pleased that they spoke. I also realized, listening to the students, that for them—college freshman from not particularly privileged backgrounds looking ahead to a lifetime of work—the idea of affirmative action had a very different meaning than it did for me, a tenured professor with a secure job. If they saw affirmative action as unfair, it was at least partly because they feared the possibility of their losing out on jobs they were qualified for, and in a time when all around them were warnings of a diminishing job market, downsizing, and economic instability. Moreover, for these students coming of age during the time of affirmative action, the policy was itself seen as part of institutional power and authority, not as helping the powerless. They considered themselves rebels for opposing it.

Reflecting about these matters, and about the lack of support for Wilder from any student in the discussion, I wondered if I should perhaps speak. I waited as long as I could to hear if any student would speak up in support, but none did. Sherry also was silent, seemingly preferring to let students make up their own minds. I, however, felt the need to have at least one other voice enter the discussion that was not so hostile to everything that Wilder represented. After some internal debate about whether or not it was appropriate for me to speak out, I decided to do so. Just as discussion was petering out and Wilder was preparing to leave, I raised my hand and got the floor. I talked about the long history of discrimination in the United States and the lack of opportunity

for the victims of discrimination. I mentioned that, as a faculty member,
I had been involved in a number of searches for new faculty and had
had contact with the affirmative action office. I stated that, in my experience, what the acting director was saying had been true. Qualified
people had been hired, and minority candidates were only hired when
they were at least as qualified as anybody else in the search. I asked James
Wilder if that had been his experience as well, and he said it had. No
students responded to my comments, and he wrapped up his presentation and left the room.

There were only a few minutes remaining in the class, and Sherry
decided to use the time to go over what we had all just experienced. She
asked if there were any further comments, and this time, one of the African American students, Latecia, who rarely spoke in class, raised her
hand. Though silent while Wilder was in the room, she had clearly been
thinking hard about what he had said, and about how her classmates
had responded to it. Latecia now said, in a quiet but very determined
voice (in fact, much the same way that other students had made their
comments and asked their questions) that she supported affirmative
action because she felt that, "without it, I just don't think I could get a
fair shake in applying for a job." No one responded to her comment,
perhaps because students were emotionally drained from the tense class
session, but also, it seemed, because students had made an implicit pact
not to argue with one another in class discussion. And on that note,
Sherry reminded students of their journal and reading assignment for
the next session and dismissed class.

While the class went on, I thought it a bit strange that Sherry was saying very little. Indeed she was unusually quiet, though normally ani-
mated and comfortable about using her position as teacher to explain,
clarify, probe, extend, and counter in class. On this day, however, aside
from introducing James Wilder, calling on students who wanted to ask
a question or make a comment, and initiating the debriefing session after he left, Sherry made very few points of her own. Particularly for such
a sensitive topic, and given the strong feelings and strongly conservative views that were dominating the discussion, I had assumed she
would have a fair amount to say. Yet I also knew how reluctant she was
to try to ram her own views down students' throats, preferring instead
to let statements of various sides of the issues develop from the students
themselves. But Sherry had her own reasons for contributing little to the
discussion, which she explained when I asked her to assess the visit and
its impact upon the class. Here are some of her comments:

> Before Mr. Wilder's visit, students often relied on "affirmative ac-
> tion" bashing to express their disconcerted relationships with group

politics and social inequalities. They struggled to mediate between their individual experiences and accountabilities and their sense of community wellness. In journals or conferences, when discussing issues of race, they would make comments along the lines of 'I'm not the one who made [African Americans] slaves. Why should I be blamed now and why should I be deprived of opportunities if I'm more qualified?' Honestly, that argument has become a traditional response, a classifiable folk motif arising from the English 102 situation. I'm fascinated—and threatened—by it.

What especially haunted me was the silence of minority students in the class, and the utter disparity between what was said in journals and what was actually uttered inside the whole group. I am sensitive about forcing minority students to represent the struggles of their entire race, ethnicity, sexual orientation, class, so I tried very hard not to single those students out for counterpoints. Here is where I really feel conflict: even while I am a teacher with a mission to foster critical literacy and seize moments for the sake of a lively classroom experience, I am a person first. I am relatively comfortable drawing attention to problematic signifiers and cultural assumptions during group discussion—much more so than I am putting a minority student up as "front man" for fairer, more tolerant class readings of social problems. Any argument coming from a 'real' black/gay/poor student carries more weight than all of my preaching or 'leading' put together, but I see a real danger in demanding dissensus over silence in certain situations. This isn't to say that I'm not seeking an effective, useful, and humane way to go about opening up a space for them; it's just to say that creating student-based heteroglossia and polyvocalism in a predominantly white, conservative, middle class heterosexual classroom is much easier said than done . . . .

Sherry goes on to examine her own complex responses to the session, reflecting on what she viewed as a lack of true interchange and possible reasons for her disappointment.

I was nervous during Mr. Wilder's visit. I thought his approach toward affirmative action—his experience and his authority—would help move students past a binary way of thinking, that it would complicate our ways of seeing specific social situations raised by the text, by our lives, and by our discussions and interests. My predictions, however, were mostly wrong. I don't say all wrong because who knows what each student carried away that day, perhaps to draw upon later in life. What happened, for the most part, was a good, mostly understandable history and explanation of affirmative action and a follow-up Q and A period where students slowly, bravely began half-voicing their "gripes" with Affirmative Action. When you [Russel] asked your question (made your comment), I interpreted an 'academic' affirmation of the Affirmative Action mission, a program director and minority reinforcing its value; when Mr. Wilder responded to student concerns (which of-

ten masked their struggles with prejudice and group identity), I interpreted yet another 'academic' and political affirmation of the
Affirmative Action mission. What never happened, to my mind, was
real talk about real struggle (me included). I deeply appreciated Mr.
Wilder's willingness to visit and involve himself in a real campus
context; at the same time, I was disappointed by his obvious distance from the students, including the minority students. (I felt disappointed in what I read as a lack of energy and articulate questioning on the part of most students too). Your [Russel's] participation,
because of its clearly authoritative, in-group connection to Mr.
Wilder, frustrated me. My own uncharacteristic fear of speaking frustrated me. Later, I even challenged myself regarding my disappointment and frustration. For example, could I compare my disappointment over Mr. Wilder's coat and tie approach to the question and
answer session to a situation where a teacher EXPECTS a minority
to represent his or her entire race before a largely hostile group?
Was Mr. Wilder any different than the minority students I couldn't
help but protect?

Thus Sherry, during the class and even afterward, felt almost paralyzed
by what she saw as a near obligation not to impose her own views upon
the students, while feeling at the same time that the views students were
expressing were extremely problematic. The hoped-for discussion among
students, with all views represented, never really took place, though one
minority student did weigh in with an impassioned comment supporting affirmative action, but none of the other students would touch it with
a ten-foot pole. This class clearly did not like to argue among themselves.
In addition, she felt that James Wilder and I as well were such clear representatives of the establishment, and thus so distanced from students,
that we could do little if anything to help students reconceptualize these
complex issues and feelings they were dealing with.

The result was that students' anger continued to smolder over such
controversial issues as affirmative action. Disagreements were not being resolved, though it is possible that different positions were at least
being clarified. Later, in a case-study interview, Joshua voiced frustration over the way he and his friends found themselves positioned in the
discussion of affirmative action: "We're not racists at all, but this topic
almost forces us into that label. I know there are people out there who
would never hire a minority unless they had to. But I also know that as
a white male I'm the last one hired, and that doesn't seem fair either."
Louise was perturbed that Wilder had begun by referring to the youth-
fulness of the class and by stating that, unlike him, students were not
old enough to remember the overt discrimination which had existed in
Cincinnati until the 1960s. She had interpreted his comment much differently than I had: "When he came in the room, the first thing he said
was something like, 'I hope there's no one over thirty in this classroom.'

I felt he said that because younger students would be more likely to accept what he said, and older students would be more likely to question him." The class as a whole was clearly not placated, and possibly even more upset after the visit. And in this tense atmosphere, students began the next unit of the course, focusing on ethnicity, group membership, and diversity in the United States.

Homogenous Writing about Diversity

Many students made a potentially dangerous topic safe by steering away from controversial subject matter in their essays. The third writing assignment of the quarter focused on group membership in the United States and the nature of prejudice and diversity. This unit in the textbook centered around what the authors referred to as "The Myth of the Melting Pot," or the idea that immigrants came to this country with distinctive cultures only to lose their own ethnicities and blend into a unified American culture. The book presented readings that challenged this pervasive notion, with essays on the nature of prejudice toward "outsiders," the social construction of racial categories, what it is like to be a member of a particular group or of several different groups at the same time, and the nature of American racism toward African Americans. The section thus provided an opportunity for students to confront their own attitudes toward group difference, attitudes that had been much on people's minds throughout the quarter, and to learn more about group formation and diversity in American culture.

The key essay in the unit, "Formation of In-groups," was the psychologist Gordon Allport's classic study of the nature of prejudice and group formation, published in the 1950s. It introduces such concepts as "ingroup" and "out-group" and examines the ways in which loyalty to one's own community can often contribute to suspicion and negative feeling toward members of other groups. After having students read and discuss the Allport essay several times over the course of a week, Sherry passed out the next essay assignment. This prompt asked students to write a narrative about their own membership within a group, then to explain how their own experience related to Allport's theory.

Rather than a purely narrative, autobiographical account of their backgrounds and upbringing, this assignment asked students to apply concepts from Allport's theory of prejudice to an examination of some aspect of their lives. Yet the assignment gave students a good deal of scope to write about a particular in-group that they belonged to. It did not force students to write about, say, an ethnic or racial grouping. One of the important ground rules that Sherry had been working hard to inculcate in students throughout the two quarters was an ability to deal more comfortably with abstraction and theory. She reasoned that this ability would come more easily were students able to use theory for the purposes of self-examination. A preparatory journal entry she had asked students to write involved "a profile of yourself. Who are you as an in-group member? How does this group benefit you?" She further asked students to "describe in detail what kinds of people represent your out-group and why? Which group(s) do you consider to be your reference groups? Why do you want to be like them?" Sherry planned several class activities in which students could further reflect on and discuss the Allport system. This reflection would then be part of the essay required for the unit.

While students had read about different kinds of minority experience in their textbook, Sherry wanted them to hear firsthand from minority peers about the nature of their group membership and the ways they had been treated by members of the majority culture. For this activity Sherry had recruited two former students: Louis, an African American who had come from an urban ghetto background in which few of his peers had gone on to college, and Su Lin, a Korean student. She asked Louis, who was an articulate and confident speaker, to lead a discussion with several students, including Su Lin; one of her current students, Clarissa, from an Appalachian background, who had had a baby at fifteen; plus Randy and Denise. Louis, Su Lin, and Clarissa had each had the experience of being an outsider, to some degree discriminated against or excluded. Randy and Denise, white, middle-class suburban students, had volunteered to be part of the discussion because several other minority students intended to be part of the discussion had not shown up for class. Sherry organized the discussion as a fishbowl, in which the discussants would sit and talk in the middle of the room while the rest of the class sat in a circle around them and listened in. Following the small-group discussion, the class as a whole would have the chance to consider further the issues raised by the small group.

I found the small-group discussion riveting, and many of the other students appeared to as well; they listened intently. Louis spent a few minutes at the outset talking about how he had some difficulty relating to his former peers, and they to him, as their interests had diverged. Louis rather quickly moved from talking about himself to asking questions to the other panelists. He encouraged Su Lin to discuss how she had adjusted to living in the United States and how she was able to interact with Americans. He asked Clarissa what it was like to be stereotyped as a teen parent. This part of the discussion was particularly interesting, because only the previous quarter Clarissa had left class in tears when the subject of teen pregnancy came up, unable to speak about her own situation or even to hear others talk about the issue in more general terms. This time, however, Clarissa was much more composed as she talked about how a number of her friends dropped her after she became pregnant, while others stigmatized her as a "slut" and assumed, wrongly, that she must be a weak student. She talked about how it was in part this stigmatization that strengthened her resolve to stay in school, graduate with honors, and go on to college. The discussion, with its immediacy, seemed to have an impact on students beyond that of the textbook essays. During the large-group discussion about the fishbowl, a number of students stated that they now felt they had a better understanding of what members of minority groups experience. As students packed up their books to leave, I could hear them saying to one another that this had been one of the most interesting classes yet.

During the next class session, after scheduling two out-of-class workshops for students trying to revise their previous papers, Sherry announced that "We're going to do some writing today." Specifically, the activity involved "situating your beliefs and making connections between the readings." As she explained,

> That's been a big problem in your essays. We want to do more than just find the good quote that sounds right or that supports your argument. We want to see relations between what someone's saying in one essay and what someone else is saying in another essay, and how all that relates to what you or someone else may be experiencing.

In the class session that followed, with papers now due in less than a week, Sherry asked students to continue the work of the previous day but this time in the context of their own rough draft. Specifically, she wanted students to do what they had been having the most trouble doing throughout the quarter, that is to relate their experiences, this time their experiences of in-groups, more directly to the readings, particularly the Allport essay around which this assignment was organized. Sherry gave students a number of options. They could simply read part of their essay, raise issues about the reading, discuss a problem experienced while writing, or pretty much go in any direction they chose, as long as it was relevant to this writing assignment about the nature of their in-groups. The plan was to go around the room, student by student, with each taking one of the options listed on the board, so that all students could take part in a way comfortable to them.

Katie began class by reading part of her essay, which was about genetic screening. Her essay quickly moved from genetic screening to the "evils" of abortion, discussing a family whose children all have a genetic problem that causes them to have deformed hands, though they are otherwise healthy. During her reading, Katie never mentioned the Allport essay or the concept of in-groups. Responding to the draft, Sherry asked, "How does this story relate to the Allport essay?" Donna replied, "People want to treat her as an out-group member because of her hand. But because she's not bothered by her handicap, she doesn't see people without deformities as her reference group. She's not trying to pretend like she's just like everybody else. She knows she can do whatever she wants as long as people don't discriminate against her because of her handicap." Sherry affirmed that a good connection had been made between the story and the essay.

Next Clarissa, the teen mother, read part of her piece about the death of her grandfather. However, unlike most such essays, hers was not a sentimental discussion of cherished memories. Rather, and surprisingly, she described her grandfather as a nasty, abusive, alcoholic ne'er-do-well who treated his family miserably and was especially disliked by Clarissa. In her closing sentence, she said that she felt nothing when he died, no emotion except perhaps relief that he was gone. No student chose to comment on this stark piece, so Sherry moved on to the next student. This was Mary, one of the nursing students. Rather than read a piece, she chose to comment on Clarissa's essay, saying how shocking it was and how it went against the normal way people are supposed to feel about their grandparents but they do not always. She said she felt badly for Clarissa. Then, pausing and clearing her throat, Mary added, "My uncle just died of AIDS. And I wasn't sad for him, because he had it coming, but I was sad for my father." The room was silent as students took in what Mary had just said. After a few seconds, Randy raised his hand and tentatively asked for clarification as to why Mary was not sad. She replied in essence that her uncle was gay and he deserved to die. It is not clear that everyone in the class agreed with her. In fact, surely some did not. Several had written journal entries in support of the notion of gay families and of gays adopting children. And one student had even written that his own father was gay but that he was still a good father, active in his children's lives. However, as before, students appeared eager not to argue among themselves, and therefore no one chose to take issue with Mary's comment.

Also eager not to provoke controversy in her essay, Louise was quite nervous about this writing assignment after her difficult experiences with the first two papers. In particular, she knew that she had a great deal of trouble bringing the textbook readings into her essays. At a basic level, it was difficult for her to understand the more theoretical readings, and each essay assignment highlighted at least one of these. She had never done this sort of reading before, and had a difficult time figuring out the argument the writer was trying to make, though she would read the text-book pieces over several times and even had her husband reading and discussing the essays with her. Moreover, once she felt she had made some sense of the readings, it was still very difficult for her to figure out how she might bring them into her own essay. She felt she knew how to tell a story and, though more difficult, to make an argument. But she was very unconfident about how to use written source materials in the ways Sherry was encouraging students to do, as means of reflection, explora-tion of ideas, and critical thinking, not only as support for what she wanted to argue in her essay. Just as important, she felt the assigned read-ings had extremely little to do with what she wanted to talk about in her own essay, and it therefore seemed like an artificial task for her to bring an apparently irrelevant reading into her own text. Sherry would have said there were many ways in which the textbook essays were in-deed quite relevant to Louise's writing, but Louise herself, try as she might, had trouble seeing the connections.

In addition, like many of the other students, Louise did not particu-larly want to write about the issues of race and prejudice that the writ-ing assignment was not so subtly pushing students toward. She was uncomfortable broaching such threatening topics in the semipublic do-main of an essay. After the Affirmative Action director's visit, students had said little about issues of race, downplaying their significance and focusing instead on other, safer topics. Moreover, many students were from largely unintegrated worlds, practically all-white suburbs, small towns, and neighborhoods. They had had little experience with people from very different backgrounds, as a number of students commented in their own essays. Thus, rather surprisingly to me, very few students chose to examine questions of racial discrimination or prejudice against a particular ethnic or religious group in their essays. One student from a small, almost all-white town, wrote about her experiences meeting (and being largely suspicious of) people from other ethnic backgrounds for the first time here in college. Having had one negative experience, she was essentially suggesting that this experience seemed to be confirm-ing her initial prejudices. But she was in a distinct minority in choosing to focus on the race question. Instead, many chose to write about cher-ished in-groups they belonged to or had belonged to, which were more like social, recreational groupings. For example, a number of students wrote about their high school friends and what belonging to a clique was like.

It appeared to me that students were finding ways of making the as-signment safe for themselves by avoiding minefield topics such as ra-cial difference, though case-study students disagreed with this assess-ment. As Louise put it, "I was just writing about what I was interested in, and race wasn't such a big issue with me." Joshua, citing his experience as a student in racially integrated schools in Memphis, said, "I never would have picked a topic on race because, growing up where I did, I never thought about race as an in-group/out-group thing." Yet in focusing on their own peer groups, students were writing about what they knew best and cared about most, and were avoiding the potentially explosive topics of race, discrimination, and prejudice. They were uncomfortable considering such topics, had generally thought very little about them, and in many cases felt they had had little direct experience with them. They were also clearly afraid of sounding racist and, though Sherry had been extremely careful not to reward or punish any particular views, students were also afraid of running afoul of Sherry and her beliefs. They tended to feel that the book was radical and that Sherry shared the book's views, even though she was almost never explicit about her own beliefs. Thus, students used the flexibility inherent in the assignment to steer clear of controversial topics and to write about topics that appealed to them more and interested them more. As more than one student explained to me, they just were not that interested in writing about diversity and prejudice; these were not topics that they considered very important.

One subject many students did have experience with and interest in was belonging to a particular religious group. Religion was a fairly popular topic for this assignment, with more than half a dozen students writing about some aspect of their church membership. Louise was one of this group. Indeed, religion and church membership were among the most important parts of her life. Early on in the unit, she had considered writing about growing up in a working-class neighborhood and feeling somewhat inferior to her classmates who came from a more middle-class neighborhood and tended to look down on her and her peers. However, she said that the subject of church membership was really on her mind these days, as she and her husband were considering finding a new church, and therefore she chose to write about her current situation. There was also an element of instrumentalism to her choice of topic. Whether or not to change churches was an important decision she was to make, and rather than write about the, to her, more abstract issues of racial membership and attitudes toward other groups, she would much rather focus on a topic more closely related to her day-to-day life. Also, the choice of topic gave her an opportunity to apply the Allport categories to her own situation in a way that was nonthreatening and unlikely to expose anything about herself that she did not wish to.

11:00 A. M. Sunday Morning

"C'mon Mike, Let's go we're gonna be late." I yelled as I paced up and down the room looking for my purse. "I'm coming," he snapped as he entered the room. It was Sunday morning and I couldn't wait to get to church. Our thirty-minute drive always seemed like three hours.

At that time we were going to Longview Baptist Church. The church had about 150 members. The members were elderly people, single people of all ages, young married couples with and without children and teenagers. The diversity in people didn't seem to matter. I felt like we were all one big happy family. It was a place where I felt acceptance, love, warmth and a genuine concern for me. The people had no trouble showing feelings that were sincere.

The pastor was a young man in his thirties with a family of his own. He had lived a poor, hard live as a boy. His family was from the lower-class part of Kentucky. His father was an abusive alcoholic. Coming from this type of background he could relate to just about everybody in his congregation. Every Sunday morning he brought to us a sermon from the bible that you could apply to your everyday living. He addressed problems that we encounter in our basic lifestyle. He made it plain and simple that everybody could understand the point that he was trying to get across. The way he delivered his messages amused us, humored us, at times it angered us, and he always challenged us to improve ourselves and our lives. When he was on a one on one bases with me he could make me feel like I was such a unique person. It was like I was the missing piece to the puzzle that was needed to make it complete. His leadership and personality reflected in the membership of the church.

That pastor and the members is what I called my place of refuge. I contribute my individual growth to the experiences with my in-group. I needed the people as much as they needed me and I needed that type of leadership. Within my in-group there was a reference group. I would watch the people that were more mature in their Christianity than I was. They appeared to be wise and confident in their relationship with God. They were busy doing active service for God toward others. I would think to myself, I want to be just like that.

That five years was about the best time in my life. I felt part of something and I felt the church was a part of me. I loved those people and the pastor. When "we" were together I felt like I was somebody special. I felt at ease, like being at home in your most comfortable chair.

All good things at some point and time must come to an end. I'm no longer part of that group. At the new church I now attend I feel a part of the out-group. I feel like I don't fit in there. The people are not as warm and accepting as the other group of people were. It's almost as if they are trying you on for size to see if you're going to fit into their group, if you fit into the group then there is a sense of bonding.

Why is it I feel like I'm in the out-group? We have the same basic foundation of religious beliefs. Allport states that the in-groups preferences must be his preferences, it's enemies his enemies. One strong point in favor of this statement is that I don't have the same feelings for the pastor as the in-group does. My opinion of him is not as favorable as some of the others, therefore I don't support him in quite the same way as the in-group does. I feel that he is lacking in some areas of his way of teaching. He is a good pastor, but he's not what I'm use to. He delivers his message in a different style than I prefer. He is not as grounded in the bible as my other pastor was. His personality is more geared towards the group as a whole rather than the individual.

Another point, is that I don't have the same feelings toward the members of the church as I did at Longview. At Lonview it was easy to bond with it's members, at Faith it's not so easy. The people are hard to get to know on a personal level. The members are just a different group with different characteristics.

In essence, I guess I have some prejudices against the in-group at Crestmont. In my eyes they don't live up to the same level as my previous in-group. My attitude toward the pastor is not going to conform to the attitude of the group. I only "share" their feelings toward the leader.

Allport states, no individual would mirror his group's attitude unless he had a personal need, or personal habit, that leads him to do so. My personal needs are not that of the in-group. Just because I feel a part of the out-group I'm not going to leave the church, it has a lot of positive factors that I like and haven't been able to find anywhere else. If my needs ever do change I feel certain that I would be welcome into the in-group.

Clearly, Louise produced an essay about her feelings toward her previous church and current church, and then shoehorned a minimal consideration of the Allport categories into this other discussion. For Louise, as for many students, it was very difficult to write the kind of exploratory, multivocal essay that Sherry was encouraging. The framing of the essay with an Allportian analysis seems artificial and peripheral to the main issues of the paper. She does not refer to any other essay in the unit, and she does not deal at all with the racial and ethnic issues regarding "the myth of the melting pot" that the unit itself focuses on. When I asked her what was most difficult about writing the essay, she said it was "tying in the *Rereading America*, tying in Allport." To do so, she said she "was trying to find something that Allport had written backing up the way that I feel, or maybe trying to make some kind of connections between the way that I feel to what he writes." She ended up finding a minor point in the Allport essay concerning the tendency of individuals to mirror their group's attitudes out of a personal need to do so, and highlights this notion of personal need in the last paragraph of the essay. But she almost completely ignored the overall thrust of the Allport essay in its focus on prejudice and group-identity formation, preferring to emphasize issues both safer and closer to her own interests. With flexibility of topic built into this assignment, most students likewise chose to avoid writing about what they saw as the boring and also dangerous issues of race and ethnicity.

Conclusion

Throughout the 102 course, students strongly resisted the textbook's questioning and critical attitude toward United States culture. They defended and affirmed the existence of the traditional family; expressed faith in the idea that, with hard work and a good attitude, anybody with talent and desire can become successful; and voted with their feet by avoiding the potentially controversial topics of racial difference and prejudice. The one student who did deal with prejudice wrote about how she had encountered African Americans for the first time at the University, anxious but open and hopeful, but then a negative experience with one such student confirmed her suspicions that she would have difficulty relating to minorities. To the end, students complained that the text and the course were trying to "cram these liberal ideas down our throats," as Joshua put it. Not that surprisingly, then, this critique of students' values was not received with much sympathy by students. To the contrary, "My conservative ideas have mainly been solidified," Josh asserted.

Yet if the class did not appear to change students' minds about such issues, it did at least expose them to some ways of thinking that they may not have encountered or carefully considered previously. They read pieces reflecting alternative points of view, wrote journal entries about them, talked about them in class, and in a number of cases wrote essays about them. Looking back on the quarter, Louise sums up her own ambivalent attitude toward the course: "While 102 was going on, I felt I didn't like it at all. I always worried if you didn't take the same point of view as the teacher, you'd be wrong. I'm conservative, and the class was

very liberal, so we were constantly going in opposite directions. But looking back on it, there were things I really liked about the course. I liked
the open discussions we had. I liked the conflicts we had."

As a beginning point in a college education, then, the course may not
have been such a failure after all. It did seem to help students become
more aware of and sensitive to cultural and political issues which at the
outset they were extremely distanced from. For example, despite the
homophobic sentiments often expressed in class, Wendy, herself part of
the group of conservative students who often dominated discussion,
ended up writing her research paper, the last paper of the quarter, on
the topic of AIDS. Much affected when her classmate said that her uncle
had deserved to die of the disease because he was gay, Wendy concluded
in her paper that that idea was wrong. Her essay bespoke a difficult internal struggle against her own feelings of prejudice and intolerance, with
a more tolerant and accepting attitude winning out. And Louise, probably the most outspoken of the conservative students, told me that the
class, while not changing her conservative beliefs, had "made her more
aware of different points of view" on issues that she had previously considered simple and straightforward. Perhaps understanding is the first
step toward larger changes. Or perhaps it is unrealistic to expect such
large changes. What we see in students' writing after two quarters of
college writing instruction is a mixed picture, with improvements no-
ticeable both in students' comprehension and their production of texts
but with rather significant problems remaining, particularly in incorporating written sources into their own writing, in doing the kinds of activities typically included under the rubric of critical thinking. In the
following chapter, Sherry Cook Stanforth critically examines her own
teaching, as well as my interpretation of it.

7 The Dangerous Intersection of Home and School

Sherry Cook Stanforth

Several years have passed since I sat in that circle trying to make sense of their friendly resistance. Dissertation work and a new daughter have kept me busy. Now, pausing to think and write about an important teaching experience, I am surprised to find that in many cases, the pseudonyms are starting to take over. I struggle for that feeling of being there again, for knowing details about my students' projects and their "out-of-class" lives. A while back, I passed Louise on a campus sidewalk. We stopped to talk for a few minutes, sharing stories about our progress through the system and wondering about other members of the group. When we parted, I carried away a memory of good relationships.

But even with the atmosphere of camaraderie established in English 101, I realize now that by the end of second quarter most of my students were simply surviving my class. They were all biding time, waiting for release from a situation that seemed to operate on "no pain, no gain" principles. The curriculum in English 102 involved getting "outside your own skin" to "examine the world from multiple perspectives" (Colombo et al., *Rereading America*, p. 2). For me, that meant helping writers develop strategies for navigating the critically challenging, "other-oriented" discourse posed by the reading assignments. First, they needed to work through the complexities of language to understand central ideas and arguments. Then they needed to develop the level of critical awareness that would allow them to join an ongoing social conversation with some authority. Not so far away from what I had been doing as a graduate student, really. Initially, *reading comprehension activities + general writing instruction + energetic class discussion = effective teaching* seemed like a good formula.

However, textual involvement in English 102 threatened an exposure different from the kind represented in essays on dying grandparents, drunk-driving accidents, and family discord. Most of my students neither expected nor wanted to address gay marriages or theorize about sexual and racial injustice in a writing class. After the period, a small group of students would gather at Mr. Jim's Grill to debunk the "left wing" "politically correct" *Rereading America* textbook with its deceptively polite introductory invitation: "You may have to reexamine your relationships to family, friends, neighborhood, and heritage" (p. 2). Translated into the pragmatic language of studenthood, this "reexamination" activity really meant dissecting personal values for the sake of a grade. Here—in the classroom of all places—was a concrete example of the bad "outside" influence parents warned about. Writers saw themselves as victims, forced to argue "against" either the authority of home or that of the academy. Thus, first-year composition became a paradoxical friend-enemy, the evil means for achieving a necessary end. Unit by unit, my students perceived me as the emissary of suspect knowledge and they wondered how to respond.

Of course, I didn't hear any of the conversations shared over post-class coffee but I imagine the clipped, frustrated interjections: "What does she want from us? I mean, how are we supposed to write about this stuff?" "This isn't what I came here to learn. I don't see how this is going to help me in the real world." "So what happens if you just don't agree with the book or the teacher?" In turn, I would climb the two flights to my office and find empathy with colleagues, who, like me, constantly struggled to find a locus of authority inside a tangle of institutional, cultural, and individual agendas. Part teacher, part student, we were liminal personae, figuring out how to *be* within an institutional hierarchy. "There's nothing more terrifying than the tenuous position of a graduate student," my friend Brad once commented during lunch. Another friend, Tami, offered the insight, "Every time we open up our mouths and talk about our students, we talk about ourselves." Office conversation reflected a contagious feeling of inadequacy. I am reminded of Richard Hoggart's reference to community life and the "authority which has its eye" on "Us," the working class (1957, p. 49). In his description, middle authorities tend to act more sharply toward the working class simply because they want to "feel more securely separate from them" (p. 50). When students openly rejected the curriculum or simply failed to rise to the intellectual challenge of our pedagogy, we secretly feared blame. Their deviance perpetuated our performance anxiety. Someone had to carry the burden of education missing its mark. Would it be the administration? The book? Our students? Ourselves?

Despite the deep commitment many teachers made for their students, the way to address intolerance for the curriculum seemed to be heading toward intolerance of its recipient. So normal from the vantage point of social theory, stock representations of consistently "bad" students contributed to a disturbing occupational dynamic. Almost daily, teachers lamented the horrific ignorance of individual writers who misapplied citations or misinterpreted the central idea of an argument. Born-again Christians, especially, became the target of over-the-desk jokes, "sickening" their teachers with myopic rhetoric. The seminar discussions and disciplinary texts might address "concerns about the critical development" of such students, but in the daydream, teachers leapt up from the desk and slapped duct tape over their mouths. Cultural literacy was a hot topic, too: today's students didn't listen to National Public Radio. They'd never heard of *The Atlantic Monthly* or opened a copy of *The New Yorker*. In journals and class discussions, they desecrated the holy trinity of race, class, and gender. Their sparse knowledge about canonical texts, local government, educational issues, social politics, and fine arts set them apart as "bottom" members of the academy. Mention of English 102 or *Rereading America* in a social gathering of writing teachers or students consistently inspired dark narratives of struggle in the writing classroom. Really, the trick was to avoid teaching the course altogether if you could. Even those of us who cared deeply about "cultural investigation" within composition pedagogy hoped to find some other, less painful way to lead students to critical awareness in their thinking and writing. Helping them evolve as socially just citizens seemed overwhelming, especially for first-year teaching assistants. In between conferences and classes, they sat around the office together, pondering the ongoing confusion of their work. Was the goal to teach them better values or better writing or both?

My own teaching wasn't going so well either, despite several years of experience and a thick file of "difference-based" writing activities I had designed and successfully implemented in other forums. The sudden apprehension I held for my work bothered me. Three times a week, I walked into my basement classroom and tried to "speak in ways that challeng[ed] but [did] not diminish" students (hooks,1988, p. 132). Usually, Russel sat across the circle near Chuck and Latecia, making notes in his legal pad. I'd known him for years—in fact, he was the first person I spoke with about my professional goals in composition studies. As my academic advisor and director of the composition program, he had witnessed my teaching and writing on numerous occasions outside of the scope of the study. I trusted his evaluations of my work. Now, in a setting where I was a living example of putting program theory into practice, I felt vulnerable. When confusion or tension surfaced during class discussion, I heard the vigorous scribble of Russel's pencil. How was he interpreting the situation?

Trouble lurks in places where truth is negotiable. James Zebroski notes that "it is not possible or desirable to pretend that politics do not exist in the very pores of the classroom, the curriculum, and language studies" (1992, p. 93). My classroom, with its symbolic convergence of program administrator, teaching assistant, and twenty-five undergraduate writers, reflected the messy, multiple translations of the academic chorale. "My family and I feel that there is absolute right and wrong, no grey areas," Joshua wrote in a research paper on "situational ethics." In it, he described the human tendency to deny personal responsibility in outcomes and expressed his deep mistrust of situations "where there is no definite answer to the question" of values. For most of my students, facts "proved" the case while questions only weakened it. In their eyes, arguments and the values they represented were black and white, two-sided constructions. The object of writing was to champion the "right" side of the issue. It was a matter of common sense.

Yet, I kept sending them into the grey territory. I emphasized argument as a more "round" dynamic—a creative, intersubjective act inspired by competing and overlapping voices. When students labeled a reading as "boring" or "impossible" or "too political," I challenged them to work through the ideas together until they found the "personal" relevance. A friend and I began conducting informal workshops for students who felt lost in the assignments. We wanted them to develop a stake in their academic reading and writing activity and to see it as a "real" component of everyday living. The "birth control in school" fishbowl activity I initiated in the first quarter (despite the fact that it began falling apart even before Clarissa left the room in tears) modeled the complications of mediating personal and social policy. Individual beliefs and opinions and stories *mattered*. Still, I pushed students to explore the limitations of their own experience so that they could begin imagining other politics of location (Rich, 1986, p. 215). I foregrounded dissensus in discussions and assignments and tried to present consensus "not as the goal of the conversation, but rather as a critical measure to help [them] identify the structures of power that inhibit communication" (Trimbur,1989, p. 614).

On drafts, I offered some advice about improving surface presentation, but more often, I tried to engage writers in the kind of conversation that would lead to more thoughtful arguments. "Louise," I might scribble in the margin of a draft, "how would a single parent trying to stay off of welfare respond to your views regarding daycare?" Or, during a conference about his research proposal on transfusion-acquired AIDS, I might challenge Denny to investigate his comfortable use of the phrase "innocent victims" when referring to hemophiliacs. The image of Clarissa walking away as her peers joked around about unplanned pregnancy followed me into English 102, reminding me of my accountability as her teacher. I could never fix the painful moment that silenced her important perspective, and, possibly, inhibited her ability to develop critical skills from the activity. Still, by emphasizing the inseparability of language and action, I might have led students to recognize their own accountability within dialogue. Instead of trying to change their beliefs, I encouraged them to adopt a reflexive stance regarding their own political situatedness.

To draw on an academic proverb, things get lost in translation. Perception mattered, and my audience didn't buy most of my attempts to inspire critical investment. Being a scholar is different from being a student. As a scholar, I might choose to stay behind, "learning for learning's sake," defining this and redefining that at the seminar table or computer, appreciating the indeterminacy of social politics, playing creatively within the grey areas, rattling off paradigms of belief, dissecting others, overturning the "myths" of my daily living. But for most students school was only a stepping stone. They perceived me as a public servant whose job it was to teach the kind of literacy that would allow them to "get through" college and into their profession of choice. I paced around the room, trying to startle them with profound questions. They sat quietly at their desks, waiting for the answers to follow.

I sift through a stack of cover letters I received from Rachel, a nursing student, during the first quarter of composition. While many of her classmates jotted down brief apologias or blandly summarized the approaches they took with assignments, Rachel always fashioned professionally "appropriate" documents that contained rich examples of her writing process. Beneath her "sincerely" closure, she included a determined signature, her professor's last name, her social security number, and the course title. On the surface, she appears to be the "cooperative, if not compliant" writer Russel describes. Our conversations together often included that familiar "just tell me what to do and I'll do it" moment. Though savvy about the codes of writing presentation, Rachel ultimately resisted the less cut-and-dried task of *making* knowledge in an academic context. Within the tidy structure of her work, I recognize her growing unhappiness about the unknowns associated with writing in my class.

"I didn't like this type of essay." "I wouldn't like to write another paper like this one," Rachel writes in her cover letters. Her problem-solution essay, entitled "The Misunderstood Procrastinator," presents a defense of the "poor working student" who must "get an education" in order to "go anywhere in the world." In it, she suggests that too many teachers are blind to the "multidirectional pullings" of their students' lives. They simply don't realize how hard their students are willing to work in order to succeed in college. One of the student "types" Rachel describes uses procrastination as a "coping method" for being "afraid to ask about something he/she doesn't understand." Reading between the lines, I see a young woman on her way to becoming a nurse. My classroom is only one of the many involved stops she must make to achieve her goal. She desperately wants me, her English teacher, to understand her position: she is trying very, very hard to produce exactly what I want her to produce. She visits my desk at least once a week, draft in hand. She is asking and still not understanding.

I imagine more scenes at Mr. Jim's Grill. Talking and laughing together, the group approaches a maroon vinyl booth decorated by a bigger-than-life poster of Marilyn Monroe. Louise volunteers to get a round of coffee and Michelle follows, finishing up her scathing review of the Carnegie and Lasch articles assigned earlier in the quarter. "My roommate and I read them *three* times trying to get the point. We were completely lost. No one ever really talks that way . . . ." Her voice fades into the murmur of people wait_ _g in line.

Sighing, Candy unzips her backpack and shuffles through a worn, blue folder. She hands Joshua her not-yet-passing draft about reverse discrimination in a local police department to see if he can make sense of the feedback. "It seems like she just comes back asking questions. But she doesn't tell us how to fix it."

Joshua shakes his head as he skims the conversational notes I've penciled in the margin of Candy's draft. An engineer in the making, Joshua looks for consistent rules and efficient routes for solving problems. Composition is a game of indeterminacy. He smiles and plays along but he wants writing to work like math. He values certainty, especially when it comes to human agency. "Hey, don't feel so bad," he finally tells her, biting into a muffin. "You should see my draft. I think she does that to everyone."

In the ideal "problem posing" classroom described by Ira Shor in *Empowering Education* (1992), no one feels "bad" or browbeaten by academic challenges. Whenever I felt haunted by the negativity in English 102, I reflected on "good" teaching moments from my past. Jim, a white student who wrote passionately about the evils of affirmative action in his journal, hears a black student, Rose, critically analyze a potential employer's racial attack. Dale and Johnna, two middle-aged business majors, study a Quiche-Mayan creation myth in order to discuss it as "literature." After reading Alice Munro's "Boys and Girls," Carol and Steve generate a list of stereotypes assigned to men and women, then speculate about how their lives would be different in the "other" gender. Wendy, who admitted her struggle with homophobia to me in a conference, decides to pursue a research project examining relationships between homophobia and AIDS awareness in high school students. Et cetera.

I remember a profile Louise wrote, praising an elementary school teacher for her ability to make students "feel good about themselves." This particular teacher put "a lot of emphasis on positive reinforcement" and "rarely [said] anything negative." Evidently, she helped her students believe that school—and her classroom—was a good place to be. They *liked* learning. I'm not suggesting that we should measure our success as teachers in terms of popularity. We owe our students the experience of intellectual struggle more than we owe them that feeling of "liking" their education. As a teacher of writing, I live for those invigorating moments when, as bell hooks describes it, students seem to be "coming to voice in an atmosphere where they may be afraid or see themselves at risk" (hooks, 1988, p. 132). That kind of work can be revealing; it can lead participants to a good place, somewhere that they really want to be. But the balance between useful struggle and invitation is so delicate. I continue to stumble across more questions than I do answers in my day-to-day work. What do we, as writing teachers, specifically value about shifting old paradigms, about asking our students to "talk back" to authority? Who should hurt to learn and why?

Maxine Hairston's angry critique of composition "radicals" who lead students to "suspect there is a correct way to think" (1992, p. 189), reminds me of the difficulty involved in managing the friction points that emerge in a "political" writing classroom. More than once, sitting in my circle of students, I sensed close calls with disaster and hid from uncomfortable conflicts. Like them, I feared the exposure involved in getting outside my own skin. Yet, as their teacher, I believe it is my responsibility to "striv[e] always to see the learning event from the standpoint of the student" (Witherell & Noddings, 1991, p. 7) and to foster the kind of interpersonal reasoning activity that is "guided by an attitude that values the relationship of the reasoners over any particular outcome" (Noddings, 1991, p. 158). The critical task of reexamining my own relationship with academic authority begins with the willingness to risk situating myself within the "other" knowledge raised by my students.

Home voices call, warning me not to forget the hold of other places, other times. "You've turned into some sort of troublemaker," a family member once told me after a heated political discussion. "Since you've gone away to college, you've changed." Some of the cultural questions raised by *Rereading America* would have held no place in my family core of values. I wasn't so far from my students once. I, too, carried the codes for Hairston's "fake discourse" (1992, p. 189) after my "reeducation" as a citizen in college classrooms. But I also grew in my thinking about that which was "not me." I never told my own students that as an eighteen-year-old freshman, I received an earth-shattering "D minus" from an Honors Philosophy professor on an essay assignment addressing the question, "Is Homosexuality Wrong?" Personally uncertain of whether homosexuality was wrong or not, I assumed the binary stance implied in the prompt and drew on the less difference-embracing ideas of my home culture. An academic authority challenged my reasoning and reduced me to angry tears. After a tense office conference, I revised somewhat thoughtfully and redeemed my grade but not my confusion. My appreciation of the conflict came a year or so later, when I realized for the first time that one of my childhood friends was gay. Only then was I able to see with the double vision of someone who had traveled through the dangerous intersection of home and school.

Perhaps I should have shared more stories in the circle, struggled more with my students instead of against them. *Mary dismisses her uncle's death from AIDS as deserving. Shaken by her comment and the ensuing silence, I say weakly, "We need to remember that not everyone feels that way."* Close call. The stranger's story comes from "the edge between her unique world and the world of others that she has just entered" (Shabatay, 1991, p. 136). Stories can be a comfortable resting place, easy in their voicy, familiar unfolding. But they can also mark experience—or its absence—in ways that startle us into careful listening and learning. I remember my parents warning me about the dangers of my new pocketknife, purchased in the Smoky Mountains with allowance money when I was seven. No one wanted me to own that knife: it was risky. My mother shook her head and said, "You'd better watch out." My father kept turning in his seat by the campfire to remind me of potential hazards. Finally, I said to them, "Look. It isn't that sharp." I ran my thumb across the blade to demonstrate until the shine of my own blood startled me into silence. I won't forbid my daughter to buy a pocketknife and I won't enforce theories of danger upon her. I will simply tell my story.

Maybe our students aren't really resisting school but its habit of insisting that they compartmentalize their lives. In the introduction of his essay "You Can Study at Home and Earn Your Degree! Call Now!" Joshua describes his grandfather's dreaded "Sunday-drive-college-degree-lecture," which argues for the necessity of obtaining a college degree in order to "get anywhere in life." Reading this particular piece for the first time, I felt tugged away from teacherly evaluation, toward something more uncomfortably "personal." I grew up hearing similar dialogues from my father, who spent the first part of his childhood with four generations of family in an East Tennessee farm house, logging trees and baling hay to help make ends meet. As an adult, he struggled for thirteen years in evening college to get a bachelor's degree and become a mechanical engineer. He was self-made, loyal to an ethic of hard work. But shifting economies in the 80s threatened his job security on a regular basis. During every Milacron lay-off season, he sat at the supper table, tense-faced, predicting that it was only so long before "they" caught up with him. The "bean counters" in upper management were blind to the value of hard-earned experience—how one looked on paper mattered more. Engineers who'd invested decades of their lives in Milacron were disappearing, being replaced by people with PhDs and multiple degrees. My father doubted he'd ever make retirement and the "degree-lecture" he sometimes offered me was tinged more with cynicism than pride. "Just don't forget that integrity comes from within" was always his closing remark.

Asked to situate his views within several textbook arguments around the "Myth of Individual Opportunity," Joshua wrote a passionate defense of his "successful but degree-less father." Instead of developing the hints he made about a cultural infatuation with post-secondary education, he (uncritically? critically?) selected a handful of well-stated phrases from each author and artfully wove them into a personal commentary on his colliding worlds of home and school. Family politics inspire most of the content for the essay. Joshua's father chooses not to climb the prestigious educational ladders in the fashion that Joshua's uncles do: instead, he cares more about "well brought up children" and "what type of man he is on the inside." By investing in family instead of social status, Joshua's father achieves a kind of greatness that Joshua's grandparents "fail to see."

College, insists Josh in his essay, "does not teach wisdom." Wisdom is something "gained through personal experience in life . . . ." My father would agree. The idea that wisdom might come from a home place and into the classroom challenges institutional authorities to join in the intellectual discomfort by acknowledging the presence of competing "outside" knowledge. Inside the circle, the student who holds the opinion that we should enforce seat-belt laws more stringently is always a safer bet than the one who talks disparagingly about her gay uncle. The subject matter feels less personal and therefore less dangerous. I never use teachers' manuals but I did leaf through the *Rereading America* "Resources for Teaching" guide provided by St. Martins Press, which emphasizes the pedagogical aim of "shift[ing] the emphasis from personal opinions, ideas, and beliefs and refocus[ing] the class on the ideologies that help shape us and our experiences." One example of this "shift" suggests that a class discussion of gender roles should consider "perceptions of the dominant society's attitude toward or portrayals of women, not [students'] personal opinions about what women should or shouldn't do, think, say and so on." This, notes the guide, is a "subtle difference in approach" which the teacher must "take the time to clarify" (p. 3).

During the first week of the second quarter, Joshua wrote in a journal: "Men and women should have equal rights, but I still believe in the stronger and weaker sexes and the abilities and responsibilities associated with each." Somehow, as his writing teacher, I was supposed to lead him to separate his *belief* from a critical analysis of cultural knowledge regarding men and women. From his own position within the circle of composition theory, Richard Marius declares that we "should not be engaged in teaching students to understand their psyches"(1992, p. 476). Lamenting the critical ignorance represented by just-another-student-writing-about-divorce, David Bartholomae (1995) asserts: "I don't want my students to celebrate what would then become the natural and inevitable details of their lives" (p. 71). Richard Penticoff and Linda Brodkey shake their heads in consensus, adding that a writing curriculum should discount "personal opinions as irrelevant to the practice of conducting rhetorical inquiry, however important they may or may not be to the writer's own experience" (1992, p. 141). In their course, "Writing about Difference," they highlight Stephen Toulmin's terminology of "claims, grounds and warrants" and the idea that argumentation is "a prologue to further inquiry" (p. 132). Yet, even as Penticoff and Brodkey attempt to move away from a narrow definition of literacy pedagogy, they "prohibit" their students from using "personal" writing when responding to issues related to cultural difference (p. 141). Writers' lived experiences do not count for anything in the academic arena; instead, argumentative authority comes from the ability to set aside everything "personal" and methodically analyze social discourse. Western civilization has a long history of reading the world through objective-colored lenses. Images of robed Greek men still plaster the front cover of writing textbooks that are packed with rules for how to mask one's subjectivity. All the while, my students sit at a booth in Mr. Jim's Grill, making personal knowledge over steaming cups of coffee.

I agree with Russel that composition professionals often taint the goal of introducing important political ideas in writing contexts with a destructive "intellectual elitism." Opinions and beliefs lie at the core of all ideologies, including those sanctioned by the academy. So many times, I've read about how teachers of writing are in one of the best positions to lead students to an awareness of "civic responsibility." There is contradiction, though, in the idea that we can somehow achieve this goal without addressing the presence of feelings and experiences (including our own) in the classroom. If writers sense unchallenged myths about The Student in Need of Moral Transformation, they won't respond to educational invitations to look past comfort zones and "re-see" their most cherished values. Like the pragmatic working class Hoggart describes, our students are "generally suspicious of principles before practice . . . ." (1957, p. 65). Outside of school—at the family dinner table or work, at church or in a group of friends—what people think *counts* for something. Bartholomae's stock student, in writing about her parents' divorce, exists apart from Bartholomae's arena of cultural skepticism, offering much more than convenient evidence for his argument against traditional humanism in composition pedagogy. As a thinking, feeling individual, the student confounds theory in her desire to reflect on a disturbing change in her immediate social structure. Whether or not someone labels the product of her thinking as trite, it still counts as cultural evidence for something that *she*—not Bartholomae—knows about living.

When I decided to become a writing professor, my grandmother gave me a hand-painted heart-shaped plaque that says, "To teach is to touch someone's life forever." She told me to treat the people I met in my classroom with understanding, compassion, and encouragement. "Listen to their stories," she said. Her advice has not always come easy. I am both composition teacher and graduate student in composition. As I learn "inside" voices, I am trying not to forget the sound of outside voices that will contribute to the "making of knowledge in composition," with or without my critical investment. Teachers have everything to gain by caring more about student affect and its place in writing classrooms and research. The student who resists the disassembly crew comes from somewhere. Maybe her father has calluses on his hands instead of an article on post-structuralism. A getting-outside-my-own-skin approach means that I will always have more questions than answers, more reflexivity than exigency. But I know something now: I know that *how my students perceive my teaching* will ultimately become the "pedagogy" that teaches them.

8 Conclusion: Reflective Instrumentalism and the Teaching of Composition

Who are our students? What do they want? And what should we teach them? I use these overarching questions to frame this final chapter, which examines how findings from this study relate to current approaches to teaching composition and to the formulation of a new curricular model. A recent profile of the nation's college freshmen, from an annual survey based on responses by more than 250,000 students at two- and four-year institutions, helps to answer the first two of these questions. Linda J. Sax, director of the survey for the academic year 1997–1998 concluded that, on the whole, "incoming students showed unprecedented levels of academic and political disengagement" (quoted in Gose, 1998, p. A37). The survey of freshmen found that 74.9 percent of students listed "being very well off financially" as an essential goal. In contrast, 40.8 percent chose "developing a meaningful philosophy of life," and just 26.7 percent mentioned "keeping up-to-date with political affairs." Three-quarters of the students surveyed planned to major in pre-professional fields. Such findings are consistent with the strongly pragmatic attitudes and approaches shown by Sherry Cook Stanforth's students as they worked their way through the composition sequence.

I would suggest that students' lack of political and academic interest and their strong pre-professional orientation are no aberration, but reflect firmly rooted tendencies in American culture and history. They spring from a pragmatic, hands-on, careerist emphasis in the country as a whole, first identified by the French observer Alexis de Toqueville in his 1835 book *Democracy in America* and discussed in chapters of the book such as "Why the Americans Are More Addicted to Practical Than to Theoretical Science," "Commercial Prosperity and Future Prospects of the United States," and "What Causes Almost All Americans to Follow Industrial Callings." These pragmatic tendencies have continued up to the present day, and seem to be increasing in intensity as students and others focus more and more on issues of financial security and worries about economic uncertainty. Yet composition specialists, as well as other academics, have been slow to consider how the pervasive pragmatism of college students, and of U.S. society more generally, relates to our classroom approaches. In discussing the role of colleges and universities in

170

their book *The Good Society*, Robert Bellah and his co-authors (Madsen, Sullivan, Swidler, & Tipton) assert, "The fact that most of our students have no intention of devoting themselves to clear critical inquiry but are concerned primarily with pursuing economic advancement is seldom taken into account by the professors" (1992, pp. 156–157). Where composition teaching is concerned, I would suggest that this charge has considerable merit indeed.

Current approaches to composition frequently ignore or dismiss as an irritant students' pragmatic focus, even as proponents of these approaches encourage teachers to "prophesy for social change" (Bizzell, 1992, p. 295) or to help their students "imagine themselves as intellectuals" (Harris, 1997, p. 19). Though well-intentioned and justified in challenging students intellectually and politically, these writers, when presenting their pedagogical frameworks, seem not to consider seriously the likelihood that most students have no interest in being activists or intellectuals, nor the possibility that the teaching approaches might need to be rethought in some way that addresses this mismatch of teacher and student goals.

Some authors do actually address this mismatch, if only briefly. Such writers generally present student pre-professionalism and political conservatism or lack of interest as a pedagogical challenge to be overcome, a problem to be solved by the resourceful teacher. Students emerge from these discussions as potential converts to be won over to a cause. The editors of the popular collection, *Left Margins: Cultural Studies and Composition Pedagogy*, draw attention to "that moment of (sometimes profound) rhetorical conflict between the teacher's articulation of an oppositional stance—an agenda that moves against the political grain—and the student's resistance to it" (Fitts and France, 1995, p. x). Yet instead of dwelling on that crucial moment and exploring the reasoning behind these teacher-student differences, the editors quickly move past the idea of student resistance, not asking why this opposition exists, nor considering if students' views possibly have any merits, nor examining how these views may influence student learning. Rather, the authors highlight their book's overall intention "to make available compelling examples of writing instruction that facilitate political demystification and social change" (p. xi). Such transformative approaches fail to appreciate or even to interrogate in a systematic manner students' essentially pragmatic reasons for studying composition—and going to college—in the first place.

Those few authors who do actually stop to examine this pragmatic orientation in any depth are generally scornful of it, finding little or nothing of value. And nowhere is this attitude more clearly expressed than

172 Collision Course

in Kurt Spellmeyer's book *Common Ground: Dialogue, Understanding, and the Teaching of Composition* (1993). Spellmeyer critiques what he terms "instrumentalism," by which he refers to the dominance of "[a]n ethic of production and exchange, an ethic of calculating reason" in the teaching, learning, and use of written language. Such an instrumentalist emphasis in the teaching of composition, he argues, leads to "the study of language by appeal to its vocational utility; the reduction of language itself to a system of functional conventions; the valorization of persuasiveness, the smooth, salesmanlike 'presentation of ideas,' at the expense of theoretical reflection, the thinking we do about ideas" (1993, pp. 8–9).

In putting forward a rationale for the pedagogy of cross-cultural awareness and critical self-reflection which forms the subject of his book, Spellmeyer presents a dichotomy between two classroom approaches. On the one hand, he posits an uncritical instrumentalism—the clear villain of this set piece, and a villain with enormous powers. Such a teaching approach, he suggests, may help students succeed in business by developing certain communicative and persuasive skills, but it involves no serious analysis and perpetuates blindly the ills of society. The marketplace ethos embodied in this approach, laid out in influential textbooks during the early twentieth century, has, according to Spellmeyer's hyperbolic prose, "defined for composition teachers ever since an absolute horizon, beyond which they cannot, or must not, lift their eyes" (p. 10). On the other hand, as an alternative to this reductive though apparently dominant approach, he offers a sophisticated, self-conscious, theoretically aware, and politically progressive pedagogy of "understanding." This more theoretical approach offers the best means at our disposal not only to teach writing in an intellectually challenging and satisfying manner, but also to work toward comprehension and transformation of existing conditions—the "demystification and social change" endorsed by Fitts and France (p. xi). To support this dichotomy and to undergird this pedagogy of understanding, Spellmeyer cites philosopher and educator John Dewey. In *Democracy and Education*, Dewey argues against a purely vocational approach to schooling "as a means of securing technical efficiency" (1916, p. 316, quoted in Spellmeyer, p. 12), and in favor of a pedagogy of empowerment, self-reflectiveness, and transformation. Once Spellmeyer establishes his framework in the first chapter, the pedagogy he elaborates in close to 300 densely written pages never again discusses the relationship between composition instruction and the kinds of work students might be doing for the forty or so years in which they will presumably be employed after college.

In the context of college composition, a choice between instrumentalism and understanding as mutually exclusive, polar opposites is, of course, no choice at all. What composition teacher today could argue against a pedagogy of understanding, reflection, dialogue, and transformation, the critical literacy equivalents to motherhood, apple pie, and the flag, and in favor of a skills-oriented, anti-intellectual, vocational approach designed only to enhance "the smooth, salesmanlike 'presentation of ideas'"? Leaving aside the dubious accuracy of Spellmeyer's characterization of composition teaching throughout much of the twentieth century as wholly untheoretical or reflective, I would point out that he stacks the deck here by presenting a caricature of an approach that would attempt to help students in their subsequent careers. He denies this sort of pedagogy any possibility of intellectual value or means of promoting critical reflection, presenting readers with an overly simplified, either/or choice. Consequently, his absolute rejection of instrumentalism allows him to propose a way of teaching writing that is decidedly non-instrumentalist, an interpretive, theoretical, and politically aware pedagogy purified of the noxious ills of the marketplace, and with far loftier aims. On the other hand, I would suggest that Spellmeyer is too quick to condemn instrumentalism. Despite his strong advocacy of "theoretical reflection, the thinking we do about ideas," he gives the idea of instrumentalism short shrift, hustling it offstage as quickly as possible in order to present his own approach. Yet there are serious considerations to address regarding Spellmeyer's (and other critical literacy theorists') dismissal of student careerism as a legitimate concern in the teaching of composition. Before consigning instrumentalism to the dustbin of composition history, let us examine more thoroughly this concept and its relation to what we do in the classroom.

From our vantage point as academics and as college teachers, students' strong instrumentalism clearly does have a major down side. Students are badly served indeed, not only in our classes but in all classes, even in their major, when they allow their intellectual and political development to be short-circuited by the attitude that college is *only* a means to job skills and financial security. This point is so evident that it barely needs mentioning, except that I do not want readers to think of me as an apologist for grade-obsessed, single-mindedly careerist, and otherwise disengaged students; an advocate of a pedagogy that caters to such students; or an opponent of critical reflection, political awareness, questioning of the status quo, and social change. Rather, I very much want students to develop their critical tools, to think of themselves, not as Hobbesean free agents out to get as much as they can for themselves, but as members of a larger society with rights and responsibilities. I want students to learn to write in ways that not only help them achieve the desired financial security but also provide intellectual development and strategies for addressing public issues. I stand united with critical literacy theorists on these matters. However, I think theorists have been far too eager to advocate approaches that fail to consider adequately the issue of student instrumentalism, and far too quick to condemn this instrumentalism as wrongheaded and in dire need of correction.

I would argue that instrumentalism, broadly defined as an emphasis upon the world of work and career advancement, is too deeply ingrained in U.S. culture and history to be so blithely ignored or dismissed in composition pedagogy. It is a fundamental characteristic of our students. Yet it is also a fundamental feature of many of us, if we are honest about our own aspirations and careers. I want to be successful in my work partly for intrinsic reasons of personal satisfaction in promoting my ideas about composition teaching, which I have worked hard to develop and believe in strongly. I want to be successful partly for political reasons in hopes that my work will benefit students from all backgrounds and possibly even contribute to a more just social order. But I also want to be successful partly for reasons of ambition. I readily confess to a desire to do well in my career, write successful books, be respected in my field, raise my salary, better provide for my family. I do not think such careerism is wrong, particularly when balanced with these other goals, and I think many other people in the field share this view. In any case, these careerist urges are not going to go away—either in our students or ourselves—even if we really wanted them to go away, which most of us do not. Rather than condemn instrumentalism in students, then, I believe we need to find ways to make sense of and come to terms with this instrumentalism, and, ultimately, to develop means of making better use of it in the classroom.

But first of all, I believe we need to recognize that students' pre-professional orientation and their emphasis on future careers is in many ways a positive quality. As individuals, students are motivated in their studies in large part by a desire to achieve the level of academic success necessary to enter their chosen fields, and also by the related (though, admittedly, often subordinate) desire to learn what they need to know for their future work. Yet members of particular professions are by no means the only ones who benefit from the work of that field. As a society, we all benefit from the work of engineers, architects, computer hardware and software designers, accountants, business managers, scientists, pharmacists, teachers, health care professionals, and artists of various kinds. Every time I log onto my computer, search the Internet, ride my bicycle, watch a film, listen to my compact disk player, cross a bridge, take an elevator, or relax in my own home, I am enjoying the fruits of instrumentalism. Most of the people employed in the professional fields that make these activities possible prepare for their work in college, and part of their preparation generally involves studying composition. Regardless of the kinds of political changes one would like to see in this country, we still need talented, qualified people working in these fields, and students come to college specifically to receive the education and credentialing they need to enter such fields, including writing instruction. Jeff Smith makes this point very strongly in his 1997 *College English* article, "Students' Goals, Gatekeeping, and Some Questions of Ethics." And it is not only the politically conservative or apathetic students who are career-minded. Smith points out that, "Even politically activist students, like those profiled in Paul Rogat Loeb's *Generation at the Crossroads*, speak with pleasure of the upward mobility they hope to gain from being in college (Loeb, 1994; Smith, 1997, p. 86)." There is more than a hint of intellectual elitism—a belief in the superiority of the critical, intellectual work of academics over other kinds of work—in the pervasive dismissal of student careerism that one finds in the composition literature. Why, we seem to be asking, can't students be like us? What we should be asking is whether or not it makes sense for us to design composition curricula as if students were indeed going to become critical intellectuals.

In truth, very few of our students are going to become critical intellectuals, such as academics, writers, or social critics; they have very different reasons for coming to college. I would therefore suggest that it is a mistake for us set up our classes as if they were. Even John Dewey, whom Spellmeyer cites as a key opponent of instrumentalism in education, while opposing an uncritical vocationalism, did recognize the importance of preparation for the work world in the education of all students. In the words of Lawrence Cremin, author of *The Transformation of the School: Progressivism in American Education 1876–1957*, Dewey did not by any means reject instrumentalism. Rather, he "believed that democracy necessitated a reconstitution of culture, and with it the curriculum, that would conceive of scientific and industrial studies as instruments for making the great body of the people more aware of the life around them. This meant introducing vocational subjects not merely to build utilitarian skills, but as points of departure for increasingly intellectualized ventures into the life and meaning of industrial society (1964, p. 124)." As Dewey himself framed the issue of vocational studies in his book, *Democracy and Education*, "The problem of the educator is to engage pupils in these activities in such ways that while manual skill and technical efficiency are gained and immediate satisfaction found in the work, together with preparation for later usefulness, these things shall be subordinated to education—that is, to intellectual results and the forming of a socialized disposition" (1916, p. 231; quoted in Cremin pp. 124–125). Thus, far from rejecting instrumentalism and banishing vocational concerns from the classroom, Dewey recognized the work world as a key element of society, and believed that students' education should provide them with the skills they need not only to critically analyze the work world, but also to function effectively within it.

By contrast, today's politically oriented composition pedagogies seem to place exclusive stress on the importance of developing tools for critical analysis but reject the idea that we are also preparing students for occupations. Yet as this study has shown, students tend to interpret such a critical literacy approach as pessimistic, negative, and accusatory, and at a time when they are trying hard to sustain the optimism and motivation necessary to do the hard work being asked of them. Students then go on the defensive in ways that make them even more likely to resist the instruction.

I therefore believe that we need to show greater respect in composition pedagogy—and find a place in our course designs—for the more instrumentalist orientation of most of our students. We create a large gulf between ourselves and our students by not respecting their goals. And in the process, we lose a substantial amount of students' cooperation, and of our own credibility in the classroom.

Students' pragmatism seems particularly understandable these days given the way in which our society increasingly depicts a college education as a required credential for the job market. In other words, most of our institutions mandate that the experiences of a college education are crucial for entering most jobs. Then, in the composition class, we turn around and critique students as anti-intellectual and/or reactionary if they fail to endorse other, less pragmatic agendas in the classroom. We set up our classes by asking students to critique and resist authority; we just don't want them to question *our* authority as we ignore or dismiss their own goals. A pragmatic justification undergirds our courses, and by extension our own existence as professional academics, yet we are reluctant to acknowledge this justification. Is it any wonder, then, that students fail to embrace our curricula with anything approaching enthusiasm and often with genuine reluctance?

In many ways, promoting teaching approaches that emphasize critical inquiry and political analysis and action serves our interest and self-image as academics and as intellectuals. Influenced as we are by critical developments in the English departments where most of us received our education and in which most of us reside professionally, we have taken the dominant cultural and political emphasis of much contemporary work in English studies and applied it to our ways of thinking about the teaching of writing. Such course frameworks fulfill certain personal and professional needs, particularly given that, as composition specialists, we operate in intellectual environments where the complexity of our work is often misunderstood and devalued. Even today, many of our literature colleagues and other faculty throughout our institutions seem to imagine that our professional life is still dominated by such issues as correcting sentence fragments and run-ons, teaching formulaic ways to organize essays, or helping students get in touch with their personal voice. Through these more theoretically sophisticated courses, we position ourselves as operating on an elevated critical plane, drawing on complex notions of discourse and culture. In the same vein, we construct ourselves as politically astute agents of change, fostering in our students progressive, questioning attitudes—"a teacher of virtue," in the words of Patricia Bizzell (1992, p. 283), drawing upon the sophist philosopher Isocrates. Put simply, our work seems much more challenging, interesting, and important when we define ourselves as teachers of theory and activism.

But despite the obvious attractions of these approaches, I would suggest that setting up composition curricula that ignore or dismiss student instrumentalism has serious negative consequences in our courses, often leading to student alienation, hostility, disengagement, avoidance behavior, and unproductive conflict. In Sherry's writing class, students used up a good deal of their time and energy complaining and becoming frustrated about the lack of fit between the course and their own goals. They also spent considerable time finding topics to write about that would allow them to avoid engaging (and possibly running afoul of) what they viewed as the political and ideological emphasis of the class. In denying the legitimacy of students' pre-professionalism, we risk losing something very important: the cooperation of our students. We often end up fighting with them, and I believe this is a fight we ultimately cannot win. Students will give us what we want, albeit grudgingly, for the few months we have them. But then they will move on, and our efforts to transform them will have served to increase their cynicism. A different approach is needed.

I am not suggesting a return to the purely vocationalist emphasis caricatured by Spellmeyer—if such an approach ever really existed. Rather, as an alternative to a critical pedagogy that devalues students' pre-professional orientation, I would like to propose an approach to teaching composition that attempts to foster what I call "reflective instrumental-

ism." This approach preserves the intellectual rigor and social analysis
of current pedagogies without rejecting the pragmatism of most first-
year college students. Instead, the approach accepts students' pragmatic
goals, offers to help them achieve their goals, but adds a reflective dimension that, while itself useful in the work world, also helps students
place their individual aspirations in the larger context necessary for critical analysis. This pedagogy seeks to establish a truly common ground
between student and teacher by welcoming, incorporating, and then
building upon students' primary reasons for coming to college and
studying composition. As a composition teacher and administrator, I
want my students to learn ways of thinking and writing that help them
do well in their studies and in their careers. I also want them to gain
personal satisfaction, interest, and enjoyment in reading and writing. At
the same time, I wish to cultivate a critical aspect within this instrumentalist framework. I believe that an important part of teaching involves
persuasion, specifically convincing students that it is worth their while
to engage seriously with a course of study. Rather than alienate students
by pushing a classroom agenda that fails to take their goals seriously,
this approach offers teachers a greater opportunity to gain students'
cooperation.

As an example of reflective instrumentalism in the classroom, I have
developed a course for our first-year writing program that focuses on
the topic of higher education (Durst, 1999). However, the course does
not attempt to position students as critics of the academy and of the society in which it operates, a role they are in any case loath to fulfill as
they struggle to enter the academy successfully. Rather, the course provides an opportunity for students to better understand what college can
offer them and to take greater responsibility for their own learning. An
important purpose of the course is to assist students as they clarify their
own educational goals by reading, thinking, talking, and writing. This
idea of having first-year students study college itself is related to the
pedagogical approach Shirley Brice Heath articulates in her book *Ways
with Words: Language, Life, and Work in Communities and Classrooms* (1983).
Heath outlines a curriculum in which students become ethnographers,
examining both their home cultures and the very discourses they will
have to learn in order to succeed in school. Similarly, in this composition class, students learn new academic literacy strategies even as they
develop a deeper, more varied sense of what it means to be a college student.

Grounded in this reflective instrumentalist approach, course readings
for the composition class present students with diverse points of view
on many of the central issues that have shaped contemporary thought

about higher education. Though students at my university declare a major upon arrival and tend to be very eager to specialize in their pre-professional classes, they generally—in my experience—think of their intended major more as a set of classes or a compilation of course credits than as a field of study. Accordingly, a research project for the course asks students to investigate their intended major through examining documents relating to the course of study (such as the department's description of the major), reading about the field, interviewing a professor as well as a professional in the area, and conducting field observation at a work site. Through this project, students should learn that a major is more than a set of courses leading to certification and employment, that it constitutes a body of knowledge and a set of problem-solving strategies, that it promotes particular ways of thinking and acting, that it has a history, and that it performs certain functions in the larger society. Such learning is very useful to students in a pragmatic sense, yet it also provides a foundation for more critical analyses of a multitude of issues, including relationships between schooling, work, culture, and politics. Ernest Boyer, in his book, *College: The Undergraduate Experience in America* (1987), advances the notion of an "enriched" major providing social, historical, and philosophical grounding for the increasing numbers of students who choose to specialize in pre-professional areas. Boyer argues that such grounding is frequently absent or inadequate in undergraduate career-oriented majors. A reflective instrumentalist framework in first-year composition, drawing upon this notion of an enriched major, takes advantage of the motivation students bring to their areas of specialization, provides students with useful knowledge, and engages students in critical scrutiny of schooling and society.

While not attempting to position students as opponents of inequities in higher education or in society as a whole, neither should the course be viewed as supporting an oppressive status quo. The status quo depends on an uncritical, unquestioning acceptance of current conditions. This course provides numerous opportunities for students to question and begin to develop critical perspectives, but in an environment where students need not feel guilty or defensive about wishing to be successful in their lives and careers. At the same time, as the course progresses, the very idea of success can itself be critically examined and complicated as part of an analysis of school and career issues.

In his article on gatekeeping, Jeff Smith argues that, for composition teachers, taking students seriously "means honoring the choices they make and, indeed, deferring to those choices if at all possible. To do otherwise is undemocratic at best, if not infantilizing and frankly oppressive." And he adds that, "we are ethically bound by students' own aims"

(1997, p. 317). I disagree with this view if it means, for example, that teachers have to accept students' aims uncritically and to help them achieve those aims and those alone. As college teachers, an important part of our work surely involves helping students see and come to terms with the complexities in what may appear to them as fairly straightforward issues, and perhaps we should include here students' own reasons for coming to college. But at the same time, let us accept the fundamental reasonableness of students' desire to gain practical expertise in their college coursework; and let us help students do so, even as we attempt to foster greater reflectiveness and engagement with the world.

Works Cited

Allport, G. (1992). Formation of in-groups. In G. Colombo, R. Cullen, & B. Lisle (Eds.), *Rereading America:Cultural contexts for critical thinking and writing* (pp. 292–306). New York: Bedford Books of St. Martin's Press.

Austin, J. L. (1962). *How to do things with words: The William James lectures delivered at Harvard University in 1955.* New York: Oxford University Press.

Axelrod, R. B., & Cooper, C. R. (1993). *The concise guide to writing.* New York: St. Martin's Press.

Bartholomae, D. (1985). Inventing the university. In M. Rose (Ed.), *When a writer can't write: Studies in writer's block and other composing-process problems* (pp.134–165). New York: Guilford.

Bartholomae, D. (1995). Writing with teachers: A conversation with Peter Elbow. *College Composition and Communication, 46,* pp. 62–71.

Belenky, M. F., Field, M., Clinchy, B. M., Goldberger, N. R., & Tarule, J. M. (1986). *Women's ways of knowing: The development of self, voice, and mind.* New York: Basic Books.

Bellah, R. N., Madsen, R., Sullivan, W. M., Swidler, A., & Tipton, S. M. (1992). *The good society.* New York: Vintage Books.

Bennett, T. (1990). *Outside literature.* London: Routledge.

Berlin, J. A. (1987). *Rhetoric and reality: Writing instruction in American colleges, 1900–1985.* Carbondale, IL: Southern Illinois University Press.

Berlin, J. A. (1996). *Rhetorics, poetics, and cultures: Refiguring college English studies.* Urbana, IL: National Council of Teachers of English.

Bizzell, P. (1992). *Academic discourse and critical consciousness.* Pittsburgh: University of Pittsburgh Press.

Bleich, D. (1978). *Subjective criticism.* Baltimore: The Johns Hopkins University Press.

Bogdan, R. C., & Biklen, S. K. (1982). *Qualitative research for education: An introduction to theory and methods.* Boston: Allyn and Bacon.

Bourdieu, P. (1974). The school as a conservative force: Scholastic and cultural inequities (J. C. Whitehouse, Trans.). In J. Eggleston (Ed.), *Contemporary research in the sociology of education* (pp. 32–46). London: Methuen.

Boyer, E. L. (1987). *College: The undergraduate experience in America.* New York: Harper & Row.

Britton, J., Burgess, T., Martin, N., McLeod, A., & Rosen, H. (1975). *The development of writing abilities (11–18).* Schools Council Research Studies. London: Macmillan.

Brodkey, L. (1996). *Writing permitted in designated areas only.* Minneapolis: University of Minnesota Press.

Brodkey, L., & Penticoff, R. (1992). Writing about difference: Hard cases for cultural studies. In J. A. Berlin & M. J. Vivion (Eds.), *Cultural studies in the English classroom* (pp. 123–144). Portsmouth, NH: Boynton/Cook-Heinemann.

Brooke, R. (1987). Underlife and writing instruction. *College Composition and Communication 38,* 141–153.

Bruffee, K. A. (1984). Collaborative learning and the "conversation of mankind." *College English, 46,* 635–653.

Chase, G. (1988). Accommodation, resistance, and the politics of student writing. *College Composition and Communication, 39,* 13–22.

Coles, W. E. Jr. (1974). *Composing: Writing as a self-creating process.* Rochelle Park, NJ: Hayden.

Colombo, G., Cullen, R., & Lisle, B. (Eds.). (1992).*Rereading America:Cultural contexts for critical thinking and writing* (2nd ed.). New York: Bedford Books of St. Martin's Press.

Cremin, L. A. (1964). *The transformation of the school: Progressivism in American education 1876–1957.* New York: Vintage Books.

Crowley, S. (1991). A personal essay on freshman English. *Pre-Text: A Journal of Rhetorical Theory, 12,* 155–176.

Crowley, S. (1995). Composition's ethic of service, the universal requirement, and the discourse of student need. *Journal of Advanced Composition, 15,* 227–239.

Derrida, J. (1981). *Dissemination* (B. Johnson, Trans.). Chicago: University Press.

Detterman, D. K., & Sternberg, R. J. (Eds.). (1993). *Transfer on trial: Intelligence, cognition, and instruction.* Norwood, NJ: Ablex.

Dewey, J. (1916). *Democracy and education: An introduction to the philosophy of education.* New York: Macmillan.

Durst, R. K. (1994). Coming to grips with theory: College students' use of theoretical explanation in writing about history. *Language and Learning across the Disciplines, 1,* 72–87.

Durst, R. K. (1999). *You are here: Readings on higher education for college writers.* Needham Hts., MA: Simon & Schuster Custom Publishing.

Edmundson, M. (1997, September). On the uses of a liberal education: As lite entertainment for bored college students. *Harper's Magazine, 295,* 39–49.

Ehrenreich, B. (1989). *Fear of falling: The inner life of the middle class.* New York: Pantheon Books.

Elbow, P. (1973). Writing without teachers. New York: Oxford University Press.

Elbow, P. (1995). Being a writer vs. being an academic: A conflict in goals. *College Composition and Communication, 46,* 72–83.

Emig, J. (1971). *The composing processes of twelfth graders.* Urbana, IL: National Council of Teachers of English.

Fish, S. (1980). *Is there a text in this class? The authority of interpretive communities.* Cambridge, MA: Harvard University Press.

Fitts, K., & France, A. W. (Eds.). (1995). *Left margins: Cultural studies and composition pedagogy.* Albany: State University of New York Press.

Flynn, E. A. (1988). Composing as a woman. *College Composition and Communication, 39,* 423–435.

Foucault, M. (1972). *The archeology of knowledge; and The discourse on language.* (A. M. Sheridan-Smith, Trans.). New York: Pantheon.

Freire, P. (1970). *Pedagogy of the oppressed.* (M. B. Ramos, Trans.). New York: Continuum.

Fulkerson, R. (1996). *Teaching the argument in writing.* Urbana, IL: National Council of Teachers of English.

Gale, X. L. (1996). *Teachers, discourses, and authority in the postmodern composition classroom.* Albany: State University of New York Press.

Gilligan, C. (1982). *In a different voice: Psychological theory and women's development.* Cambridge, MA: Harvard University Press.

Giroux, H. A. (1983). *Theory and resistance in education:A pedagogy for the opposition.* South Hadley, MA: Bergin & Garvey.

Giroux, H. A. (1988). *Schooling and the struggle for public life: Critical pedagogy in the modern age.* Minneapolis: University of Minnesota Press.

Goldstein, R.(1992). The gay family. In G. Colombo, R. Cullen, & B. Lisle (Eds.), *Rereading America:Cultural contexts for critical thinking and writing* (pp. 477–491). (2nd ed.). New York: Bedford Books of St. Martin's Press.

Gose, B. (1998). More freshman than ever appear disengaged from their studies, survey finds. In *The Chronicle of Higher Education,* January 16, 1998, A37.

Greene, S. (1995). Making sense of my own ideas: Problems of authorship in a beginning writing classroom. *Written Communication 12,* 186–218.

Grice, H. P. (1975). Logic and conversation. In P. Cole & J. L. Morgan (Eds.). *Syntax and semantics, vol. 3: Speech acts* (pp.126–149). New York: Academic Press.

Guth, H., & Rico, G. (Eds.). (1993). *Discovering literature: Fiction, poetry, and drama,* pp.127–133. Englewood Cliffs, NJ: Blair Press.

Hairston, M. (1992). Diversity, ideology, and teaching writing. *College Composition and Communication, 43,* 179–193.

Hall, S. (1980). Cultural studies: Two paradigms. *Media, Culture, and Society, 2,* 57–72.

Harkin, P. (1991). The postdisciplinary politics of lore. In P. Harkin & J. Schilb (Eds.), *Contending with words: Composition and rhetoric in a postmodern age* (pp. 124–138). New York: Modern Language Association of America.

Harkin, P., & Schilb, J. (Eds.). (1991). *Contending with words: Composition and rhetoric in a postmodern age.* New York: Modern Language Association of America.

Harris, J. (1994). From the editor: CCC in the 90's. *College Composition and Communication, 45,* 7–9.

Harris, J. (1997). *A teaching subject: Composition since 1966.* Upper Saddle River, NJ: Prentice Hall.

Heath, S. B. (1983). *Ways with words: Language, life, and work in communities and classrooms.* New York: Cambridge University Press.

Higher Education Research Institute. (1998). *The American freshman: National norms for fall 1997.* Los Angeles: Author.

Hillocks, G. Jr. (1995). *Teaching writing as reflective practice.* New York: Teachers College Press.

Hofstadter, R. (1963). *Anti-intellectualism in American life.* New York: Vintage Books.

Hoggart, R. (1957). *The uses of literacy.* New Brunswick, NJ: Transaction Publishers.

hooks, bell. (1988). *Talking back: Thinking feminist, thinking black.* Boston: South End Press.

Horowitz, H. L. (1987). *Campus life: Undergraduate cultures from the end of the eighteenth century to the present.* New York: Alfred A. Knopf.

Iser, W. (1989). *Prospecting: From reader response to literary anthropology.* Baltimore: The Johns Hopkins University Press.

Jacoby, R. (1994). *Dogmatic wisdom: How the culture wars divert education and distract America.* New York: Doubleday.

Jarratt, S. (1991). Feminism and composition: The case for conflict. In P. Harkin & J. Schilb (Eds.), *Contending with words: Composition and rhetoric in a postmodern age* (pp.105–123). New York: Modern Language Association of America.

Kirsch, G. (1993). *Women writing the academy: Audience, authority, and transformation.* Carbondale, IL: Southern Illinois University Press.

Knoblauch, C. H., & Brannon, L. (1984). *Rhetorical traditions and the teaching of writing.* Upper Montclair, NJ: Boynton/Cook.

Knoblauch, C. H., & Brannon, L. (1993). *Critical teaching and the idea of literacy.* Portsmouth, NH: Boynton/Cook.

Langer, J. A., & Applebee, A. N. (1987). *How writing shapes thinking: A study of teaching and learning.* Urbana, IL: National Council of Teachers of English.

Lapointe, A. E., et al.(1989). Educational Testing Service. *A world of difference: An international assessment of mathematics and science.* Princeton, NJ: Author.

Levinson, S. C. (1983). *Pragmatics.* Cambridge: Cambridge University Press.

Loeb, P. R. (1994). *Generation at the crossroads: Apathy and action on the American campus.* New Brunswick, NJ: Rutgers University Press.

Macrorie, K. (1970). *Uptaught.* New York: Hayden.

Marius, R. (1992). Composition studies. In S. J. Greenblatt & G. B. Gunn (Eds.), *Redrawing the boundaries* (pp.466–481). New York: Modern Language Association of America.

Marzano, R. J. (1991). *Cultivating thinking in English and the language arts.* Urbana, IL: National Council of Teachers of English.

McLaren, P. (1994). *Life in schools: An introduction to critical pedagogy in the foundations of education* (2nd ed.). New York: Longman.

Mercer, N., & Edwards, D. (1987). *Common knowledge: The development of understanding in the classroom.* London: Methuen.

Miles, M. B., & Huberman, A. M. (1994). *Qualitative data analysis: An expanded sourcebook* (2nd ed.). Thousand Oaks, CA: Sage Publications.

Moffatt, M. (1989). *Coming of age in New Jersey: College and American culture.* New Brunswick, NJ: Rutgers University Press.

Moffett, J. (1968). *Teaching the universe of discourse.* Boston: Houghton Mifflin.

Murray, D. M. (1968). *A writer teaches writing.* Boston: Houghton Mifflin.

Murray, D. M. (1982). *Learning by teaching: Selected articles on writing and teaching.* Upper Montclair, NJ: Boynton/Cook.

Naipaul, V. S. (1987). *The enigma of arrival: A novel.* New York: Alfred A. Knopf.

Nelson, J. (1990). This was an easy assignment: Examining how students interpret academic writing tasks. *Research in the Teaching of English, 24,* 362–396.

Newkirk, T. (1997). *The performance of self in student writing.* Portsmouth, NH: Boynton/Cook-Heinemann.

Noddings, N. (1991). Stories in dialogue: Caring and interpersonal reasoning. In C. Witherell & N. Noddings (Eds.), *Stories lives tell: Narrative and dialogue in education,* 157–170. New York: Teachers College Press.

Perry, W. G. (1970). *Forms of intellectual and ethical development in the college years: A scheme.* New York: Holt, Rinehart, and Winston.

Petraglia, J. (Ed.). (1995). *Reconceiving writing, rethinking writing instruction.* Mahwah, NJ: Lawrence Erlbaum Associates.

Piaget, J. (1959). *The language and thought of the child.* (3rd ed.) London: Routledge.

Postman, N., & Weingartner, C. (1969). *Teaching as a subversive activity.* New York: Dell.

Rich, A. (1986). Notes toward a politics of location. In *Blood, bread and poetry:Selected prose, 1979–1985* (pp. 210–231). New York: Norton.

Rosenthal, R. (1995). Feminists in action: How to practice what we teach. In K. Fitts & A. W. France (Eds.), *Left margins: Cultural studies and composition pedagogy* (pp. 139–156). Albany: State University of New York Press.

Rorty, R. (1979). *Philosophy and the mirror of nature.* Princeton, NJ: Princeton University Press.

Rothschild Ewald, H., & Wallace, D. L. (1994). Exploring agency in classroom discourse or, Should David have told his story? *College Composition and Communication, 45,* 342–368.

Shabatay, V. (1991). The stranger's story: Who calls and who answers? In C. Witherell & N. Noddings (Eds.), *Stories lives tell: Narrative and dialogue in education* (pp. 136–152). New York: Teachers College Press.

Shaughnessy, M. P. (1977). *Errors and expectations: A guide for the teacher of basic writing.* New York: Oxford University Press.

Schorer, M. (1961). *Sinclair Lewis: An American life.* New York: McGraw-Hill.

Sheeran, Y., & Barnes, D. (1991). *School writing: Discovering the ground rules.* Milton Keynes, England: Open University Press.

Shor, I. (1992). *Empowering education: Critical teaching for social change.* Chicago: University of Chicago Press.

Shor, I. (1996). *When students have power: Negotiating authority in a critical pedagogy.* Chicago: University of Chicago Press.

Skolnick, A. (1992). The paradox of perfection. In G. Colombo, R. Cullen, & B. Lisle (Eds.), *Rereading America: Cultural contexts for critical thinking and writing* (pp. 402–409). New York: St. Martin's Press.

Smith, J. (1997). Students' goals, gatekeeping, and some questions of ethics. *College English, 59,* 299–320.

Spellmeyer, K. (1993). *Common ground: Dialogue, understanding, and the teaching of composition.* Englewood Cliffs, NJ: Prentice Hall.

Spradley, J. P. (1980). *Participant observation*. New York: Holt, Rinehart, and Winston.

Sullivan, P. A., & Qualley, D. J. (Eds.). (1994). *Pedagogy in the age of politics: Writing and reading (in) the academy*. Urbana, IL: National Council of Teachers of English.

de Toqueville, A. (1835/1964). *Democracy in America*. (A. Hacker, Ed.). New York: Pocket Books.

Tobin, L. (1993). *Writing relationships: What really happens in the composition class*. Portsmouth, NH: Boynton/Cook-Heinemann.

Trimbur, J. (1989). Consensus and difference in collaborative learning. *College English, 51*, 602–616.

Trimbur, J. (1994). Taking the social turn: Teaching writing post-process. *College Composition and Communication, 45*, 108–118.

Vygotsky, L. (1934/1986). *Thought and language*. (A. Kozvlin, Ed. and Trans.). Cambridge, MA: Massachusetts Institute of Technology Press.

Zebroski, J. T. (1992). The Syracuse University Writing Program and cultural studies: A personal view of the politics of development. In J. Berlin & M. Vivion (Eds.), *Cultural Studies in the English classroom* (pp.87–94). Portsmouth, NH: Boynton/Cook-Heinemann.

Index

Author

Russel K. Durst is Acting Head of the English Department at the University of Cincinnati, where he was previously Director of Composition. He has served as Chair of the NCTE Standing Committee on Research and as an editorial board member for the journals *College Composition and Communication* and *Language and Learning Across the Disciplines*. His research on critical literacy and on writing assessment has appeared in numerous journals and edited collections. He is co-editor of *Exploring Texts: The Role of Discussion and Writing in the Teaching and Learning of Literature* (1993).

Contributor

Sherry Cook Stanforth is a doctoral candidate in English at the University of Cincinnati. Her work has appeared in *Indiana Review, MELUS, Language and Lore*, and in the NCTE publication, *Ethics and Representation in Qualitative Studies of Literacy*. Her dissertation project draws on folklore theory and ethnographic data to examine the built-in dialectics of oral writing lore (experience narratives, proverbs, and recurring conversational motifs) informally exchanged among teachers and students in a local writing community. Her community involvement includes collecting family-oriented folklore and performing regionally in an all-women's Appalachian folk band.

This book was set in Palatino and Helvetica by Electronic Imaging.
Typefaces used on the cover were Crackhouse, Goudy, and Officina.
The book was printed on 60-lb. offset paper by Versa Press.